+HV5822 .H4 C6

COLLEGE FOR HUMAN SERVICES
LIBRARY
345 HUDSON STREET
NEW YORK, N.Y. 10014

Connections: Notes from the Heroin World

CONNECTIONS

NOTES FROM THE HEROIN WORLD

Leroy C. Gould

Andrew L. Walker

Lansing E. Crane

Charles W. Lidz

New Haven and London, Yale University Press, 1974

Copyright © 1974 by Yale University.
All rights reserved. This book may not be
reproduced, in whole or in part, in any form
(except by reviewers for the public press),
without written permission from the publishers.
Library of Congress catalog card number: 73-86896
International standard book number: 0-300-01731-6

Designed by John O. C. Mc Crillis
and set in Times Roman phototype.
Printed in the United States of America by
The Vail-Ballou Press, Inc., Binghamton, N.Y.

Published in Great Britain, Europe, and Africa by
Yale University Press, Ltd., London.
Distributed in Latin America by Kaiman & Polon,
Inc., New York City; in Australasia and Southeast
Asia by John Wiley & Sons Australasia Pty. Ltd.,
Sydney; in India by UBS Publishers' Distributors Pvt.,
Ltd., Delhi; in Japan by John Weatherhill, Inc., Tokyo.

Contents

	Glossary and Abbreviations	vii
	Acknowledgments	xi
	Preface: Technical Notes for Social Scientists	xiii
1.	Introduction	1
2.	Street Life	19
3.	A Cop's View of Narcotics Work	69
4.	A Hell of a Night	85
5.	O. Ryan's Day in Court	102
6.	Defending Drug Cases	119
7.	All in a Morning's Work	138
8.	Different Strokes for Different Folks	153
9.	Methadone Maintenance	183
10.	Zeta House: A Humanizing Community	209

Glossary and Abbreviations

acid:	*d*-Lysergic acid (LSD), a hallucinogen. Originally a white street-culture term.
agreed rec:	Agreed recommendation; the agreement reached between defense and prosecution on the disposition to a case or related cases.
ARCH:	Addiction Referral Community Help agency.
boost:	Steal, usually from a parked car or a store.
broad:	1, A prostitute; 2, police term; any female suspect or potential suspect.
burn:	Cheat. The term primarily refers to economic exchanges in which one party does not meet the conditions after the other has committed himself. There is some tendency to generalize the term to include any kind of interaction in which one party bests another through reneging.
cold turkey:	To stop using opiates abruptly and without the benefit of medication. Has been part of the lexicon of the addict subculture at least since the 1940s.
crib cracking:	Burglary. "Crib" is a term for apartment.
CSH:	Central State Hospital.
dealer:	A person who sells any drug on a regular basis.
detox:	Detoxification. The term is sometimes used in a generic sense and refers to medically supervised withdrawal from any addicting drug, but usually it refers to detoxification from heroin or methadone.

dime bag:	A glassine envelope containing heroin retailing for $10, larger than the standard "bag" which retails for $6 in Riverdale.
dirty urine:	A urine specimen which has been found by the testing laboratory to contain traces of illegal drugs or quinine.
downer:	A class of either barbiturates or tranquilizer-based drugs; originally a white street-culture term.
dude:	A black subcultural term. 1, An adult male; 2, a male addict.
half load:	A wholesale unit of heroin—usually 15 street bags.
horse:	Heroin; an old term for heroin, not used very often except to bring out specific imagery.
joint:	1, A marijuana cigarette. This use is largely white street-culture. 2, prison (or occasionally jail). This use is largely black street-culture (syn: slammer).
jones:	(Opiate) habit. Heard more often among black opiate users than white.
make:	Recognize. Implies "seeing through a cover."
medical exam:	A courtroom term referring to the medical examination for venereal disease required in prostitution cases.
MHC:	See RMHC.
NAU:	Narcotics Addiction Unit.
nolle:	1, To conditionally dismiss a prosecution without a finding of guilt or innocence. Technically, the prosecution may be reinstated within one year. 2, A disposition to

GLOSSARY AND ABBREVIATIONS

	the criminal charges. From the Latin *nolle prosequi* (unwilling to pursue).
OD:	Overdose. To take too much of any drug. Can be used to suggest fatality, more often either advanced narcolepsy or simply overindulgence.
OPT:	Outpatient therapy.
PD:	Public Defender.
piece:	A wholesale quantity of high-quality heroin; often about four cubic inches.
PO:	Probation officer; parole officer.
pre:	See PSI.
p.r.n.:	According to need (*pro re nata*).
pross:	Street term for prostitution.
PSI:	Pre-sentence investigation. 1, An investigation performed by a probation officer to provide facts which aid in the sentencing of a person who has pleaded guilty to or been convicted of a serious misdemeanor or a felony. 2, The report that results from such an investigation.
reefer:	Marijuana. Can mean either the plant substance or a marijuana cigarette. (Syn: joint; generally used in the former sense.)
ripoff:	Steal, exploit. The term probably originated in the radical politics of the 1960s meaning exploitation or counterexploitation and gradually came to its present meaning.
RMHC:	Riverdale Mental Health Center.
ROR:	Release on recognizance. A form of pretrial release conditioned on a written promise to

	appear (PTA). Given to "good appearance risks," ROR allows release without financial security (bail).
set:	A system. May be used to designate either the entire heroin subculture or a particular ongoing social situation (e.g. "the set at Fatty's").
skag:	Heroin; largely a black street-culture term.
smack:	Heroin. A term used more in the white sub-street-culture than in the addict subculture.
speed:	A class of amphetamine-based drugs; originally a white street-culture term (syn: ups).
split:	Leave; a term used at least since the 1950s by both blacks and whites.
stone, stoned:	Designating drug influence.
strung out:	Addicted. Used by both blacks and whites, usually with specific reference to opiates, but occasionally generalized to mean a type of dependence relation.
stuff:	Heroin.
the Man:	Usually the police or other agents of legal authority, but sometimes generalized to any authority figure. Seems to be of black ghetto origin.
trick:	A prostitute's customer.
violate:	To revoke someone's probationary status and thus reimpose a suspended sentence.
works:	The equipment necessary to prepare and inject heroin. Usually an eyedropper and hypodermic needle, but can be a syringe. There are many street terms for this equipment: e.g. guns, gimmicks.

Acknowledgments

We are indebted to many people for helping us in many different ways over the last few years. Unfortunately, we can do little to repay them except give them credit here for the help they gave us.

We owe a very special debt of gratitude to all those people who talked with us and allowed us to observe their work and play. Anyone who has ever done field research knows that one cannot possibly succeed without the active support of the people he is researching. It is their memories, stories, scene interpretations, and motivational accounts which are the core of this book. They have given us help far beyond the requirements of office or interest. We have refrained from thanking them each by name, but they know who they are and we wish to express our heartfelt appreciation to them.

Another type of support has come from other members of our research team who have contributed directly to this work. Ernest Badger, Miguel Figueroa, the Rev. E. Benjamin LaFrazier, and Robert Logan have been particularly helpful in depicting the worlds of the addict and treatment patient. Thomas Muskelly and the late Dolores Outlaw deserve special thanks. They oriented us to the addict's world when we knew nothing about it. Barbara Clinton, a former nurse in the Methadone Clinic, provided us with many important insights into the world of treatment and patients. Her experience was invaluable.

At another level we received advice and counsel of the highest order from a group we designated our Research Advisers. They included Egon Bittner, Albert Cohen, Kai Erikson, Abraham Goldstein, Stanislav Kasl, Stanton Wheeler, Gerald Klerman, and Thomas Levin. They met with us on weekends and holidays, sometimes coming many miles. They waded through pages of manuscript and papers. More important, their advice was, without exception, careful and thoughtful. They provided experience and wisdom to a group made up largely of interested field workers. We hope this and succeeding works will justify their efforts.

We owe a particular debt of gratitude to people who have read all or parts of this manuscript and gave us their advice: Michael G. Haggerty, Mattie Holloway, Vincent Nuzzo, Donna Smith, Donald Wright, Anthony Williams, Michael Perlson, James Coleman, Fred Enslign, Francis DeGrand, Alan Postman, Lawrence Dragunoff, Arthur Joseph, Jonathan Silbert, Thomas Corradino, Robert J. Mulhern, Jr., David Marcucci, and Kathy Sheehan.

During our years on this research project, several students worked with us, providing significant contributions: Esther Heen, Morgan McCall, Marcia Brick, and Katherine Kiene. Special mention should go to Alan Wichlei and Ira Bergman for collecting direct source material for some sections of this book.

Other colleagues who merit thanks are Eileen Saper and Mary Jo Shepard, who shared a common burden with us as part of our research staff. Steven H. Lewis, who worked closely with us on this project, has provided comments and insights that have been most helpful.

Leah Ambrose, Mary Tucker, and Jan O'Shinsky did typing and ran our office. Without them the work would never have got done.

Further, we wish to thank Herbert Kleber for his support and the National Institute of Mental Health, which partially supported this project under Narcotic Addict Treatment Program Grant No. 1 H17 MH 16356.

Finally, we want to thank Anne Wilde for copyediting and Jane Isay, our editor, whose faith, assistance, and encouragement helped us immensely.

Preface: Technical Notes on Subjective Perspectives as Data for Social Scientists

By the prevailing standards of contemporary social science, this is a rather unorthodox book. As will be discussed in the introduction, this volume is deliberately and radically nonanalytic. The presentation of actors' perspectives makes important and valid information available to the general and professional public on a subject of considerable concern. As such, we intend the substance of this book to stand on its own.

Our decision to present one portion of our data in an unorthodox fashion was made after considering a number of significant theoretical, methodological, and philosophical issues. To the extent that the general reader needs to be familiar with these issues and our resolutions of them in order to assess the realiability and validity of our data, they will be discussed in the introduction.

We believe, however, that these issues are acquiring increasing significance for contemporary social science. Since we have not only ruminated on them but also worked out some practical solutions which eventually led to this volume, we decided to add a technical preface to the substantive perspectives. By elaborating our methodological stance from a sociological perspective, we hope to provide additional orienting information for professionals as well as contribute to the ongoing methodological discussions in the social sciences.

In the last fifteen years there has been a remarkable change in the theoretical treatment of deviance by sociologists. This shift began with the rise of "labeling theory" which identified a new unit of analysis for the study of deviance.[1] Parsons (1949),

---

[1]. This case is an interesting confirmation of the paradigm proposed by Kuhn (1962). No new theory has emerged which explains all the inadequacies in the old theory systematically, but there seems to be growing consensus about what the major elements of such a theory would be.

Cohen (1956), Sutherland (1956), Merton (1957), and others working within an older theoretical framework all asked some variant of the question: "What factors (conditions, attributes, pressures, strains) induce a person to commit a deviant act?" [2] The concern was basically etiological: "What *causes* deviance?"; the unit of analysis was the person, the deviant. Newer deviance studies, by Becker (1963), Erikson (1966), Cicourel (1967), Lemert (1967), and many others, have revolved around the question: "What are the characteristics of situations in which people are treated as if their identity or behavior were at variance with what people 'should be' or 'should do'?" The concern is basically phenomenological: "How is a particular element of the social world constructed?"; the unit of analysis is the social situation.

This theoretical shift has been accompanied by shifts in research strategy. Following the older paradigm, the most common strategy was to identify a deviant population and determine in what ways that population was different from a "normal" population. Difference, of course, depended upon the etiological factors that researchers wished to probe. The finding might be that the deviant has a different body type, different perceptions of opportunity, different super-ego formation, different peer groups, or even different genes. But the basic research strategy was to find out *how* deviants are different, and then theorize how this difference *produces* deviance.

This strategy is incompatible with newer deviance theory for several reasons. Such research is almost inevitably carried out in a context in which the definition of the research subject as deviant or nondeviant is nonproblematic (that is, the "deviantness" of the subject is taken for granted by the researcher), and the situational grounding of the behavior in question is left out.[3] The context in which the data are generated may be the psychiatrist's couch, a penitentiary, a courtroom, or even a clinic, but rarely the setting in which the behavior typically occurs. Furthermore, such data:

2. This "older theoretical framework" is basically *positivism*, as Matza (1964) uses the term.
3. This point is strongly argued by Polsky (1966, chap. 3).

are much too heavily retrospective; data from people who aren't really free to put you down; data often involving the kind of "cooperation" in which you get told what the criminal thinks you want to hear so you will get off his back or maybe do him some good with the judge or parole board; data from someone who is not behaving as he normally would in his normal life-situations; and above all, data that you cannot supplement with, or interpret in the light of, your direct observation of the criminal's natural behavior in his natural environment. [Polsky 1966, p. 123]

Becker's work (1963), stressing the importance of imposing labels on the deviant's identity and behavior, required not only a shift in research objects toward the procedures of control agencies that apply the labels but also a shift in research strategies. Questions about the mechanisms whereby labels are imposed simply could not be answered by studying the characteristics of "label imposers." Recently, then, deviance research has moved toward what might be called a naturalistic approach, with the research goal a more "faithful rendering of natural phenomena" (Polsky 1966, chap. 3; Matza 1969, chaps. 1, 2). But, faithful rendering of natural phenomena is easier to talk about than to accomplish, even though it seems mandated by various theoretical developments in the field.

Erikson's (1966) study of deviance in Puritan Massachusetts gave further support to the new focus on the total situation in which deviance and control are acted out by pointing to the importance of the religious and political crises of a community in producing the appearance of "crime waves." Erikson also reemphasized Durkheim's (1938) observations on the "functions" of crime for the larger society. Becker and Erikson, as well as the important works of Matza (1964), Cicourel (1967), Gould (1969), and many others, have driven the issue of the differences between deviants and nondeviants well into the background of deviance research.

Thus, instead of documenting or analyzing differences, contemporary deviance theory has assumed a more ecological approach to the occurrence of deviance. Rather than seeing it as a characteristic of behavior or identity, it is seen as a process, during which various roles and interests come into play.

This process consists of a series of situations analytically bound together by virtue of the contribution of each to the establishment of the "fact" that something "wrong" was done and is being responded to.

The empirical researcher, though, finds himself in a difficult position. He can no longer orient himself to the question, "What factors make these people do these things?" Instead, he must gear his observation to the question, "How is this situation managed so as to produce an instance of deviance?"

We were interested from the beginning of our work in analyzing the "drug problem" as a case study of a type of deviance, but in accordance with our theoretical disposition we were concerned with the operation of the system whose output is the complex of phenomena which the public recognizes as the "drug problem." In retrospect, it is apparent that drug use—as a particular form of deviance—acquired a special status in the late 1960s and early 1970s. Like the Puritans whom Erikson studied, modern America has its "crime waves." In Puritan Massachusetts the crises were Quakerism, Antinomianism, and witchcraft. Communism, delinquency, and drugs have probably played similar roles in contemporary America. We believe that "epidemicness" is an important parameter of the "Drug Crisis," but epidemicness is largely constituted through political, journalistic, and community activities whose description goes well beyond the scope of the present volume. While the processes through which epidemics and crime waves are generated, maintained, and finally dissipated are important research and analytic topics, this volume is addressed to the more "primitive" question of how the behavior in question (drug taking) is generated, identified, and dealt with, not in terms of statistics and abstractions but as the process occurs naturally.

So in setting the boundaries of the phenomenon to be researched, we first had to establish the core personnel in the deviance-control process. It seemed reasonable to assume that a population of deviants, or at least people accused of the deviation in question, was essential to the generation of the phenomenon. There also seemed to be no doubt that the police, the courts, and the rest of the legal apparatus were also intimately involved in the process. And while it might be less obvious on a priori grounds, there were good empirical reasons for suspecting that the medical and paramedical programs dealing with drug abuse were also essential to the generation of the phenomenon. Thus we defined our research interest as the chain of situations in which the deviance-control process is worked out, and consequently the populations we selected to study were drug users, law enforcement machinery, and treatment agencies.

Our second problem was to establish what kinds of data would shed light on the deviance-control process itself. There were compelling reasons to adopt Matza's "naturalistic sociology"; put simply, we felt that the existing literature on drug abuse and control was dated, contradictory, fragmented, and heavily weighted toward analysis at the expense of description. Since we felt that not enough was known about the whole phenomenon to support the kind of theorizing and polemicizing that we found in the literature, we set out to construct an account of "what's going on out there." But what kind of data are relevant to what is going on? Data such as psychological tests and questionnaire surveys were immediately discarded as being more relevant to the positivist understanding of the world of deviance than to naturalistic accounts. Clearly we needed data that are more grounded in the "real world." [4] But the methodology literature, which is generally more concerned with theory verification than description, offers few guidelines for finding out what's going on out there.

We did find good methodological advice, however, from some vintage sociologists, particularly Max Weber and W. I. Thomas. In the convoluted methodological debates that characterized early twentieth-century German social science, Weber took the position that the proper objects of sociological analysis are patterns of social action.[5] But Weber had a specific meaning

4. We are using "grounded" in somewhat the same sense as Glaser and Strauss (1966).
5. This was in opposition to those who were arguing that the object of analysis should be cultural spirit (*Geist*) or essences. See Schutz (1967, xvii–xxi, chap. 1); also Parsons (1937, chap. 13).

of "action" in mind. He was concerned with much more than the overt physical movements of a person's body. In fact, he based his entire theoretical work on the concept of social action as *meaningful* behavior (Weber 1957). Thus in Weber's "interpretive sociology" (*verstehende Soziologie*) the primary data are actions—in the sense of behavior situated in a meaning-providing subjective context—which are social in nature. The intricacies of this position are difficult, but what is relevant to our research is that data should not be mere recordings of what is done (in the sense of overt behavior) by the people in whom we are interested, but should include both their outward behavior and the "sense" they make out of these actions and the world around them.

Thus, through Weber, we were led into the admittedly slippery terrain of subjective data. One point that was understood from the beginning, though, was that the "subjectivity" of the accounts we would collect should belong to the subjects of our research, not to us, the researchers. In other words, we were constrained to follow rules of observation, such as value neutrality as specified by Weber, in gathering data.[6] If we admit to the essential subjectivity of our data, however, what then is its epistemological status? Are we forgoing all claims to grasp the "reality" of the drug problem and merely cataloging the dreams and fantasies of the people who are involved in some macabre ritual? This question keeps reappearing whenever it seems that the beliefs of our research subjects contradict our own or other observers' knowledge of the world, and it must be handled very carefully.

It has been nearly half a century since W. I. Thomas first formulated his famous dictum that, "If men define situations as real, they are real in their consequences" (Thomas 1928, p.

---

6. "What is really at issue is the intrinsically simple demand that the investigator and teacher should keep unconditionally separate the establishment of empirical facts (including the 'value-oriented' conduct of the empirical individual whom he is investigating) and *his* own practical evaluations, i.e., his evaluation of these facts as satisfactory or unsatisfactory (including among these facts evaluations made by the empirical persons who are the objects of investigation)." (Weber 1949, p. 11).

584), yet the social sciences still have not accommodated their methodology to this axiom. The point is that at the descriptive level, the only reality we need concern ourselves with is the reality that is experienced by the research subjects. For example, street addicts believe that methadone and heroin are two different drugs. These drugs have certain effects in common (e.g. they are both "addicting," they both alleviate "dope sickness"), but one is essentially "medicine" and the other is a drug to get high with. And when we look at the way the two drugs are used on the streets, we find markedly different patterns. Methadone generally gets used as a "fall-back" drug. That is, it is taken to keep one from getting sick because heroin cannot be obtained (due to scarcity or financial problems) or in order to cut the addict's habit down to manageable size. Heroin, on the other hand, is taken in order to get high, feel good, enjoy life, or whatever. Pharmacologists generally believe that the two drugs are essentially quite similar and note that experienced addicts cannot even tell the differences between them when they are administered under "double-blind" conditions (Martin, 1971).[7] But addicts usually do not take the drugs under double-blind conditions and do not share the pharmacologists' belief. And it is the addicts' beliefs, not the pharmacologists', that determine the usage patterns of the drugs. The addicts' beliefs, then, were real, *as reality is understood on the streets for normal purposes,* and we take it as our research mandate to discover *these* realities.

From Weber and Thomas, then, we began to arrive at some formulation of the kinds of data we needed. Those data would be the actions—taken as overt physical behavior situated in conjunction with its subjective meaning context—of people who are involved in producing the deviance-control process. The problem for a researcher, however, cannot be solved by simply stating what sort of information is desirable. There is still a series of problems about how to find this information.

One major problem is how to discover the "subjective mean-

7. See also Goldstein et al. (1968) and DeLong (1972) for extended psychopharmacological discussions of the comparison between heroin and methadone.

ing" of any act. Weber recommended the *Verstehen* (which literally translates as "understanding") method but failed to spell it out in any detail.[8] We have no simple answers to how to understand what is going on in someone else's mind about a particular activity. As a first step, however, we have employed the "direct contact" method (or participant observation as it is sometimes called) on the assumption that, whatever the problems of understanding someone else's perspective, they are less serious if the researcher is close to the subject, both physically and emotionally, while the subject is engaged in the activity in question (Schutz 1967, pp. 129ff).

Deciding to establish direct contact with our subjects provided us with an overall strategy but did not solve all our problems. Even if we knew what sort of information we were looking for, and how we were going to look for it, we still needed to know how to go about finding the people who would "give" us that information. Thus we had to confront sampling problems which are as fundamental to direct-contact methodologies as to any other.

Sometimes researchers can establish contact with the entire population about which generalizations are intended, but usually they cannot.[9] Where such contact is impossible, they must instead deal with a subset, or sample, of this population. When membership in that sample is determined by explicit rules, those same rules guide generalization from the sample to the population; and when the data being collected are quantitative, and the sample-generating rules are amenable to mathematical formulation, then the rules of standard sampling and inferential statistics determine the process of generalization. In

8. Weber developed his notion of *ideal type* in order to deal with some of the problems of subjectivity. Its value, however, is heuristic and lies in its ability to synthesize and unify a plurality of concrete individual phenomena. It is not a tool that aids the researcher to apprehend those concrete individual phenomena (Weber 1949, pp. 90–104). See Schutz (1967, chap. 3) for an extended discussion of the establishment of intersubjective understanding.

9. It should be clear that we are using population in the formal sense of the universe of people (units) who meet specific membership criteria for the group in question.

our case, however, it became clear that there was no mathematical solution to our sampling or data-gathering problems. We would have to develop qualitative rules.

In studying the addict–street "focus of interest," we used a loose form of stratified sampling to ensure contact with as wide a variety of heroin users as possible. From the very beginning we recognized that, as in "straight" society, there are very pervasive racial cleavages among addicts. In addition, we were led to believe that age grading was also a significant factor in addict "street culture." Crossing race with dichotomized age yielded six sociodemographic quasi-strata: young black, young white, old black, old white, young Spanish-speaking, old Spanish-speaking. Within the scope of our resources, we have treated these groups as autonomous. We used separate researchers for each group and generalized from one group to another only with great caution.

As originally suspected, and as our work in the streets made evident, there is no single "addict community" in our city, but rather a series of enclaves which were loosely knit together by a somewhat more centralized heroin distribution network and shared experiences at the hands of the control agencies. To accommodate our design to this situation we used an informal kind of cluster technique: we attempted to make contact with members of every enclave within the metropolitan area. It was neither possible nor necessarily desirable that the members with whom rapport was first established be representative of the membership of their respective enclaves. Ideally, these members merely provided an entry point into the enclave for the researcher; in practice they provided information, entry, and support, and occasionally they put their own reputations on the line to ease the suspicions of their peers.

While it would be child's play for an individual heroin user to have avoided our scrutiny, we feel confident that we were able to cover most of the major enclaves. Without reliable estimates of population parameters, it was impossible to "weigh" particular observations in any rigorous fashion, but at least we have good reason to believe that our addict sample captured the diversity of the population. It would have taken considerable time and effort to gain access to a random sample, and the returns would have been slight.

Efforts to study legal-control agencies entailed a somewhat different problem. We rapidly discovered that our entrance into agencies involved more time than the actual observation. Random sampling was discarded; given the difficulties of actually getting into an agency, it was feasible only to concentrate on those sections of the target groups which were actually doing the "drug work." In other words, a random sample of legal and law enforcement personnel in Riverdale (the pseudonym adopted for our city of study) would yield a sample of traffic cops, corporation lawyers, civil court judges, law professors, and so on who have very little to do with the legal control of narcotics. Gaining access to all these people would be tremendously difficult, and very little important information would be gained. Therefore we could concentrate only on those lawyers, policemen, and other legal personnel who were actually involved in the processing of drug cases.

We broke the process of legal intervention into three parts —arrest, court processing, and post-conviction—and tried to observe the agencies involved in those three processes as completely as possible. At the arrest level, since there are numerous police forces in our metropolitan area, we were forced to sample and, based on data on where arrests were most common, we decided to concentrate on the Riverdale Vice Squad, which makes a great majority of the drug arrests in our area, and the juvenile officer of a suburban police department who makes all the drug arrests in his town.

The courts were first entered by observing the work of the attorneys who handle most of the drug cases for the local legal aid organization. Having thus gained entry into the court, we were able to spend considerable time observing the prosecutors, public defenders, private attorneys, clerks, and court reporters without any further problems of entry. The State Department of Probation, which has an important contact with the drug problem, was handled by observing intensively three of twelve officers chosen at random, and spending a lesser amount of time interviewing the others.

Treatment control research focused on only one agency, the Narcotics Addiction Unit (NAU) of the Riverdale Mental Health Center (RHMC). Since it was the only sizable addiction treatment center in the city we studied, sampling was never an issue. As can be seen in chapters 8, 9, and 10, though, the Narcotics Addiction Unit is made up of a variety of different therapeutic programs. In addition, each of the programs underwent considerable revision during the four years we observed them. To gather data on the operation of the clinic, we were forced to employ a variety of techniques. At one time or another, researchers sat in on almost every aspect of the NAU operation. Researchers developed and administered the computerized system of clinical records, thereby monitoring the "official" data, and researchers participated in most of the NAU-wide staff meeting structure. But perhaps the most important research tool was good rapport between the research staff and all levels of clinical staff, which facilitated the flow of information between the two staffs.

Our research, then, was not to be conducted in the atmosphere of methodological naiveté that characterizes many participant observation types of studies.[10] It was our intention to use our data to generalize to a population, which we defined as the addicts, law enforcement personnel, and medical personnel who, among them, produce, identify, and deal with drug abuse in a particular metropolitan area. Whatever the sampling techniques adopted to peer into one or another segment of this population, every effort was made to ensure the representativeness of the sample and the validity of the generalizations.

It must be emphasized, however, that our generalizations pertain to the population we studied, which was limited to one metropolitan area. Thus, in a sense, our work is a case study of the "drug problem" in one city. Patterns of drug use and control may be quite different in different metropolitan areas. Proximity to major heroin distribution centers, organizational characteristics of the police, funding available to addiction treatment programs, the prevalence of organized crime, the or-

10. See Liebow (1967, pp. 14–15) for an honest statement of the naive position.

ganization of the court system, and the racial structure of the community are only some of the factors that probably influence the nature of the drug problem. Needless to say, our research was not designed to evaluate the differential impact of factors such as these. Instead, we were interested in documenting one concrete case of these patterns.

But the generalizability of any study is limited to the population from which the sample is drawn. A survey given to a sample drawn from the Metropolitan Boston telephone book would yield results generalizable only to telephone subscribers in Boston; a questionnaire given to a random sample of welfare recipients in Phoenix would yield results generalizable only to welfare recipients in Phoenix. So the fact that our generalizations are limited to Riverdale does not imply a methodological flaw; it is a limitation intrinsic to any methodology that relies on some form of sampling.

Given the research strategy described above, we have still to specify what sort of information we have been seeking. To say that we were concerned with the actors' "subjective meanings" or the "definition of the situation" is vague, and the phrase "perspectives on the drug problem" is not much clearer. We may begin to clarify these terms by saying that we are concerned with the actors' experiential perspective. But this too needs specification. Let us begin by making a crucial distinction between perspectives *of* action and perspectives *in* action.

Sociologists, both lay and professional, specialize in presenting perspectives *of* action. Sociological analysis involves the construction of an account of the "essence" of an event for purposes other than those relevant to the actors who generated the event. The purpose for constructing the account may be academic explanation, moral evaluation, or developing programs of reform or control, but the event becomes an "instance" of a type of the event the sociologist wishes to illuminate. A perspective *in* action is constructed differently. It is formed for the practical purpose of accomplishing the activity at hand. Its formulation is concomitant to the production of the activity.

This does not mean that a participant who is habitually involved in an activity will necessarily produce a perspective *in* action if asked to describe that activity. A perspective provided by a participant to a sociologist interested in "understanding" his activity, for example, is not an account provided for the practical purposes of orienting his own activity. It is a perspective *of* action. The participant's motive for producing the account was not to act meaningfully in the system being described but rather to make the system meaningful to an outsider. It is because of this problem that we could not simply edit a collection of accounts written by clinicians, police, addicts, lawyers, et al.[11] Instead, we had to gain access to accounts of action which were intended to make the action meaningful to the actors themselves or to other actors in the same situation.

Another important difference between perspectives in and of activities concerns their logical structure. As a scientific discipline, sociology is expected to formulate its understanding of the world in accordance with Aristotelian logic (Zetterberg 1965, pp. 87–100). And, indeed, logic is an important tool for the sociologist. So, to the extent that one sociological perspective of action is not logically consistent with other accepted sociological viewpoints, an anomoly exists which is "in need of resolution" (Kuhn 1962, pp. 66–70). The practical actor involved in dealing with his routine world, however, does not concern himself with the logic of his perspective. His perspective in action must serve him to get through his day-to-day life; it must allow him to decide what type of event he is dealing with, what he should do in the situation at hand, who is on his side and who is not, and so on. Logical consistency is not a major con-

---

11. Indeed the sociological literature is rich with material which was produced by "deviants" as perspectives of their own activities. The classic work of this genre is Sutherland's, *The Professional Thief* (1937), an extended essay on being a professional thief which was written by a practicing thief and then annotated by Professor Sutherland. In the contemporary literature, McCaghy et al. (1968) brought together accounts from a wide variety of "deviants." In another recent book (Manocchio and Dunn 1970), perspectives of prison life by a convict and a prison psychologist are intertwined. Each of these books contains important material, but all are *explanations* of activities, not practical understandings. They may help the reader understand the phenomenon, but they do not bring him into it.

cern of practical activity. So our accounts of perspectives in action do not try to eliminate the contradictions, the non sequiturs, and other logical inconsistencies which seem to characterize common-sense understanding of the world.

In this book we have not been concerned with perspectives *of* the various activities making up the drug problem; the reader can find these in popular magazines, newspapers, and professional articles. Instead, we have been concerned with trying to faithfully record perspectives *in* action because we believe they are the closest we can actually get to the phenomenon with which we are concerned.

There are, however, several problems remaining. One of these is that the entities (law enforcement, the clinic, and the streets) which we have termed foci of interest are clearly not homogeneous. The medical/clinical sector, for instance, is comprised of people with vastly different training, resources, and goals. Among heroin users there are many kinds of people with correspondingly different understandings of the world they live in. And the law enforcement apparatus is a highly differentiated system within which highly divergent views are held.

Obviously some process of "glossing" differences between people is unavoidable if generalization is to be possible. When dealing with non-numerical material, though, it is exceedingly difficult to formulate rules for this kind of generalization. In simplified form, it is our goal to reproduce the dominant themes observable within each "focus of interest" while at the same time including enough of the variations to give the reader a feeling for the diversity inherent in the phenomena. Admittedly, such a formulation leaves much to the discretion of the researcher but, to borrow from the terminology of statistics, it is our belief that both central tendency and dispersion are useful guides to formulating any description. We have tried to approximate this in our accounts.

Another problem closely related to generalization is typification. Perspectives in action can be thought of as knowledge that is focused for the purpose of behaving meaningfully in a situation, but just as every individual is unique, so is every situation. To deal with this uniqueness, people habitually typify situations by categorizing any particular situation as a case at hand of some more general type of occurrence (Schutz 1964, pp. 37ff; McHugh 1968, p. 43). If this were the end of the story there would be no problem for the researcher, for he could simply lump together all the situations that were defined as similar and describe a typical occurrence of that sort. Unfortunately, though, situations are not defined simply as "a case of this," but are subject to an open-ended (and emerging) list of modifiers. For example, "making a bust" is a routine "type" of occurrence for the police. But every bust is different: "good" or "bad," with or without a warrant, involving "friends" or "strangers," emerging from immediately preceding events or planned, and so on. In situating the perspectives of our subjects, we have tried to perserve the integrity of the situational definition developed by the subjects, but we were forced, for clarity, to truncate some of these modifiers. Once again we are painfully aware of the discretion being exercised by the researcher and have tried to reproduce the variations we observed in "essentially similar" situations.

If the distinction between perspectives in and of action is understood, we can finally specify the meaning of perspective as it has been employed in this volume. A perspective is the background information employed by a participant in rendering situations meaningful enough to act intentionally within the parameters of that situation. We have been concerned here with reproducing the perspectives of a limited number of people: those who play specific roles in a specific process of deviance control. Therefore, the perspectives we have sought to reproduce are characteristic *of actors,* not unique individuals.[12] Since the amount of personal information available to an actor in a particular type of situation is vast, we have excluded from our accounts of perspectives those elements of the background knowledge that we feel are common to the parent culture of American society. For example, we describe how an addict

12. This qualification can be expressed as: our interest is in *members'*, not *people's*, perspectives. Although we would prefer this phrasing, it requires one to understand the ethnomethodological concept of membership. See Garfinkel and Sacks (1971, pp. 342ff).

deals with the problem of keeping policemen from arresting him, ignoring how he tells a policeman from a fireman, since this latter knowledge is well recognized in the parent culture.[13]

To summarize, we have formulated the following rules for the reproduction of subjective perspectives.

1. THE SOCIOLOGIST'S UNITIZATION OF BOTH SITUATIONS AND TIME MUST BE IDENTICAL WITH THOSE EMPLOYED BY THE SUBJECT. all communication is categorical in nature and reproducing perspectives (as a case of communication) is no different in this respect. We insist that our account of a perspective be true to the concrete categories which the subject employs in day-to-day life. Categories such as "latent pattern maintenance," "mechanical solidarity," and even "interaction" are not appropriate in an account of a perspective, unless it is the perspective of a sociologist which is being reproduced.

2. ANALYSIS OF ACTIVITY OR PATTERNS IS APPROPRIATE ONLY WHEN IT IS THE ACTORS' OWN. Our subjects, to be sure, seek to "understand" the world, and such understanding entails analysis. But the understanding is through "lay physics," "lay psychology," "lay sociology," "lay pharmacology," etc. Clearly it is not only appropriate, but also necessary, to include their lay analyses in our accounts of perspectives. But whatever analysis the sociologist performs belongs in his own work, not in his reproduction of someone else's perspective.

3. PERSPECTIVES ARE NOT CONCERNED WITH THE "OBJECTIVE" TRUTH ABOUT EVENTS. The researcher must present the real story as the subject sees it, not colored by the researcher's "insight." In insisting on this we depart radically from a major tradition in participant-observation research—"muckraking," which appeals to some sociological observers, perhaps because of the inherent ambiguity of most social events. While participants are caught up in their inter-

---

13. One problem with this systematic omission is that it accentuates the differences between the perspectives of our subjects and the view of dominant American culture. It would be equally possible to emphasize the similarities between them, and the resulting accounts would look completely different from those we have presented. This bias can be partially corrected by the reader's assuming commonality of perspectives between our subjects and the dominant culture in areas we have not touched on.

pretation of what is going on, it is possible for the muckraker to see through the facade, into what is *"really* going on." The problem with this sort of enterprise is that what anyone sees in a situation is a function of his own value orientation and goals, and so the muckraker merely substitutes his values and goals for those of his subjects. It is our contention that the world or any of its elements cannot be simply described "as it really is." The muckraker's conception of the truth about the world may be adequate for journalistic purposes, but not for sociology.

4. AS MUCH AS POSSIBLE, THE IDEATIONAL CONTENT OF PERSPECTIVES SHOULD BE PRESENTED AS CONCOMITANT TO CONCRETE ACTIVITIES. Perspectives are not abstractions; they are generated by and for the process of practical action. Thus it is important, when writing an account of a perspective, to show which aspects of an actor's perspective are related to which of his activities. For instance, clinicians have to be aware of the many state and federal regulations covering the operation of a treatment facility, but that information is relevant only to grant applications, on-site visits, and quasi-political interest groups, not to doing therapy with patients.

5. THE USE OF VOICE AND STYLE OF PRESENTATION SHOULD PARALLEL THAT EMPLOYED BY THE SUBJECT. This is perhaps the hardest of the rules to specify, but it is our feeling that much of the way a person thinks is communicated by the way he talks. Within the limits of clarity we have tried to reproduce characteristic styles of presentation—both through the extensive use of quotations and through modifications in our own writing styles which we hope will give the reader a better feeling for the subjects than would be possible by using more conventional academic orthography.

6. VALIDATION IS GRANTED BY THE LAY EXPERTS, NOT THE PROFESSIONAL LITERATURE. The process of reproducing a perspective is necessarily creative. No matter how assiduously the author works within the boundaries of his data, his presentation will go beyond the utterances of any particular subject. Consequently, validation is a significant issue. As a solution, we have taken our reconstructions back to the subjects—the addicts, police, clinicians, etc.—for validation. In order for this to be effective, the reviewer should be told that his judgment as an expert on "the streets" (the police, or whatever) is important and valid, since there is a tendency on the part of most people to defer to academics in reviewing the quality of written material.

Conclusion

Sociological analysis, as Weber noted, depends on the value orientation of the analyst, and conclusions depend on the types of questions one chooses to ask about the world. The scientist is not exempt from this law just because his paradigm directs him to focus on certain questions and to ignore others (Parsons, 1967). To the contrary, the more highly developed a scientific discipline, the more the content of a scientist's analysis will be determined by the paradigm he employs. Nor is this book exempt from this rule. It started with the basic orientation provided by Weber and Chicago symbolic interactionists. Nevertheless, the purpose of this study has not been to present a symbolic interactionist or Weberian analysis, but the kind of data and other information that any number of different analyses of the drug problem could use, depending on the sorts of questions one seeks to answer.

We hope this book has broken new ground in the procedures of reporting field observational studies. We do not claim that it brings sociology up to the status of the physical sciences, but we believe that this method of data reporting will prove useful.

Andrew L. Walker
Charles W. Lidz

References

Becker, Howard S. *Outsiders: Studies in the Sociology of Deviance.*
1963   New York, Free Press.

Cicourel, Aaron. *The Social Organization of Juvenile Justice.* New
1967   York, Wiley.

Cohen, Albert. *Delinquent Boys.* New York, Free Press.
1956

DeLong, James. "The Drugs and Their Effects," in *Dealing with*
1972   *Drug Abuse.* Drug Abuse Survey Project, New York, Praeger, pp. 62–122.

Durkheim, Emile. *The Rules of Sociological Method,* S. Solovay
1938   and J. Mueller (trans.), G. Catlin (ed.). New York, Free Press.

Erikson, Kai. *Wayward Puritans: A Study in the Sociology of De-*
1966   *viance.* New York, Wiley.
Garfinkel, Harold, and Harvey Sacks. "On Formal Structures of
1971   Practical Action," in *The Phenomenon of Sociology: A Reader in the Sociology of Sociology,* Edward Tiryakian (ed.). New York, Appleton-Century-Crofts, pp. 338–66.
Glaser, Barney, and Anselm Strauss. *The Discovery of Grounded*
1966   *Theory: Strategy for Qualitative Research.* London, Weidenfeld and Nicolson.
Goldstein, Avram, Lewis Aronow, and Sumner Kalman. *Principles*
1968   *of Drug Action.* New York, Harper and Row.
Gould, Leroy. "The Changing Structure of Property Crime in an
1969   Affluent Society." *Social Forces* 48(1), 50–60.
Kuhn, Thomas. *The Structure of Scientific Revolutions.* Chicago,
1962   Univ. of Chicago Press.
Lemert, Edwin. *Human Deviance, Social Problems and Social Con-*
1967   *trol.* Englewood Cliffs, N.J., Prentice-Hall.
Liebow, Elliot. *Tally's Corner: A Study of Negro Streetcorner*
1967   *Men.* Boston, Little, Brown.
Manocchio, Anthony, and Jimmy Dunn. *The Time Game: Two*
1970   *Views of a Prison.* Beverly Hills, Calif., Sage.
Martin, William. Personal communication to Leroy Gould.
1971
Matza, David. *Delinquency and Drift.* New York, Wiley.
1964
———. *Becoming Deviant.* New York, Wiley
1969
McCaghy, Charles, James Skipper, Jr., and Mark Lefton. *In Their*
1968   *Own Behalf: Voices from the Margin.* New York: Appleton-Century-Crofts.
McHugh, Peter. *Defining the Situation: The Organization of Mean-*
1968   *ing in Social Interaction.* Indianapolis, Bobbs-Merrill.
Merton, Robert. "Social Structure and Anomie," in *Social Theory*
1957   *and Social Structure,* rev. ed. New York, Free Press.
Parsons, Talcott. *The Structure of Social Action.* New York, Free
1937   Press.
———. *The Social System.* Glencoe, Ill., Free Press.
1949
———. "Evaluation and Objectivity in Social Science: An Inter-
1967   pretation of Max Weber's Contribution," in *Sociological*

Polsky, Ned. *Hustlers, Beats and Others.* New York, Free Press.
1966

Schutz, Alfred. *Collected Papers,* vol. 2: *Studies in Social Theory,*
1964   A. Brodersen (ed.). The Hague, Nijhoff.

——. *The Phenomenology of the Social World.* G. Walsh and
1967   F. Lehnert (trans.). Evanston, Northwestern Univ. Press.

Sutherland, Edwin (ed.). *The Professional Thief.* Chicago, Univ. of
1937   Chicago Press.

——. *The Sutherland Papers.* A. Cohen, A. Lindesmith, and K.
1956   Scheussler (eds.). Bloomington, Indiana Univ. Press.

Thomas, William I. *The Child in America.* New York, Knopf.
1928

Weber, Max. *The Methodology of the Social Sciences,* E. Shils and
1949   H. Finch (trans. and eds.). New York, Free Press.

——. *The Theory of Social and Economic Organization.* T. Par-
1957   sons and A. Henderson (trans. and eds.). New York, Free Press.

Zetterberg, Hans. *On Theory and Verification in Sociology.* 3rd ed.
1965   Totowa, N.J., Bedminster Press.

1 Introduction

The decades since the conclusion of World War II have not been easy times for American society. In that period America has seemed beset by a myriad of internal crises. The cessation of foreign hostilities in 1945 marked the beginning of a period of economic instability that appeared ominous to many Americans. As that crisis passed, the Cold War gained momentum, and the "police action" in Korea fanned the flames of political fear. When the shooting in Korea abated, our hysteria over Communism took the form of witch hunts, led on the international front by John Dulles and on the domestic front by the House Un-American Activities Committee, J. Edgar Hoover, and Joseph McCarthy. The internal Communism crisis burnt itself out by the mid-fifties and the nation had a breathing spell before being hit with Sputnik and the "technology gap" of the late fifties. As if that were not crisis enough, school desegregation and racial discrimination burst into American consciousness via the ugly episodes at Little Rock and Birmingham. On top of all this, urban hoodlums seemed to be banding together into gangs and engaging in violent terrorism. The juvenile delinquency crisis ran out of steam in a couple of years, but the fledgling racial confrontations of the 1950s grew into one of the major crises of the sixties. During the Kennedy administration the crisis took the form of the southern problem, but by 1965 racial strife had assumed a dramatic new pose: urban rioting. The "long hot summers" of 1965, '66, and '67 were periods of national agony which few who were in the cities at that time will ever forget.

Then by 1967 a new problem emerged, one that threatened to shake the structure of American society as fundamentally as did the racial crisis. Significant numbers of the nation's youth and young adults began to turn their backs on America's most cherished ideals and instututions. And they were not just the children of America's outcasts; they were the sons and daughters of bank presidents, professors, union officials, and politicians. They were our nation's future. Their rebellion has crystallized into three major crises: the hippie phenomenon, student disruptions, and the drug epidemic. By 1973, each of these crises was on the wane.

DRUGS

Each crisis generates its own literature. The bargain shelves of bookstores are filled with books on Communism, juvenile delinquency, civil rights, and other now discarded issues from our recent past. Some of these books were written for the general public, others for the professionals that America generally relies on to "deal" with problems. The aim of most of these books was to define the "real" nature of the problem and then suggest the appropriate remedy.

The Drug Crisis is no exception to this pattern. The number of books dealing with drug abuse has swelled in the last four years, and the torrent continues. These books take several forms. One common type is written by a medical doctor and is geared to the parents of adolescents. It contains descriptions of various drugs used by adolescents today, a "symptomology" for each drug so the parent can recognize what his child is using, and some advice on how to deal with the child once the parent suspects he is using drugs.

Another type presents accounts of the drug scene which range from lurid, largely fictional sensationalism to the results of social scientific studies. The purpose of these books is to "tell it like it really is." They go "where the action is" to bring back the "often shocking truth about drugs in America." Their value to the public lies in their attempt to look at drug usage as it occurs and where it occurs, not as it is reported in a doctor's or lawyer's office.

A third type deals with the way our society has responded and should respond to the drug problem. Since most responses at the official level have been legal, medical, or educational, these books focus on the legal status of drugs, medical systems for the treatment of drug abuse, or educational approaches to the prevention of drug abuse.

Although these three kinds of books differ radically in goals and styles of presentation, they share at least one important feature. In each, the author attempts to give the reader certain "facts" about the reality of drug use. The referent of these "facts" varies from book to book. In one book the reader may be told that one symptom of heroin use is chronic drowsiness. In another he may learn that at present there are between twelve and fifteen million marijuana users in the United States or that barbiturates present a far greater abuse potential than opiates, yet they are subject to only cursory legal control. These statements, which are presented as facts, are nothing more than conclusions which are the end product of a long process of "intellectual digestion" on the part of the "expert."

The existence of books by experts hardly needs justification. Indeed it is the role of the expert to reach conclusions in specialized fields and then communicate those conclusions and attendant facts to either the general public or a special audience. But this presents the reader with a mixed blessing. To be sure, the picture he is getting is being drawn by an expert who has had some experience with the subject matter being portrayed and thus may be assumed to be competent to draw conclusions on the basis of that experience. But on the other hand, the reader is not being exposed to the subject matter itself so much as to the conclusions of the writer.

This model of the author–reader relationship is well entrenched in contemporary society and works quite well when the reader is more interested in the experts' conclusions than in the everyday events that make up the subject matter itself. But it has one inherent limitation. Since the presentation of data is structured to support the generalizations the author is presenting as facts or conclusions, the reader is offered only the possibility of either accepting or rejecting the author's generalizations. It is a rare book about crises that permits the reader to reach any of a number of conclusions for himself.

A New Approach

This book represents a new approach to the Drug Crisis. Basically it is an attempt to describe, rather than analyze, the routine events which made up the heroin problem in one particular metropolitan area in the late 1960s and early '70s. Writing a description, though, is much easier said than done. First we had to establish what should be included in a description of the heroin problem. Clearly the behavior of addicts and other heroin users should be described. But there had to be more than that because numerous cases can be cited of large groups of people routinely doing illegal things which never become a "problem" as drug taking has. So we had to include the people whose job it is to define and cope with the problem: the legal and medical agencies which identify and process the wrongdoers.

Taken together, these three groups—addicts, law enforcement personnel, and clinicians—constitute a system in which events are generated, recognized, and responded to as "drug related." Other groups obviously are also involved in the Drug Crisis—parents, lawmakers, students, media personnel, social scientists, and so on, but their contribution to the phenomenon is largely transmission and interpretation of information, rather than production of the events in question.

Deciding to focus on the system composed of heroin users, agents of the law, and treatment personnel gave us a cast of characters for our description, and ensured that the description would include accounts of the way "problem-indicative" events are dealt with. But this still did not tell us what a good description of the system would look like. Two important questions remained: What is the goal of such a description, and out of what kind of information is such a description constructed? The answers to these questions provide the key to the rest of this book.

THE GOAL OF DESCRIPTIVE ACCOUNTS

Since it was our concern to provide information about the heroin problem in such fashion that the reader could form his own impressions and conclusions, it followed that the goal of our account would be to reduce the distance between the reader and the phenomenon itself.[1] Upon reflection, most readers

---

1. We are not using distance to mean linear space, but to mean "that which stands between two objects (or a subject and an object)."

should see that not only are they denied direct access to the world of heroin use and control, but also that their ways of finding out about that world are limited to channels which provide only abstractions, not representations. In other words, the events of heroin use and control occur in shooting galleries, alleyways, patrol cars, treatment clinics, criminal courts, and other places that most citizens never see. So how is the citizen to find out about those events? He must rely on newspaper stories and articles, speeches by public officials, word-of-mouth stories, books by experts, and other haphazard sources. The specific information presented by these sources may be more or less true, but each step in generating and transmitting puts more distance between the reader and the subject matter. At each step the initial information is abstracted, generalized, interpreted, or put into some other context. When it finally reaches the citizen (general public, policy makers, and even most social scientists), the information has lost most of its descriptive value (however great its interpretive power).

Our goal of reducing the distance between the reader and the subject matter aims to bypass this process of digestion and provide information the reader might gather if he had direct access to the system itself. Needless to say, complete elimination of the reader–phenomenon distance is impossible, since we, the authors, necessarily stand between them. And it is impossible for us to act as mere windowpanes, since we must transform real, tangible, living situations into sequences of words, which is not a passive transmission of information but an active creative process. But we, as authors, have tried to reduce as far as possible the distortion and information loss which would be introduced through interpretation and analysis.

A Revaluation of Subjective Data

The goal of reducing reader–phenomenon distance raises some important issues about the kind of data we can use to create our description. Any description is necessarily a reproduction of the appearance of the thing being described. This simple statement, however, carries a hidden question which is seldom explicitly realized: "Appearance *to whom?*" In other words, although we are used to thinking of a thing's appearance as belonging to the thing and independent of whatever observer there might be, upon closer consideration it becomes clear that appearance is not a passive characteristic but more a relational "appearing to someone." So our description of the world of heroin use and control is necessarily a reproduction of the way that world appears to someone. But to whom?

It would be possible for us to fill this hypothetical observer role in a number of ways. We could describe the heroin world as it would appear to a research sociologist, an informed citizen, a newspaper reporter, a black militant, or even an interested foreigner. Each description would be different because each of these hypothetical observers would see (and find interesting) different aspects of the subject matter. But to describe the heroin world as it would appear to *any* hypothetical external observer is to put that hypothetical observer between the reader and the subject matter itself, which runs contrary to our primary goal.

Therefore we find ourselves in what appears to be a difficult situation: we propose to describe the appearance of a social system but preclude any hypothetical external observer to mediate the appearance. There exists, however, a perfectly reasonable solution: we can describe *the phenomenon as it appears to itself*. The events of the world of heroin use and control are all generated by people, and those people have an intimate understanding of the events they generate. Their understandings of that world, although different from the understandings which any hypothetical external observer might reach, are nonetheless equally valid. Validity, however, comes to mean different things to an observer and a participant. For the observer, the validity of information is determined by the way it was collected, while for the participant it lies in its relation to practical activities. In compiling our description, then, we decided to use only the information (be that specific or general) which is used by the participants in the system we were describing to understand that system.

But, it may be pointed out, such information is essentially subjective, and any good description should be objective. This presents a serious problem which requires serious consideration. Debate on the relative merits of subjective versus objective data is especially difficult, because both these words are somewhat ambiguous. The term objective commonly has two meanings: it is a synonym for "real," or (in its more sophisticated form) for "information whose value is independent of the foibles of the person(s) who collected it." Subjective has the opposite meanings: "biased," or "impressionistic." So the statement, "He seemed to be a pretty bright guy," would be termed subjective, while "He scored 125 on the Stanford-Binet Test," is objective.

This example illustrates the problem with objective description. In order to produce an objective account it is necessary to use "standardized" categories to describe subject matter and it is precisely this standardization that we wish to avoid. In other words, the Stanford-Benet Intelligence Quotient Test makes a complicated series of assumptions about what intelligence is and how it is best assessed. Someone who is well versed in the use of such a test is presumably familiar with all these assumptions and would give any objective score a specific, limited meaning. For those who are unfamiliar with intricacies of the instrument, however, the meaning of a score is vague at best and more often lost.

So to use objective data about the world of heroin use and control would be to use categories of description which are alien to those who live the phenomenon, and thus to increase the distance between the phenomenon and the reader. We have therefore avoided all descriptive categories that are not used specifically by those who make up the drug world to understand that world.

An Objective Description of Subjective Phenomena

If we admit, even proclaim, that the information we have used is uncompromisingly subjective, what is the status of our completed description? Is that, too, subjective? Since the objectivity of a study is determined not by the kind of information used but by the way that information is collected, compiled, and presented, an answer to this question entails a detailed discussion of our research methods.[2]

The authors of this book were all on the research staff of a large, federal- and state-financed drug abuse treatment clinic (the Narcotics Addiction Unit, or NAU) in a moderately sized metropolitan area (which we have called Riverdale) during the period 1969–73.[3] Three of the authors (Gould, Lidz, Walker) are sociologists; the other (Crane) is a lawyer. The task of the research staff was to evaluate the impact of the treatment clinic on the heroin problem in the Riverdale metropolitan area. Toward that end we organized our research to determine the everyday appearance of the system and to monitor changes in the functioning of the system; we then related these changes to the presence of the clinic in the system. It should be emphasized, though, that the present volume is *explicitly nonevaluative*. In producing evaluations, a specified set of criteria is applied to data which have been tailored to meet the requirements of those criteria. Needless to say, this kind of categorization is not appropriate in this descriptive undertaking.

Our first step was to organize the research staff into three divisions—one to study the narcotics users, another to study the law enforcement and correction agencies, and the third to study the clinic. In nontechnical terms the goal of each of these study groups was to arrive at the broadest possible understanding of the system of heroin use and control from the point of view of the participants they were studying, consistent with a sound methodology. The basic elements of that methodology were:

2. A more technical discussion of our methodology can be found in the preface to this volume.
3. Throughout this volume we have used pseudonyms for both people and places. The decision to do so was not easy because they necessarily add an element of artificiality to our description. Still, many people gave us information on the assumption that their identities would never be disclosed. And since some of them could possibly be identified if even the geographic location were given, we were forced to use pseudonyms even for locations. In an area as sensitive as narcotics use and control, few of the participants have anything to gain from publicity.

1. Sampling design, the specifics of which is left to each division, should ensure contact with as wide range of subjects and situations as possible.
2. Information should be so collected that the researcher has some idea of both the situation in which it was generated and the intentions of the subject(s) who produced it.
3. Contact between researcher and subject should be recorded verbatim and as quickly as possible in order to minimize pre-interpretation or selective recall by the researcher.

Given these guidelines, each division set about organizing its own research efforts.

For researching street users the initial problems were twofold: How do we locate the heroin-using population, and how do we get information from users once we have located them? Neither of these problems admits to a simple solution, but both are mitigated by using ex-addict researchers. Judicious selection assumed, the advantages of ex-addict versus naive professional researchers are:

1. They have considerable practical knowledge of where heroin users can be found.
2. They are far more likely to be trusted by the research subjects than a stranger would be.
3. Their presence on the streets is less disturbing to the street situation.
4. They can provide entry or vouch for other never-addicted researchers.

Needless to say, there are drawbacks as well to using ex-addict researchers.

1. They are probably more inclined than naive researchers to rely on their own pre-knowledge instead of going out to find out what is going on.
2. They are less likely to know what sort of empirical information is valuable and how to present it as such.
3. Ex-addicts cannot be expected to be comfortable and effective in dealing with all users. It is assumed they will be able to

work most comfortably with the users that were around when they were shooting heroin, and least effectively with the newcomers or drug users from other ethnic groups.

None of these drawbacks precludes the use of ex-addict researchers, but taken together they suggest that close cooperation between ex-addicts and professional researchers will enhance the probability of gathering useful information.

Eventually, the team doing street research came to include five people—four black ex-addicts (three male and one female) and one white (young, male) professional sociologist. It was assumed that black researchers would concentrate on black heroin use, and the white researcher would concentrate on white heroin use. Of course, these boundaries are not impermeable, but social segregation is almost as prevalent on the streets as in other sectors of American society.

Contact with subjects was initiated on the basis of two semi-independent criteria: geographical location, and type of user. The geographic criterion deals with the fact that, in Riverdale, heroin users are neither centrally located in one geographic area nor uniformly distributed throughout the metropolitan area. Instead, they form enclaves distributed throughout the city. The "Wylerton crowd" is largely independent of the "Regulars on the Avenue," who in turn have little to do with the "Old-Timers around South Street." It was our aim (which we largely realized) to have some contact with each enclave in the metropolitan area.

As for type of user, it should be obvious to the general public by now that heroin users do not form a single homogeneous class. Even an outsider would expect considerable differences between old-timers and newcomers, blacks and whites, inner-city and suburban, affluent and poor, addicts and experimenters. Each of these types, and others that an outsider would not expect, is recognized in the world of heroin. Our guideline was to initiate contact with as many types of heroin users as possible. For instance, when we needed data on adolescent users, we selected a high school outside the city and sent our young white sociologist to find out what was going on. He knew a few students there and explained to them what he wanted to find out. They in turn introduced him to other drug-using students to whom he explained what he was doing. Over the course of several weeks he talked with over fifty students, went to parties, learned where some of the heroin users hung out, and in general learned about the world of heroin use in a suburban high school. Although three weeks may sound like a relatively short period, it must be remembered that the researcher had by that time had several years' experience in working with narcotics users and personally knew enough figures in the local culture to command a certain amount of trust. Also, the absolute number of narcotics users in this school was less than twenty-five.

For the researcher in the field, the general question to be answered was, "How do these people understand what it is they are doing, and the social context in which they are acting?" Each researcher understood this to be an essentially open-ended question requiring him to evaluate what questions were appropriate in what setting. For example, techniques in the city for evading the police are well refined, while in suburbia there is very little to say on the topic since it is not seen as a problem. Thus it was left to the individual researcher (in collaboration with the rest of the team) to decide what kind of information was needed from each contact as long as the general methodological rules were followed.

In all, contact was established with over 250 heroin (or other opiate) users. But these contacts included many different relationships between the researcher and the subject. In some cases, contact was maintained for over three years, while for others the contact was only a ten-minute discussion. The modal contact took the form of making the acquaintance of a user and then seeing (and talking to) that person intermittently for several weeks while the researcher was probing that particular "set."

Research into the operation of the legal machinery took a different form. There was never any question about being able to locate the legal apparatus. Instead, since we had limited manpower, the problem was that only part of the entire apparatus could be studied.

Since the legal system processes only arrestees, and only the police make arrests, we decided to begin by studying the police. An analysis of police data showed that the vast majority of all drug arrests in the larger metropolitan area are made by the Riverdale Vice Squad, so we limited our observation to that particular police detail. For six weeks our observer (Lidz) spent full time with the Vice Squad. The squad consisted then of eight full-time detectives, and our observer spent time with all of them, although somewhat more time was spent with the most "active" detectives.

The next step would have been to gather data on the operation of the courts, but none of the sociologists on our staff had a working knowledge of legal procedure, so while a researcher with the appropriate skills was being sought, we went ahead to study the Probation Department. Probation was selected over either prisons or parole because a preliminary analysis showed that the Probation Department was more involved than the other correction agencies in the overall workings of the court, and in Riverdale (at least) convicted narcotics users are more likely to be given probation than a jail sentence.

So our observer (Lidz) spent six weeks collecting data on the operation of the Probation Department. This meant spending every day on a nine-to-five basis in the Probation Department offices—watching interviews with probationers, sharing coffee breaks, and being part of the office. This permitted observation of probation officers in action and extended discussions between the researcher and the subjects.

Observation of the courts began with the Riverdale Legal Aid Bureau, whose lawyers represent a large percentage of the narcotics-using defendants in Riverdale. By this time, a lawyer (Crane) had joined our staff, and he and the sociologist were in court with one or another of the seven Legal Aid criminal lawyers every day for a two-month period. This gave the researchers an opportunity to observe the operation of both the lower and superior courts. Initially, we planned to observe formally both the Legal Aid and the Public Defender's offices, but this proved unnecessary since the back rooms of the court afforded sufficient informal contact with personnel from these agencies to assess their modes of operation. The lower-court prosecutors were then observed for four weeks.

Where research takes the form of observing formal agencies, one of the researcher's biggest problems is knowing when to terminate observation. For example, the Vice Squad could be studied profitably for several years. Yet we had only several years to study a range of different agencies. As a solution to this problem we arrived at a general criterion for termination: at the point where the everyday events (as defined by the members themselves) begin to look routine to the observer, the time has come to wind up operations—fill in any missing areas of information and begin to withdraw from that agency. While this is admittedly a subjective criterion, it is necessarily so, since it is only when the researcher and the subject agree on the "routineness" of everyday occurrences that the researcher can claim an assimilation of at least the main outlines of the background knowledge the subject is using in his work.

As was the case with the street research, our observers in law enforcement and correctional agencies did not go into situations with prestructured questions. Their task was to reconstruct the way in which these agencies process narcotics users, so the principal method of collecting data was to watch the operation of the system, listen carefully to the information that was passed from one member to another, ask for explanations, and then watch to see if the explanation offered to cover one situation seemed to fit in another.

Research into the drug treatment program shared many of the problems found in the street and legal apparatus research, but had one further complication. We assumed from the onset that drug treatment would look quite different from the perspective of patients and the perspective of staff, and yet both of these groups are essential to the very existence of a treatment program. Thus our strategy had to permit the collection of data from all segments of the treatment system.

Obviously, lines of communication had to be established between the research staff and each of these segments. But maintaining adequate rapport with the various segments is not an easy task. When researchers listen carefully to patients, the clinical staff is inclined to suspect the scientific validity of the research, but when researchers collect their data from clinicians, the patients (and to a certain extent the counselors as well) come to see the research staff as part of the "clinical establishment."

As a response to this problem, the treatment research team divided responsibilities. The research director (Gould) assumed responsibility for gathering information about the policies, decision making, and inner workings of the NAU clinical power structure. Since there were strong organizational pressures for the research director to spend a lot of time with the various clinical directors, he had access to data that might have been lost otherwise. Information from the patients and some of the lower-level staff was gathered by ex-addict program members on the research staff (some of whom also worked on the street research) and by a staff member who was a former methadone nurse. Five students (two undergraduates, two graduate nursing students, and one medical student), who were not identified with either the clinical program or the research staff, collected additional information on specific questions.

Data on the NAU took several forms, most of them conventional but some unusual. One important source of information was the patient data file. The research staff designed, supervised the administration of, and processed intake questionnaires and progress reports on all patients who entered the NAU. Although the quality of the patient progress reports was variable, some of the information (especially basic demographic information) turned out to be quite reliable. Gathering this information also gave us considerable access to patients.

A second source of data, especially for the Methadone Clinic, was direct interviews. One special study involved in-depth interviews with all patients enrolled in the Methadone Program during a two-month interval in 1972. Smaller interview schedules were administered to selected patient cohorts at other times. Formal interviews were also conducted from time to time, with all segments of the NAU clinical staff (counselors, nurses, and directors of the Methadone Clinic, the Outpatient Therapy

Clinic, and the Screening Unit). As described in chapter 10, only in Zeta House were formal interviews impossible. However, it was possible to interview Zeta House members and former members in other settings.

Notes from participant observations were, in most cases, our richest source of data about clinic operations. Observation of the Methadone Clinic was conducted by the former clinic staff and patients. Other members of the research staff spent from two weeks to several months as participant observers in the Outpatient Therapy Clinic, the Screening Unit, and Zeta House.

A considerable amount of data was also gathered in NAU staff meetings. Not surprisingly, various segments of the staff got together often to discuss problems. There were regularly scheduled component directors' meetings, senior staff meetings, and junior staff meetings. In addition, all three clinical components occasionally held "retreats" lasting from one day to a week, in which the "state of the program" was considered. Additional ad hoc committees were formed either formally or informally, from time to time, to deal with specific issues. Research personnel (usually the director) were often present at these meetings, for administrative reasons or "just to watch what's going on," and while others doodled, the researchers took notes.

Further information about clinical-staff perspectives on treatment came from a variety of documents written by the staff. These ranged from memoranda and clinical proposals to grant progress reports and even scholarly papers. Although these documents tended to highlight the perspective on treatment which the clinicians wished to project to the public, they are nevertheless important. It was this public image, much more than the internal family quarrels, to which other segments of the Riverdale community and the various governmental agencies responded.

The least systematic but perhaps most candid source of data about internal NAU operations came through informal social contact between research staff and clinical staff and patients. As an integral part of the NAU, research personnel spent countless hours drinking wine, going to lunch, going to parties, and hanging around the back halls where most of the intrigue and a good deal of the decision making went on. It was because of information from these sources that we were able to differentiate between "public" and "private" patient and staff perspectives on the NAU.

A Reconstruction of Subjective Phenomena

No matter how valid the data that a social scientist has to work with, it is useless unless it can be compiled and presented in a meaningful form. Thus our second major task was to convert what was in our piles of notebook papers, stacks of tape recordings, and assortments of statistics into the description that was our goal. To do so required confronting two remaining problems: reconciliation of contradictions and style of presentation.

Of these, the problem of contradictions is the more difficult. The nature of this problem is perhaps best explained by analogy. Say we are interested in producing a description of a particular person as seen through the eyes of the people who know him the best. If all of these people told us that he was really a bright guy, then the description, "He is a bright guy," would stand as a valid description. But if other people also told us that he likes to pretend he's an intellectual, then we would have to say, "According to some, he is bright, but others think he just pretends to be of intellectual status." Obviously, as the number of contradictory assessments increases, the complexity of the reconstructed account rapidly increases, unless the author takes steps to reconcile the contradictions. But the process of reconciliation generally involves either discarding one or more of the conflicting statements as false and accepting the other(s) as true, or else synthesizing the various statements into a new statement which is presumably truer than any of the original statements. Going back to our analogy, the reconciliation could take the form, "He is a bright guy, although some people don't recognize it"; or, "His intelligence is such that people form different impressions of it." But neither of these forms of reconciliation is compatible with our purposes, because each relies on the external observer (or analyst) to decide what the "true" statement is.

This problem can be mitigated, however, by partitioning the population into groups in which there is some consensus about the nature of the system of heroin use and control, and then letting each of these groups speak for itself separately. So instead of synthesizing all our data into a unified description, we have constructed a series of descriptions which taken together constitute a "nonintegrated" description of the overall system. Each description is of one aspect of the overall system, as seen through the eyes of the people who manage that subsystem. Since the system is highly differentiated, we have had to construct a number of different accounts: street life, police work, the courts, the probation office, and drug treatment as seen by several different treatment modalities. Each account offers the reader a different perspective on the overall system, while focusing on the activity that is located at that particular part of the system. For instance, the chapters on police work are accounts of the way the Vice Squad views its work, but the narcotics detective's understanding of both the clinical treatment system and the streets is included as well, since these data are important information to the narcotics detective.

Eventually, then, the reader is offered not only each actor's understanding of his own activities, but also the way his activities are understood by others who are in the same system, but viewing those activities from another perspective. So, in addition to the Vice Squad's understanding of its work, we present the clinicians' and narcotics users' conceptions of the way the police work. Where contradictions arise, it is up to the reader to cope with them. The line between fact and opinion is largely arbitrary, and in a system as differentiated as that of heroin use and control, there are bound to be differences in conceptions of the nature of things. To reconcile the differences would be to impose an unnatural order on our accounts.

We were left only with the problem of style, which is not trivial, since style is the form in which information is presented. Were our goals and data conventional, it would have been an easy matter to select a conventional style of scholarly presentation, complete with graphs and tables at appropriate intervals in the text. Such a presentation, we felt, would have forced too much structure onto our material. And yet we lacked criteria to select any single alternative. So we have written different sections in the style that seemed most appropriate to describe the subject at hand. Within broad limits of comprehensibility, we have tried to use the same vocabulary, voice, and grammar that our subjects used. For instance, when discussing topics that are emotionally charged for the subjects, we have left the emotional undertones in our accounts.

Thus the reader will encounter a number of different styles in this volume, ranging from first-person narratives and vignettes to conventional third-person descriptions. Each chapter is an experiment in the presentation of data. We expect that some styles will be more successful than others, but only time and our readers can tell us which.

Finally, in presenting the perspectives that follow, we have adopted a policy designed to guarantee anonymity and confidentiality. We have used fictitious names for all our characters, and any similarity to existing individuals is merely coincidental. Furthermore, the characters whom the reader will encounter are not existing people masquerading under fictitious names. They are composite portraits drawn from those people we came to know. We have found that this policy facilitates research, while granting a deserved measure of personal privacy to those people who so generously allowed us into their lives.

2 Street Life

Since the early 1960s Riverdale has had a large heroin-using population for a city of its size. In 1970, law enforcement and health officials were estimating the addict population at 1500 with an additional 1000 nonaddicted heroin users; by 1973 the number of addicts was privately being estimated at a much lower figure, but most officials agreed that there was still a large number of nonaddicted users. This chapter is about the way these people understand themselves and their world.

Gathering data from heroin users is not as difficult as many people would imagine. To the extent that the researcher is accepted as trustworthy, he has access to a wealth of verbal material. The countless hours I spent in the bars, poolhalls, back alleys, and parking lots were filled with loose, rambling conversations in which heroin users talked about everything from sex to pharmacology. Needless to say, not every user I talked with opened up but, since I was around for three years, many did. Several ex-addict research associates provided supplementary information without which this section would not have been possible.

The problem was to integrate all this material into a unified document. The way a hardened, older black addict experiences the world is vastly different from the way a white high school neophyte user does. And yet both are heroin users and each has to have a place in our description. It would have been possible to introduce a number of different "types" of users and let each speak for himself, but this would serve only to create a new set of discrete user stereotypes. Instead, I chose to phrase the entire description in the third person, which avoids the pitfalls of stereotyping and preserves a measure of continuity from subject to subject. The reader should not, however, be lulled by the style into a false sense of objectivity. Throughout the entire *account, users' perspectives are being presented, not the sociologist's version of objective reality.*

One additional stylistic element needs mention. There is no colloquial equivalent to the terms addict or narcotics user on the streets. Terms such as junkie, smack-freak, dope fiend, or chipper are used occasionally, but more often as adjectives than nouns. In fact it is uncommon to hear one user refer to another in terms of his habit (although users commonly refer to non-users as "straight"). In constructing my description, however, I needed a term for narcotics users, and since they themselves use "dope fiend" as often as any other term, that was the one I selected. In street usage, it has no pejorative connotations. Indeed, it is so ludicrous that every time it is uttered there is an implicit parody of Harry Anslinger. At any rate, value judgments should not be read into its use in what follows.

Perhaps the reader should have a warning. In this chapter, heroin is presented in a favorable, although somewhat ambiguous light. Needless to say, such a presentation is at odds with prevailing social science, legal, or journalistic accounts of heroin and the dope life. But what is being presented is the users' account, not an academic account. And it should not surprise the reader to learn that people who use narcotics generally have positive feelings about the drug. Whether this is all rationalization, self-delusion, or valid experience-based understanding is not at issue.

WE WERE sitting in a bar in a residential section of town one afternoon. When the barmaid made her way to our booth, Ronny and I ordered beers; Ellie ordered a rum-coke.

"You kids got I.D.'s?"

I started to produce mine, but Ronny (who was underage) spoke first.

"Look, sweetheart, when I come in here, I want some peace and quiet, not hassle. You run on back and ask Ernie. He'll tell you we're old enough to take care of ourselves."

The barmaid went behind the bar and said something to the bartender. The exchange was brief, and then she was fixing our drinks.

"How come the bartender will vouch for you?" I asked.

"The old bastard ought to," replied Ronny. "We sell him

cigarettes for two dollars a carton. Then he sells them to his regulars for three-fifty a carton."

By then the barmaid was back with our drinks. I started to pay, but Ronny motioned to me not to, and told her, "Tell Ernie we'll settle up later."

Ronny and Ellie were both, in their words, dope fiends. He was short, with the build of an out-of-shape athlete. She looked older than Ronny and was quite attractive. Both were dressed in nondescript fashion, he in an old army jacket and corduroy pants and she in bell-bottom jeans and a corduroy coat.

We talked for a while about recent police activity. The word on the street was that over fifty bench warrants had been handed down the day before. Ronny had been dealing heroin for a couple of months and was afraid one of the warrants had his name on it. I told him that if he should be arrested, I would do what I could to help. Then he asked:

"Why do you do it, Andy?"

"Do what?"

"You know, hang around with dope fiends and go through all the hassles."

I was taken a bit off balance. When I first started studying street culture I had developed an elaborate answer to the expected question: "Why do you do it?" But then nobody ever asked me, as though dope fiends found it perfectly natural that sociologists and psychologists should be constantly intruding into their lives. But finally, after almost a year's work, the question was being asked.

"I don't know Ron. I used to think I knew, but I'm not so sure any more. You got to admit, though, it sure beats working for a living."

"Yeah, but aren't you supposed to write papers or something?"

"I guess so," I replied.

"Well, what are they about?" Ellie asked.

"I don't know," I answered. "I haven't written any yet."

Ronny shot a look of pure exasperation at Ellie.

"No, this is square business, man," Ellie said. "What kinds of things are you going to write about?"

"Well, if you really want to know, I guess I'm going to write about heroin and being involved with drugs from the point of view of the people who use them."

"How come?"

"Why not? I mean, there's usually two sides to any story, and the doctors and politicians have already had their say. So why not ask the dope fiends about the view from the bottom?"

"I suppose so," Ronny replied, and the conversation trailed off. We sat around making rings on the table with our beer glasses, and then split up. Ronny had to make a connection over on the Avenue, and Ellie asked if I could give her a lift to their apartment. On the way over, I asked her why she had not responded when I told them what I was planning to write about.

"Well, I guess I can dig the idea, but I don't think it'll work."

"Why not?"

"Dope fiends are dope fiends and nobody wants to hear what they have to say. People close up to a junkie. They think they know what he's all about, when they really don't know shit! It used to bother me that I couldn't ever talk to anybody straight about drugs, but now I don't worry about it much. They'll never understand, but if you've got the energy you may as well try."

Looking In

Nobody is born with a spike in his arm. People might say that some kids were destined to become dope fiends from the first breath they took; it's in their genes, their *kharma,* the stars, or whatever. Everyone has a theory about why people become dope fiends, but when you're on the street, it's easy to see that dope fiends are made, not born.

Before going any further we ought to clear up what is meant by the name "dope fiend." We're talking about heroin and the people that take heroin. A lot of people are into heroin—all kinds of people—and in a sense they are all dope fiends; anyone is who is looking forward to that next taste of heroin. But a real dope fiend is someone whose life is built around taking dope. It's like being a musician: there are lots of people who play the piano or the clarinet or the guitar and they are all musicians, but when you talk about a real musician, you usually mean someone whose whole life is his music.

We were saying that nobody is born a dope fiend. Even people who eventually become users first have to see dope and the dope life from the outside. Of course it's not as if a person is completely ignorant about heroin and the people who are into heroin until the first time he sticks a needle into his arm. Heroin is part of the world that everybody grows up into. Most kids first hear the terrible stories about dope in the papers or in a lecture in school. The details are usually pretty hazy, but the message is clear: dope is slavery. The latest twist in this game is incredible: kids sit down on Monday night to watch the Dolphins play, and there is some football player—who is probably doing speed and pain killers and who knows what else—telling them that "he gets high on life and that's enough."

There comes a time, though, when heroin gets a chance to speak for itself. Most kids, by the time they are starting to grow up, have learned that heroin is so bad that they can't help having just a little curiosity about the stuff. All the talk they hear about heroin from their teachers doesn't just go in one ear and out the other; they may believe that heroin is bad just the way they believe that Communists are bad. But kids, especially as they get older, aren't isolated from dope by 10,000 miles the ways they are from Communism. Sometimes a kid only has to look at an older brother or sister to see heroin; sometimes fate takes him through a twisted path to his first meeting; and maybe a few will never see it. But when a person sees heroin and listens to it speak, he hears a very different story from what the cop who lectured at his school told him.

My father never lived with my mother, but he used to come by to visit me and my mother. I especially remember one time—I guess I was eleven or twelve—when he took me aside and told me, "It looks like you're growing up and maybe you need some spending money." So he took out his wallet and gave me all the money in it—two dollars. My older brother was living pretty good then—dealing shit and stepping fast—and he used to give me twenty dollars just to shine his shoes. It didn't take many smarts to figure out where the action was at.

For some kids, especially those from the ghetto and the ones who never have much when they're growing up, heroin tells a story of the fast, good life. The guy down the street who drives a Cadillac and never gets up before noon is a dope fiend pimp. The hustler who won $450 at the poolhall last night is a stone junkie. And the dude with the most outrageous clothes and a girl on either arm is the local dealer man.

Of course, the same kid may also see his brother stealing from his parents, or the cops working over the junkie down the hall, or an overdosed junkie lying in his own vomit in the alley. Heroin doesn't offer a sure-fire line to the top. Instead, it seduces by offering a chance—a chance to make it, to be big, and to be on top of it all.

But that's just one of the stories that heroin tells. Some other people are in their late teens or twenties before they have a chance to find out about heroin for themselves.

When I went to Boston to go to college I got an apartment with three other girls. God, we had some high times. Two of the girls were speed freaks and I had done diet pills in high school, so soon the four of us were all doing speed together. We did so many strange things and met so many strange people . . .

It couldn't last, though. One of the girls had a junkie boyfriend and he was always around leeching off us. It seems so funny now. We used to sit around, speeding at a million miles an hour, and tell this guy that heroin was turning him into a worm. I mean I was really down on heroin. But he was really cool—God, was he cool. If we had been speeding for two or three days and were frazzled into pieces, he would just be so cool and slow and saying we ought to slow ourselves down a bit. I'd tell him that I was alive and free and that he was dead, and he'd just laugh and say that we all start dying the day we're born.

This is another story that heroin tells. A lot, maybe most, of the people who first become involved with drugs do so with every intention of never touching heroin. Maybe they take diet pills or smoke reefer for three or four years and they realize that it hasn't done them any harm. In fact, it starts to look like their parents and teachers had no idea what they were talking about when they gave all those lectures about drugs. But these kids still believe that heroin is one drug that can drag you under. Then they meet some people who are doing heroin and someone tells them, "Listen, you just gotta be smart. Sure heroin can fuck you up, but all you have to do is stay on top of it. You can't get strung out unless you do it every day. So be cool—just do it on weekends."

Most kids are suspicious of this kind of talk. But when they hear the same story a couple of times and when the people telling the story have just been doing heroin on weekends for maybe a couple of months and are obviously not strung out, they start to think that maybe the official line is as false about heroin as it is about marijuana or pills. That doesn't mean that they will all go out and buy some heroin and a set of works, only that heroin starts to look different.

The official line about heroin always comes back to that thing about getting hooked; the posters in school say that when you start messing around, the first thing you know, you're hooked, and then you've got no more control. But the friends who are talking from experience sure don't look like they've lost any control. In fact, they keep saying that it's easy not to get hooked, as long as you're careful. So the kid who has come this far starts to see heroin as just another drug that can be handled with a little care, instead of instant slavery. Sure, messing around with heroin is risky. There's no denying that some people get strung out. But most of the people who are fooling around with heroin *aren't* strung out. Maybe some of them are taking it every day, but even they say they could quit any time they want to. So maybe you're taking a chance when you fool around with heroin, but if you've had good advice from friends who have been trying it and haven't had any problem, you shouldn't have any problem staying on top of it. And it sure sounds like it must be an incredible high!

These are only a few of the stories that heroin tells kids. However the story is told, though, the point is that heroin is worth trying once or twice. Of course, not everybody gets a chance to hear heroin's story. Some people may never realize that they know, or have had contact with, a dope fiend. Other people might be so afraid of heroin from public propaganda that they could never listen to heroin's story with any kind of an open mind. And still others listen to what heroin has to say and then decide that heroin isn't for them.

Still, there are some people who are interested in the idea that they might try it without harming themselves. This doesn't mean that all of these people will become dope fiends. They have a long way to go before that happens. A person who is interested in trying dope still has to figure out how to get hold of some, how much to take, and how to do it up. If he knows and trusts someone who is doing heroin, simply asking for a taste solves these problems. But this may not always work since he may not be willing to turn to any of the users he knows; or the ones he knows may not be willing to turn him on to heroin. To be sure, most dope fiends are usually only too happy to satisfy other people's curiosity about heroin; but not always, either because they don't want to see that person become involved with heroin, or they're afraid that he's an informer.

What it comes down to, then, is that as a person becomes interested in the idea of trying heroin, if and when a good opportunity arises, he'll try it if he is ready to. If the kid has a lot of friends who are doing heroin and who want to turn him on to it, then it takes less interest on his part to get involved than it does for the kid who does not have much firsthand contact with users.

Eventually, though, just about anybody who is really interested gets a chance. Maybe the kid who is interested has been badgering a friend to get him some dope and that friend finally came through; or perhaps he was finally at a party where some people he vaguely knew were doing dope and they offered him some. Whatever the case, he suddenly finds himself face to face with heroin.

TRYING IT OUT

Just about everybody feels shaky the first time he is eyeball to eyeball with a bag of heroin. No matter how convinced you are that it is a good idea, you can't help having a knot in your stomach. Maybe you smoke a joint or drink a little wine, just to ease your mind a little. Then finally the guy who got you the dope says, "Look, there's nothing to it. You just snort it up." He takes out a tiny spoon, fills it with the powder, and inhales it deeply into one nostril. He repeats this a couple of times in each nostril and then sits back, relaxed. You watch him closely, trying to pick up clues, but he doesn't show anything. Then he says, "OK, you ready?" You nod. He fills the spoon, puts it under one of your nostrils, and says "Now!" You breathe in deeply and you've done it. There is a sharp feeling in your nose which, your friend explains, is caused by the quinine. Other than that, you don't feel anything else. He sticks a spoonful of powder under the other nostril and you snort it with a little more confidence.

After taking another couple of snorts, you sit back and try to figure out what the drug is doing. There is still a stinging sensation in your nose and a sharp medicinal taste in the back of your throat. Other than that, though, there don't seem to be any special feelings that come from the drug. Maybe you wonder if you've taken enough. But then, you figure, there's no sense in overdosing the first time around. So you wait. And after a while the apprehension you felt starts to fade. There's really nothing to it. You relax and start to feel confidence returning. You glance over at your friend to see what he's doing. He is sprawled in a chair, staring at the wall and tapping a slow rhythm in time with the music on the radio. You decide that he must have taken a lot more stuff than you did, but that's OK.

Then, just as everything is going so well, your stomach starts acting up. Your first thought is that it must be that wine you drank, or all the junk you had been eating earlier. As the nausea increases, you get your friend's attention and ask him about it. He waves it off, saying it just happens sometimes and not to worry about it. This isn't very reassuring, but there doesn't seem to be anything to do but ride it out. Your body is feeling funny and you decide to get up. Your legs feel a little funny, but you are more worried about the nausea, which is getting worse, so you make your way to the bathroom where you vomit. Then the thought occurs to you that maybe this stuff isn't all that it's cracked up to be.

The nausea subsides, bringing feelings of relief. You find

yourself back in a chair, feeling much better. The body problems seem to retreat a bit and you start to feel that the worst is over. Your friend asks you how you're doing and you tell him that everything is under control. He smiles briefly and goes back to his world. You withdraw too, and try to feel the changes you are going through. The feelings you have are pleasant; all your secret fears were baseless. Heroin hasn't hooked you, it just lets you relax and enjoy yourself. You feel a bit like you're not quite attached to the outside world, and when you close your eyes, all kinds of dreams float into your mind. With the exception of a nagging feeling of itchiness, a sense of peace settles over you. You go along with it until that too recedes and you start noticing things around you. Your stomach starts to feel just a bit uneasy and there is a slight tremor to your hand. You notice that it's getting late and you really should be moving along.

Of course, everybody's first time is different. The kind of advice the person has had will influence his reaction. And the more experience he has had with other drugs, the less uptight he is likely to be. In addition, both the amount of heroin and the way it is taken have an effect on the high. Sometimes an experimenter won't take enough dope to really feel any effects, and then he is left with the idea that the whole dope thing has been wildly exaggerated.

At the other extreme, some people have their first encounter by way of direct injection. They might be told by their friends that the only way to get really high off heroin is to shoot it, so they get themselves tied-off and shot-up. In this case, reactions are more immediate and extreme. Right after the dope is injected, there is a flash that cuts off almost all thought and leaves the body cold and tingling. Then a numbness starts in the pit of the stomach and works outward to the arms and legs. Nausea and stomach cramps follow rapidly and vomiting may start before you can reach the bathroom. Numbness seems to seep into the brain which is still flashing from the rush, bringing with it undefined feelings of warmth and peace.

The difference between shooting and snorting heroin is largely in the way it comes on. Snorting produces a gradual effect; shooting produces a rush. A rush is like instant orgasm. It electrifies every nerve in your body, and then slowly ebbs away, leaving you drifting along in a peaceful quiet. After the rush, the effects of snorting and shooting are about the same.

After he comes down, the experimenter is back in the same world he started in, but there's a difference: he has tried something that most people wouldn't dream of doing. All of a sudden he has had firsthand experience with something that most people just talk about. In the light of this experience, he usually rejects most of the clichés about heroin. He knows that one taste hasn't turned him into a dope-crazed fiend; it doesn't hold any magical power over him. But at the same time, it wasn't the instant paradise that some people talk about. In fact, it didn't even seem to present a very tempting challenge. In all, it's a confusing experience.

Hey, Bobby told me that you finally tried some of his smack.
Yeah.
Is that all you can say—"Yeah"?
I dunno, it's hard to say anything else. I mean, I spent the whole night staring at my shoe.
Did you find out anything interesting about your shoe?
No.
You sure sound excited by the whole thing.
Well, I guess I dug it, but I'm not sure it was worth getting excited about.

You never can tell how a person is going to react to the experience of trying heroin. Some people feel that their curiosity has been satisfied and they have no real reason to ever try it again. Others may come to feel that, on the whole, the experiment was worth it, and if it can be safely repeated it might be done again, but certainly not any time soon. Many people have a lot of trouble dealing with the nausea involved in heroin use.

Probably most of the people who try heroin for the first time interpret their experience in these ways. For these people, taking dope was an adventure that might be repeated in the future but which certainly didn't mean that the experimenter intended to get into a thing with heroin. Some may never try it again; most will.

But what really interests us is those people who interpret their first experiment as deserving another. It's not that their first experience was so pleasant or so meaningful that they simply have to repeat it; first experiences with junk are almost always hard to figure out. So these people deal with confusion about their first experience by further experience.

In talking with their friends they find their experience was fairly typical for a first try, and that when they are a little more at ease it all gets better. So maybe the next weekend they try it again. Of course, they don't want to try it again too soon because it's important not to do it often enough to get strung out; but waiting a week seems reasonable.

The second experience is likely to be different from the first in that the experimenter now has some notion of what the drug will do. So instead of simply sitting back and then figuring it out later, he can begin to understand what is happening while it's happening. When the nausea hits, he knows it will pass and he can look forward to the high that follows. When the high comes on, he can groove with it, knowing that it will end leaving him intact.

Usually, then, the second experience with heroin is more clearly enjoyable than the first. And after his second high, the user begins to gain confidence in his ability to continue heroin without picking up a jones or becoming known as a junkie. Having just become involved, he usually sees heroin as an exciting new addition to his life. There is a kind of pride and excitement in being part of something that's the object of so much attention. And at this point it seems that no real commitment or change of lifestyle will be necessary.

CHIPPING

So after a while, those who continue to fool around begin to fall into a pattern of occasional use, which is called chipping. A chipper is someone who has some kind of ongoing involvement with heroin and the drug scene, but who doesn't have a habit.

A chipper takes heroin when it is fun, easy, convenient, important, or for whatever reason—if only to relieve boredom. Getting high is a thing to do occasionally in the course of an otherwise straight-seeming life. It might be that a chipper usually meets the same bunch of kids at parties on Saturday nights and they all get high together. Or maybe a girl gets off with her sister in New York once a month. Or maybe the chipper has a friend who deals smack and occasionally gives him a bag to enjoy. The possibilities (as they say) are unlimited:

> I didn't know you had ever done skag!
> Yeah, when I first came to Riverdale I moved in with a chick who used to dip and dab and she first got me off.
> Was she strung out?
> Not when I moved in, but she picked up a jones after a couple of months and I moved out 'cause she was selling my shoes.
> Did you do any more stuff after you moved out?
> Well, you know, I'd see her around and I was working, so I'd buy a couple of bags and we'd get off together. But I didn't really have any connections so it was just when I ran into her. But then she moved in with a real heavy-duty junkie and started whoring, so we never met and I was scared to get into that whole thing, so I kinda quit using shit myself, except on rare occasions.
> You mean you just up and quit because your old lady got strung out?
> You gotta understand, man, that I really dug heroin and I could see myself sliding into the same kind of thing that Bonnie was into. It's just that she was about six months ahead of me. Plus I started playing [bass] with the Diamonds and none of them were into stuff, so I cut it loose.

To a chipper, heroin is an amusement, a diversion. He may dig stuff, but his life is mostly the same as it was before he tried it. He has a job (or is a student), plays basketball with the other kids in the neighborhood, spends money on records, and goes out with straight girls. Like the movies, heroin is fun to do when you have the time and the money.

But being a chipper also provides an entrance into the world of dope. One thing about dope is that you always have to get it from somebody else. So even the chipper has to make connections, and even though politicians say that it's easier to buy dope than cigarettes, it's not quite that simple. Probably the easiest way to get dope is to know and be trusted by someone who is a regular dealer. Failing this, it's best to know and be trusted by someone who has no problem acquiring dope and is willing to pass it along. Otherwise, the chipper is going to have to spend a lot of time in the streets finding someone who will sell him dope or else just get it when he can. The kinds of connections a chipper works out depend on his own situation and the way dope is dealt in his area of town. If three of his high school buddies are dealing steady, then he's all set; but if he's new in town and has short hair and wears suits, then it's going to be harder. In the same way, if he happens to know people who have been free of police harassment it will be easy for him to buy, while if the cops have been busy and paranoia is rampant, then there will be less loose dope around and people will be much more uptight about new faces.

One of the first things that anyone learns when he starts using drugs is that connections are necessary, so they are always on his mind. Say, for instance, Johnny connects from Bill, a high school friend. Now one day Johnny goes by, but Bill doesn't have any dope, so Bill says, "Let's go down to Split's place. He'll have some." So they both go over to Split's and get off with him. Split seems to be an up-front kind of guy, so the next time Johnny wants to get off and can't get in touch with Bill, he sees Split on the street and tells him he's looking to get high. They head back to Split's and get off. While they are at Split's, Carole shows up and wants to buy dope. She and Johnny check each other out, and the next time they meet on the streets, they go back to Johnny's and get off together.

In this fashion, a chipper learns to make his way around the set. He learns how and where to connect, who to trust and who to stay away from. A lot of the learning comes the hard way. When he is too anxious or greedy, he gets burned by receiving bad dope or no dope at all for his money. Other people leech off him. He gets set up for ripoffs. Sometimes he gets charged outrageous prices for his dope. All of this is learning, but not everybody falls prey to the same dangers. Like anywhere else, the person who knows how to take care of himself will have fewer problems than a fool. And, even more, the treatment you get depends on the friends you have.

Getting Into It

People say that once a person has shot some heroin and fooled around with street life, heroin starts dragging him down in some sort of a demoniacal way. But that certainly isn't the way it looks to the person who is living that life. From his point of view, learning about dope means learning about a bunch of new possibilities and problems. In a way, it's like a kid coming to college for the first time. There are a lot of ways that he can relate to college. He can become a gung-ho student going to all his classes and attending lectures and trying to be successful as a student, or he can try to get by with the least possible involvement, or he can decide that college just isn't his thing and drop out. But even these possibilities aren't clear-cut. At some times a college kid might be really interested in his studies, while at other times he couldn't care less about the whole thing. Or he might even drop out and then return again several times.

In the same way, a kid who is getting into dope sees that there are a lot of ways to be involved with it. If he doesn't like what he sees in it, he can just pull out. And some do. Or, if he is interested in dope, but doesn't like the "opportunities" that are open to him, he may continue to dip and dab without trying them out. Or he may feel that dope is treating him right, and slowly it becomes an important part of his life. But it's not a matter of clear-cut decisions. Sometimes a kid gets into chipping in a heavy way, but finds that after spending the cash he had around, borrowing money from friends, and maybe even ripping-off money from his parents, the well eventually runs dry. So after a run of a couple of weeks, he cuts back to a more moderate level that he can afford. Or, alternatively, a person may be using stuff for a while and then feel that his job is slipping away, or a girlfriend gets busted, and so he quits, only to end up using stuff again six months later.

What most straights don't understand is that there is no set way of life that is common to all heroin users. It's true there are some ways of life (like hustling) which many dope fiends slip into at one time or another, but for every junkie pimp in the world, there is at least one chipper who gets up at seven o'clock every morning to go to a straight job. Chippers come in all sizes and colors. One may be a brother from the blackest section of town who has a scholarship to Harvard but gets off with his high school crowd when he's back in town. Another may be a working girl who hangs around with a dope fiend and sometimes gets off with him, a white kid from the suburbs who goes downtown to cop and catch a little action on Friday night, a VW salesman, a musician in a rhythm and blues band, or a construction worker.

Heroin can be many things to many people, but each person has to figure heroin out for himself. The way a person uses it depends on what he is looking for from the drug. Some people get most of what they want from straight activities, so they only taste the stuff when they're at loose ends, or frazzled, or in some way cut loose from their normal activities.

No, heroin isn't much of a big thing for me. Sometimes when my woman and me get into a knock-down fight I head down to the Sliding Gate. And my old friend Jo-Jo shows up and he knows why I'm there. So he says, "James, you look like you need to get high." And that's about it. Like I say, it's no big thing.

Other people seem to stay involved with dope to balance off all the straight parts of their lives; they just seem to get choked up by having a job and going to school at night and trying to put a little money in the bank and so they need to be a part of something that is fast and loose. These people are in a tough spot, though. On one hand, they like the thrill of doing something illegal and glamorous, but on the other hand they've got a lot to lose, not only if they're caught by the police, but also at the hands of other addicts. So these people try to play a safe game: they seldom cop their drugs on the streets or talk dope with strangers. Instead, they buy all their dope from one discreet source (usually at higher prices) and get off only with a small circle of friends. They usually snort their dope rather than shoot it, since they wouldn't want their boss or wife to see tracks from a spike.

Another kind of chipper is a person who has a lot of contact with people who are doing drugs steadily. This might be a girl who goes out with dope fiends, or a barmaid at a dope fiend hangout, or a numbers runner whose business associates are into heroin, or even a counselor in a youth program. This kind of person may not be very interested in dope, but since he has ready connections, he takes a taste every now and then when he's in the mood.

And then there are the people—mostly kids, it seems—who really dig drugs. They start smoking reefer when they're twelve. By the time they're fourteen and fifteen they are doing barbs all week long and acid on weekends. They snort their first smack when they're sixteen and by the time they're seventeen they're chipping regularly.

Why sure, you remember last year when they busted those kids in Wylerton with the acid factory? That was my buddies—the Committee. Now that was some group of stone freaks. We were going to flood Wylerton with acid.
How come you weren't busted?
Well, I was involved in other things at the time . . .
Were you doing much acid?
Ho-ho, was I doing much acid? I was so electric that I used to be able to plug my guitar amplifier into my belly button! They used to call me Mr. Acid at Wylerton High, before I got thrown out.
Were you doing acid and smack at the same time?
Not really. I was dealing acid and smoke to the kids in school, but by then I was into stuff. See, my stepfather just couldn't deal with having an electric stepson, so they made me come to the Narcotic Addiction Unit. Now you know as well as I do what kind of drag the NAU is, *but* I did broaden my social horizons and incidentally made some dynamite connections.
So you had never gotten off before you got sent to the NAU?
No, but all I heard there was how great smack is. And it is. I really liked it. I dug the big cops-and-robbers scene. Slinking around—making furtive gestures—nodding off at parties.

For these kids, heroin is a kind of game. Of course, they are involved in a lot of different games: their family, school, the counterculture or whatever. But heroin is a particularly pleasant game. It provides a certain status, pleasant feelings, and a challenge.

For white kids in particular, becoming involved with heroin provides them with a key to a world which is normally closed to them. It brings them into contact with people who are living outside the law; people who are doing the kinds of things that parents warn their children about, and having an exciting time at it; people who have skills and knowledge that kids never learn in school.

But it is not like each chipper works his thing out with heroin once and for all, and then never changes. In the last year or so the quality of the dope on the streets has gotten so bad that a lot of people who were chipping heavily a year ago have cut down on their use. It isn't worth it any more, except on a once-in-a-while basis, they say. A chipper doesn't have a habit, so he is free to take stuff on his own terms, according to his own needs. He might get off three or four days in a row when an old buddy is in town for a while, and then not do any dope for a month. And there are a lot of people around who got into heroin a little too heavily, picked up a jones, and then got hip to what was happening and cut back to Saturday night chipping.

What it all comes down to is that a chipper is a person who has control over his heroin use. Some chippers are newcomers who haven't lost control yet, while others have been into stuff for quite a while and have seen what happens when you lose control. But however he maintains his control, the chipper is a person who gets to enjoy his drugs without having to spend all his time chasing the bag.

Getting Strung Out

From all we have said it may seem that heroin is really pretty harmless; but it isn't, mainly because it seems that way. The guy (or girl) who is fooling around with stuff starts to get in trouble when he starts to lose respect for the power of heroin. Say a person has been dipping and dabbling with heroin for a while. At first he was fearful of that white powder and had a cardinal rule that he would not do it any more than once a week. As time goes on, he finds that he has settled into a kind of routine of doing stuff just about every Saturday. He knows that he doesn't have any kind of a habit, because he is never sick on Sunday or Monday and it's not like he lives the whole week just waiting to get high on Saturday. It's just that come

Saturday night he feels good and goes out and gets high. Now after a while, he might begin to feel a little funny about being so uptight about this rule, because he gets to know a lot of people who are getting high more often than once a week, and they aren't strung out. So maybe sometime when he's on vacation, or when he has a fight with his woman, or he hits on the numbers, he gets high some time during the week. After breaking his rule once, he might get a bit worried and be sure not to break it again for awhile. But then he breaks it again and again, and he finds that it still doesn't seem like he is getting messed up. So the guy gradually comes to feel that all that talk about getting strung out is mostly just bullshit. He begins to feel that ironclad rules are unnecessary and all that's necessary is common sense and caution.

So now we have this guy who has been into dope for maybe a year, and he digs it. He thinks he has the whole thing pretty much under control. He has been regulating his use and hasn't gotten strung out. The problem is that there's always that temptation to do just a little more stuff and see if it keeps getting better. It's not something he *has* to do, just a curiosity. But usually there are checks on this curiosity. It's only possible to do a limited amount of dope and still take care of schoolwork, a job, or the responsibilities of married life. As long as a dope fiend is paying for his dope from his regular spending money, he can afford to buy only a limited amount. And it's possible to do only a limited amount of dope before straight friends, parents, teachers, or others who are in a position to make life rough, find out (or suspect), and start to make trouble.

As long as a person has these checks and responsibilities, he may never have any problem with dope. But when and if they start to lose their hold on him, heroin is always ready to move in. It can happen in different ways: heroin may sneak up on him while he's not looking, or he may go off on a long spree which ends up with him strung out.

Say this guy who has been chipping along gets laid off. His boss tells him, "No sweat, we'll take you back in a month," and gives him a small bonus. Now he knows that he doesn't have to go out and get another job, so he figures he'll just lay up for the month—take a vacation. If his woman is working, though, he can't blow town for a while, so he finds himself on the street with money in his pocket and time to burn. The most natural thing in the world is to get high! Pretty soon, two weeks have gone by, and he's been high every day and he's spent all his money. So maybe the next day he just hangs around with no change in his pocket, feeling nasty. One of his junkie friends takes pity on him and supplies him with a bag, gratis. The next day he doesn't do any dope, just to prove to himself that he isn't strung out, but the following day he borrows twenty bucks from his old lady, since it sure is a drag being on the street with no change at all. He turns the twenty into thirty at the poolhall, but spends twelve on dope. Two days later he's flat broke again, and now his wife won't give him anything. He goes three days without any dope—just hanging around, and then a junkie friend asks him if he knows anybody who wants a color TV. He finds somebody who will give him $140 for it, and the junkie will sell it for $80, so he pockets $60. That money lasts him for a week, and then it's time to go back to work. But now when he goes to work, he finds that he is really looking forward to that shot every night. A month later his wife asks him what's happening and he tells her nothing, but resolves not to do any more dope for awhile, and the next day he feels like shit—runny nose and hands shaking and his eyes hurt. He takes the day off from work but his boss is suspicious of something. He can't get to sleep that night, and he knows he doesn't dare take another day off, so he cops a bag the next morning and does it up before going to work. In this case, heroin has snuck up behind this fellow and grabbed him. He never had an intention of doing that much heroin and probably was pretty surprised to find out that he was strung out.

But take another example. Say we have a girl, call her Connie, who is maybe eighteen or nineteen. She comes from a large family—six kids—and her father left when she was four. Her mother receives welfare, but another man has moved in with them. Connie works in the laundry at the hospital and brings her check home to mama every week. Then she meets a dude named Sweet Pie. Now Sweet Pie is some kind of a flashy guy.

He's dressed to the teeth and wears a Panama hat in the summertime. Everybody in town seems to know Sweet Pie and has a word for him when he passes by. Say Connie falls for Sweet Pie in a big way, and they start spending a lot of time together. Maybe some of her girlfriends tell her that Sweet Pie is just a junkie pimp. So she asks him about all those girls he seems to know so well. Sweet Pie laughs and tells her that they are just girls that he helps out every now and then when they get in trouble. If Connie is willing to believe Sweet Pie's story, her mother isn't, and when she hears that her daughter is running around with "that pimp," she throws Connie out. After bouncing around with her girlfriends, she ends up staying at Sweet Pie's place.

Even when she was living at home Connie knew that Sweet Pie was using dope, since she had been getting off with him regularly. As soon as she moves in with him, though, she starts getting off at least once or twice a day. She stops caring about her job and gets fired. That's no problem, though, because the $68 a week that she was making was pennies compared to the money she and Sweet pie are spending. For a week or two after losing her job, they live fast—sleeping until noon every day and then cruising the city in Sweet Pie's Buick until late at night. They stay constantly high on stuff and cocaine.

Then comes the fight. Connie catches Sweet Pie with another woman and gets mad. He slaps her around and calls her a lazy, fat-ass bitch. She walks out on him and finds a girlfriend to stay with. But the next morning she's so miserable that she has to borrow money to buy some heroin. Over the next couple of days she tries to figure out what to do, and goes into debt for $75, most of which she spends on stuff. She tries to see Sweet Pie, but he tells her he's got a new woman. So after talking to some of the girls she met through Sweet Pie, she decides to try hustling. That night she turns two tricks: the first goes well, but the second one beats her and then refuses to pay. With no one else to turn to, she runs to Sweet Pie, who gives her a bag of dope to calm her down, and listens to her story. Then he explains that he has a woman, but he is willing to help her out if she is going to hustle. In fact, he tells her, she can probably do pretty well as a hustler if she has somebody to take care of her. So Connie finds herself turning tricks to support a habit.

These two stories oversimplify getting strung out, but they point out that just as there are different ways that people get into dope in the first place there are also different ways that people get strung out: sometimes a gradual, hardly noticeable increase in use up to a point where the person is forced to accept the fact that he has a habit—sometimes an extended spree which everybody knows is going to lead to a jones.

But whether it's fast or slow, getting strung out always comes down to having time, money, and connections. It's a simple fact that you can't get strung out unless you take a lot of dope on a daily basis, and in order to do so you have to have connections to get the dope, money to pay for it, and time to do it.

A connection is simply a guy to get drugs from. But there are all kinds of connections, some good, others unreliable. A good connection is easy to contact and always has dope when you want it; an unreliable connection is a "sometime" source. When he is just messing around with stuff, an experimenter needs connections, but they don't have to be very good. A sometime source is good enough for a taste every now and then. Sometimes an experimenter's connection isn't even a dealer, but a go-between, or a friend who cops an extra bag occasionally. But nobody ever got strung out with those kinds of connections. Doing a lot of stuff requires a good pipeline to the dope, and that means having at least one, but more likely two or three, steady, reliable sources.

There aren't any special rules for making connections. It is simply one of the most important things about dope use. Anybody who can't make good connections will never make it with dope. He just doesn't know how to take care of himself.

Time and money, though, are a different matter. Doing dope seriously takes quite a bit of time. There's the time it takes to cop dope, and then all the time that is spent simply being high. By and large a person who has some family obligations and holds a full-time job or goes to school has too many demands on his time to be able to do enough dope to pick up a habit. What happens then is that as a person gets deeper and deeper into dope, he cuts more and more of his straight obligations loose. For kids, the first thing to go is family obligations. They spend less and less time at home, and when they're home they are just sleeping or nodding off in their rooms. After-school activities go, and even in-school time is spent copping and doing dope.

But in cutting these obligations loose, the user is also cutting himself off from his financial resources. For kids, these are usually his family and perhaps a part-time job, while for older people they are primarily jobs, but also husbands or wives and parents. A kid can usually manage to work his parents and older brothers or sisters for a couple of bucks when he needs to, but when he's not spending much time at home and nodding out when he is home, then parents and kin get harder to hustle. They're mad at him all the time, and he's lucky if he can even get some peace and quiet at home.

Older people depend more on jobs than family for spending money, but they run into the same problem. As dope takes up more and more of their time, it is harder to take care of business on the job:

Hey Billy, I haven't seen you at the Horseshoe. Aren't you tending bar anymore?

No. I got fired.

What happened?

Oh, you know. I was just working afternoons, and Sonny was stopping by all the time and we was getting off in the back room. I guess I was fucked up a lot of the time and the boss got pissed off. Said I was giving away too much booze. So he canned me.

It is ironical that the more time a person spends copping and doing dope, the less money flows in from straight sources. Since there are very few straight sources that are fertile enough to provide for a heroin habit, anybody who is using dope on a regular basis is more or less forced to turn to the hustles to pay the bill.

But it is a lot easier to work out a hustle than a lot of people think. The entire heroin street scene is built on the assumption that everybody involved in it is hustling. So usually the deeper a person gets into dope, the more he finds himself surrounded by hustling. Naturally he will find himself being hustled more than ever, but it also means that he has a lot more opportunities to learn about hustling than any straight Joe.

Hustling is a fine art, a way of life—not just going out and ripping off an apartment every now and then. And hustlers like to talk shop together. Those nights when three or four dope fiends are hanging around drinking wine, conversation always comes around to get-rich-quick schemes and new variations on old hustles. Stories are passed around about the best way to beat such-and-such a situation, what to do when a deal goes sour, or the mistakes that so-and-so made.

For a kid who is just getting into hustling, these conversations are like lessons. He gets a chance to hear all the angles before he actually goes out to try his hand. But knowing what to do isn't enough—it takes experience to develop the nerve and reflexes of a good hustler. Fortunately, experience is as easy to come by as theory. Most hustles are run by two or more people. Crib cracking, for instance, usually takes at least two people, one acting as a lookout and one working inside, as well as a fence to move the goods and maybe somebody else to pass the checks and credit cards. Although most dope fiends have regular partners in their hustling, there is always room for a newcomer who can fill in when one of the regulars is in jail or otherwise occupied.

So someone who is starting to get into dope seriously needs more and more money, but at the same time he gets a lot of help on the street in learning to hustle for that money. Hustling isn't easy work—in fact, it's harder than most straight jobs—but it's custom-tailored for dope fiends. Hustling requires spending a lot of time on the streets, talking with other hustlers, being in the right place at the right time, and being ready for anything. But a good dope fiend is doing all these things anyway. So becoming a good dope fiend is the same thing as becoming a good hustler.

Making It As a Dope Fiend

Apart from dippers and dabbers, and chippers, and Saturday-night-get-high types, a real dope fiend is a guy who has accepted heroin as just about the most important thing in life. To understand him you have to understand how he relates to his heroin. Doctors and judges and social workers all explain this relationship as "addiction" and go on to talk about tolerance and abstinence syndromes, and all that's probably true, but it misses what the relation really is.

Take any Joe off Wall Street and ask him if he's strung out behind money, and he'll say that you can't get addicted to money, and besides he works to make money because he needs to have money in order to be able to live the best he can. But just take a look at this Joe—money is absolutely central to his way of living. Sure, other things may be important to him. He may even say that some things, like his family or his good name, are more important to him than money itself, but this doesn't change the fact that just about everything he does from day to day involves either making or spending money. And what would happen to him if he was cut off from money? He'd be a bum in no time at all. He'd be miserable. He wouldn't have any idea how to get what he wants or needs from the world.

A dope fiend's habit is the same kind of thing. Getting high is like a pivot point between the dope fiend and the world. Dope is no more of a goal for a dope fiend than money is a goal for a Wall Street Joe. Like money, dope provides the user with a way of life. Everybody, straight or hip, wants the same things: happiness, comfort, security, freedom from hassles, and respect. The big difference is how they go about getting these things. A Wall Street Joe goes out and makes a lot of money as a way to relate to these things; a dope fiend uses dope. When he's high, everything fits into place; when he's not high, he's taking care of business so he can get high again.

So whatever the medical definition of addiction, for a real dope fiend dope is a way of living, a life to lead. But this is only part of the story, because comparing dope to money doesn't do justice to the emotions an addict has for his dope.

Spider, you've seen it now. Why don't you hook up with one of those sweethearts of yours and just lay back a bit?

Can't do it; I already got a mistress.

Yeah? I didn't know that.

Sure, she comes in a bag and cost $6 a throw. Sometimes she treats me like dirt, sometimes like a king.

That's a pretty melodramatic line.

Maybe. But when she treats me right ain't a woman in the world that can stand up to her. And, when I cry, I cry for heroin.

Dope isn't just a thing, it has a personality of its own. Sometimes it plays hard to get, sometimes it's so sweet you could cry, and sometimes (when it's absent) it makes you miserable. An affair with heroin involves all the same emotions as an affair with the most desirable woman in the world: love, hate, joy, contentment, fear, desire, and longing. Being strung out on heroin isn't simply a matter of bodily needs, it's like being emotionally involved with another person.

There is a setting in which practically every sure-enough dope fiend carries out his love affair with heroin—the streets. The streets are where the action is: bars, sidewalks, candy stores, poolhalls, back alleys, rooming houses—any number of places where groups of dope fiends can get together without harassment. They are the dope fiend's territory, where he cops dope, hustles, hangs out, eats, plays, hides out, and sometimes sleeps. They are his home.

All people need places in which they can comfortably operate. Straight people have their own kinds of territories. They have private homes, office buildings, private cars, and expensive restaurants to take care of business and pleasure. But entry into these places is only for those who can buy their way in using money or prestige or background. But your standard American dope fiend blows most of his money on dope, hasn't any prestige, and trades his background away early in the game, so he is excluded from the territory of straight America.

So what is he left with? Those places where he doesn't have to buy his way in. But that still leaves a lot of room. Most cities are filled with public places where it is possible to spend a lot of time without paying for it. And these are the places that dope fiends naturally gravitate to. A bar where it is permissible to nurse a fifteen-cent beer becomes a favorite meeting point for a clique of dope fiends; a candy store owner realizes that he can make good money if he allows dope fiends to hang around; the poolhall is always a favorite because day or night there is some action; the alleys near liquor stores are almost certain to contain a few people sipping wine or rum-cokes after dark; areas of the park which are not patrolled by the police are nice places to catch a nap, read the paper, and enjoy the weather; malls of shopping centers are nice places to watch the flow of humanity and perhaps boost packages which shoppers leave unwatched while they make phone calls. And then, of course, there are always the sidewalks, where you can find almost anything if you are in the right place at the right time.

The thing about the streets which makes them so attractive is that they are always there and always open. They belong to dope fiends just the way dormitories belong to college kids. Even users who have the bread and respectability to make it in other social sets spend a lot of time on the streets because that is where the people he needs to know are. Unless he is very special, a dope fiend off the streets is like a fish out of water: he can't make connections to get dope, hustling is difficult without the various services the streets offer, it is difficult to conceal himself in a world he doesn't belong in, and (maybe most important) he can never feel comfortable and relaxed in the straight world. So a good dope fiend knows the street like the back of his hand (which he is likely to know very well, since the veins along the back of the hand are particularly accessible). This means he knows who are the people on the street, where the action is, and what will be going on.

Because of the way the police operate and the general difficulties in living outside the law, one of the first rules of street life is, "know who you're dealing with." This applies to all aspects of life: the guy you buy your drugs from (or sell drugs to), the guy you sell hot TV's to, the guy you share a bottle of wine with, or the guy you try to hustle at the poolroom. Any of these guys could well be an undercover narc or an informer, or one of the numerous junkies who support their habits by ripping off or burning fellow addicts. So in order to survive, a dope fiend has to know how far he can trust the people around him. Most successful dope fiends show an ability to size up people they meet in terms of trustworthiness and motivation, and have a good memory for people.

But simply knowing the people on the set is not enough. When a dope fiend wants to sell a hot TV, cop a couple of bags, sell a half load, find somebody to pass some hot checks, or get somebody to go downtown for a concert, he has to know where to connect with the right people. So he has to know what kinds of things routinely go on in the various spots that dope fiends frequent. If he's looking to buy or sell dope, he knows there is always a brisk trade at the poolroom, or the Horseshoe, or the candy store down by the park. He knows that he can dispose of such-and-such type of stolen goods at Pop's pawnshop or through the bartender at the Paradise. He knows that Fat Charlie's is a good place to drink beer and hustle the little college girls, and the alley behind the hospital is a good place to find a crap game.

The streets aren't just a string of all-alike "sets" where anything could go on. They're just too big for that; people would never be able to find who and what they are looking for without some idea where to find it. So to be able to use the streets effectively, a dope fiend has to develop an extensive knowledge of where special activities are likely to be going on. But knowing where to find things has to be combined with a sense of the rhythm of street life.

The streets have a rhythm of their own. They start off slow —no action at all (except for the dudes who wake up sick) until early afternoon. Then dope fiends start appearing, after taking their first hit of the day. Through the afternoon the action stays slow, with some people out hustling, mostly boosting, ripping off parked cars, and breaking into apartments of working squares. For those who will be working later it's a quiet time for hanging around with friends. Then by later afternoon the action starts to pick up. Most dealers have picked up their stuff by then, and the people who have been out hustling have gathered goods to be converted into dope. So by the early evening most of the dope fiends are on the streets, fencing their stuff, connecting for dope, and having a bite to eat. The bars and poolrooms, which have been slow all afternoon, start to fill up, and there are knots of people hanging out in front of stores and on corners. The girls who are hustling, and their pimps, move into action in the early evening. People move around a lot, looking for other people and just looking for action. Word gets around about what's happening—"Sonny has got some dynamite stuff over at the Horseshoe," or, "There's a band cookin' at Fatty's," or whatever. There are lots of things that determine what kind of a night it will be. If there is plenty of good dope in town, everybody will be high and mellow; if it's a nice warm night, people will be stretched out in the park or sitting on steps enjoying the weather; but when the weather is bad, there's no dope in town, and hustling has been bad, then people will be sick and uptight and the action will be slow. Everybody just goes to sleep and hopes tomorrow will be better.

At any rate, the action starts to slow down after midnight when places start closing and most of the squares are off the streets. The dope fiends who are hanging around are just hitting high gear, but when all the squares have gone home, the dope fiends start to feel a little exposed, since they and the police are the only people left. No dope fiend wants to get caught by the police at two in the morning on a deserted street. From midnight on, then, most of the action is in back alleys, apartments, rooms, and all-night diners. There are still a few people hustling late tricks or trying to score, but most dope fiends are off the streets and into more private things, which may go on far into the night.

So what looks like a crowd of people standing around on corners or just sitting in bars is really a well-organized scene. Actually, though, there are three scenes: soul, hip, and Spanish. Any dope fiend, black, white, or green, is only going to hang around where he can feel comfortable and take care of business without being harassed, and there are places where a white can operate, but a black would stand out too much, and vice versa. So the races generally make it in their own sets: blacks rely on the ghetto for camouflage and protection, whites gravitate toward white slums and the hip areas, and the Spanish scene is confined to a small section of town.

In addition, there is a certain amount of distrust between the races. Blacks see white dope fiends as middle-class punks who don't know what it means to be outlaws, and whites see black dope fiends as all-out junkies who would just as soon rip off a white dope fiend as any square. And each race distrusts the other as full of informers.

This is not to say there is no mingling. In fact there are places (mostly near the colleges in the city) where black and white dope fiends hang out together, and there are members of each race who spend most of their time hanging out with people of the opposite race. Furthermore, a lot of white kids cop their dope from black dealers, especially when their regular connections are dry. But by and large the races remain separate on the streets.

This isolation is even stronger in the Spanish community. There are not too many Spanish addicts in Riverdale, and they stick together very tightly. They are seldom seen in either white or black hangouts and are not even known to white or black addicts. Language has a lot to do with this, but they also have their own connections. Spanish dope fiends hardly ever cop from either black or white connections. They don't even like to be seen on the streets with black or white dope fiends, so they almost always cop in the Spanish section of the other cities near Riverdale.

It is generally true that the streets are broken up by race, even though the boundaries are not hard and fast. But there are no strong hostilities between the races. There is very little racial tension in those hangouts that are integrated, and the whites who hang around with blacks are generally welcomed once they are vouched for. A white kid will almost never be accepted in a black set, though, unless some black addict will stand up for him.

Hustling

Being a dope fiend involves a lot of money. Here in Riverdale a bag costs $6, a nickel bag costs $10, and a half load goes for anywhere from $45 to $60. While there aren't many dope fiends in Riverdale shooting more than a half load a day, that is still a lot of money to come up with on a regular basis. There are some people who earn almost all their dope money legitimately, usually by running something like a leather goods store, or working for the university. But there aren't too many jobs around that provide the kind of money, freedom, and spare time that a dope fiend needs. And, let's face it, if a guy really wanted to make it in the business world, he probably wouldn't be into heroin. So most dope fiends have to hustle for their money.

A hustler (all hustlers, not just dope fiends) is *always* on the make for money. It doesn't have to be illegal money. Welfare checks and money from parents isn't much, but it is money, so most flat-out dope fiends usually pull it together enough to go to the State Welfare Center and get a check for $72 a month. The money isn't much, but it's free. For a dope fiend, though, money is just going to go into dope anyway, so one of the most widespread hustles, dope dealing, usually eliminates this intermediate step and pays off directly in dope. What's more, every dope fiend considers himself an expert on dealing; he has to be in order to be able to connect.

So the first hustle that practically every chipper tries is dealing—stuff if he's brave, or grass and barbs if he isn't. A sixteen-year-old white kid who has connections for stuff is in a good position; his schoolmates who want dope would naturally rather cop from him than go downtown to cop from the spades on the Avenue. So as long as he is cool about his dealing, he won't have any trouble at all dealing off two half loads a week, keeping one half load for himself and breaking even. This is all well and good, because it means free dope, and there is a heavy ego satisfaction in being the candyman for your group of friends. But, a nickel–dime dealer soon learns that he gets some problems for his efforts, as well as free dope. When his customers are just kids who are fooling around, it is almost impossible to control the spread of his reputation as a dealer. So he finds more and more people he doesn't know bumping into him in the hall, saying, "Woody told me you can help me out." If he goes ahead and deals to every joker who hits on him, he soon has a clientele of total strangers, but if he plays dumb, or tells strangers that he is not dealing any more, he risks angering them. And when you're a dealer you can't afford to have people down on you—you're too vulnerable.

As everybody knows, the Man is more interested in catching dealers than users, and any time a user is caught by school authorities or the police, his dealer knows that the pressure will be on the user to reveal his sources. In the beginning a dealer doesn't have to worry about this very much, because he is only dealing to good friends he can trust, and the chances of anybody being caught are slight. But as time goes by and his clientele widens and the authorities grow suspicious, the dealer becomes paranoid. So usually a kid gets out of dealing because he gets busted or because he can't handle the paranoia. But he has had his first taste of hustling.

When he hits the streets, a dope fiend sees an incredible assortment of hustles being run around him: dealing, pimping, whoring, checks, credit cards, crib cracking, short and long cons, panhandling, boosting, mail theft, insurance ripoffs, hijacking, blackmail, smuggling, and so on. But each of these hustles requires a feeling for how things operate. So a newcomer may fall into any one of these hustles, depending on who and what he knows. If he is tight with people who are crib cracking, there's a good chance they will turn him on to that hustle. If a girl is good looking and gets hooked up with an easy rider, he'll try to teach her a trick or two and put her on the streets. Street-wise hustlers are always on the lookout for fresh blood to handle the riskier sides of their games. But the newcomer's background also qualifies him for some hustles and makes others nearly impossible.

Take, for instance, mail theft. Everybody knows that a lot of money moves through the mails, but not everybody knows when and where. If you grew up in the ghetto, though, you know that Aid to Dependent Children and welfare checks are mailed out, say, on the fifth and twentieth of each month, and social security checks arrive on the third of each month. So you keep your ears open for who is getting these checks, and pretty soon you have a nice list of where a lot of money will be at specified times, and stealing the checks from mailboxes is like taking candy from babies. But what do you do with a government check once you have it? Well, if you're from the ghetto, you know there are places that cash government checks for a fee. Or if you are well connected, you know somebody who will give you half of what the check is worth, knowing it is hot.

The point is, this is a fine hustle for someone who knows the ropes, but for someone who is unfamiliar with the whole welfare–social security system, it's a tricky business. Check forgery is another good example. It can be difficult to pass a check if the forger is not thoroughly familiar with the whole system of checking. The check may be filled out wrong, or the hustler may arouse suspicion by not filling out the stub. He may try to cash a check that exceeds the nonverification limit of the bank or store, or he might not know what kinds of identification are acceptable, or any of a thousand things can go wrong. In this case, the white middle-class kid is probably better suited to passing checks than is his black brother.

Hustles are all ways of beating the system. They all exploit some weakness, be it men's desire for sexual play, or unprotected apartments, or the fact that anybody can sign a name at the bottom of a check. But to be able to exploit weaknesses you have to develop some knowledge about how the system works. There have been dope fiends (without police records) who have gone to work for security companies in order to learn about burglar alarms—what the weaknesses are and how to beat them. A good hustler knows as much, if not more, about the system he is working and the people he is manipulating than the person he is hustling does. So naturally, newcomers start with the hustles that are the easiest for them, and then in time pick up other tricks as opportunities present themselves.

But not everyone has it in him to be a good hustler. Making money illegally is the same as making money legally; some of the rules are different but many of the problems and skills are the same. And everybody seems to have his or her own level of accomplishment. Some people, after twenty years of shooting dope and hustling, become absolutely brilliant all-around criminals; others develop a lot of skill in one or two hustles and live well off those for a long time (although this is difficult, since the police hear about them eventually and make it almost impossible to continue operations in the normal fashion). Some people develop enough of a knack at hustling to survive and maintain a semblance of stability, but a lot of newcomers just never make it. These are the ones who, instead of the real thing, boost imitation leather coats that can't be given away. When they try to pass a hot credit card they go to the one store that always calls for verification on charges over $5; they break into apartments on the morning that the owner stayed home because he was sick; when they try dealing, they get burned for their initial investment, or sell to a narc on their first day. People like this quickly slide to the bottom of the barrel of the dope world. Their inability to hustle condemns them to a hand-to-mouth existence in the underworld, and they are in and out of reformatories and prisons so often that they don't have much of a chance in the straight world either.

But the average, middle-of-the-road dope fiend is much more successful than these losers. He usually has one or two hustles which he is fairly good at, but he knows enough about other hustles to be able to boost at Christmas time, work the parking lots in June when the universities are having graduation, and deal a little dope on the side to make ends meet.

Cops and Courts

Probably the two most significant groups of people in a dope fiend's life are his connections and the police. Connections supply dope, the police supply fear. Cops come in all sizes and colors. First, there are uniformed patrol cops, called bulls. Bulls aren't much of a problem because they just ride around in their cruisers or on motorcycles trying to look like hot shots. But sometimes a bull will start making life hard on the people on his beat. Usually he'll be trying to get promoted or make a name for himself. He'll put pressure on kids to find out who is doing stuff, and then either pass the names along, or else (more likely) he'll start pushing the dope fiends around, just trying to make things difficult for them. But by and large, bulls are not the sort to make too much trouble. As long as things are kept quiet, most seem content to cruise the streets making sure nothing gets out of hand.

Another kind of cop is the plainclothes detective. Detectives work out of divisions like the robbery, fraud, or auto theft detail. Usually they are a problem only if they are working on the kind of hustles that a dope fiend is running. So if a dope fiend isn't into, say, crib cracking, then he'll probably never have any trouble from detectives on the burglary squad.

The main problem with detectives comes from their need for information. All cops, from uniformed bulls all the way up to police chiefs, are always trying to keep track of what's going on. Usually the only way they ever bust anybody is by getting somebody else to give them enough information so they know where and when to make an arrest that will stick. So cops are always on the lookout for good sources of information. And it seems like all cops believe that addicts are particularly good informants. This must be so, because whenever a detective finds out that some fellow is an addict, he starts to lean on him. He'll tell the poor guy that unless he finds out who the kids are that have been crib cracking on Rumford Street, he can expect a possession bust. In this kind of position, sometimes the only thing the addict can do is try to talk his way out of it. He can come back to the detective with a line like, "I asked around and nobody even knew that Illium Street was being worked over, so if you're gonna bust me, go ahead." More often than not, this will work.

In general, though, detectives also don't present much of a problem, as long as it is possible to stay out of their way. But one particular type of detective, the narc, is an altogether different story. Narcs are plainclothes detectives whose whole job is controlling drugs, gambling, and prostitution. So they spend their time harassing crap-shooters and dope-shooters and whores. The Vice Squad is not very large (less than a dozen detectives), but it is big enough to cover Riverdale pretty well. Because these narcs have no other duties they are free to spend all their time cruising the streets, harassing junkies and whores and breaking up crap games. Their methods are pretty crude.

Narcs make it their business to find out about everybody on the streets who is even thinking about dope, and then hassle them for information or else bust them. Their only real tool is raw power.

They know that by telling a few lies and planting some dope they have the power to send almost anybody they please to rot in prison, and they use the fear that power inspires to work people over. With some exceptions, narcs are sadistic and cunning people who seem to get some kind of pleasure out of making life miserable for people who are in no position to defend themselves. Why else would they beat a handcuffed, sick junkie half to death on the way to the police station? Why else would they torment a junkie with the sight of a bag of heroin while he is kicking cold turkey in a cell, even when they know he doesn't have any information to give up? Why else would they use threats of arrest and violence in all their dealings with addicts?

Sure, narcotics cops have a job to do, but they act as though the best way to stop heroin use is to harass and torture the little guys—dope fiends on the street who have almost no defense against the whims of the narcs. If the narcs were spending their time busting the high-level importers and distributors, it might look like they are actually trying to control narcotics use, but they never touch those people. Instead they just run around acting tough and harassing the little guy on the street.

One last thing about narcs is that they consider themselves almost totally above the law. They think nothing of kicking down doors without warrants, frisking dope fiends on the street without any cause, planting dope on people they want to bust, supplying dope to their own informants, and generally doing anything they feel like doing. Almost without exception, narcs will lie through their teeth when they testify in court against someone they really have it in for. If an addict tells the judge that the three bags of dope used in evidence against him were planted on him by the narcs, not only is he laughed at but he also knows he's in for a heavier sentence and increased hassle from the narcs when he is free again. Narcs know that they hold all the cards in the game, so they don't have to worry much about playing by the rules.

The only other kind of cops that a drug user has to watch out for are the undercover agents. These are young cops who grow their hair long, try to look like dope fiends, and then spend six months or so hanging around the dope scene. Since they don't carry any identification and don't ever make contact with the regular cops, it could be pretty hard to make an undercover agent, except for one thing: the only kind of bust that undercover narcs make is for sales. So they spend all their time on the streets buying dope from different people and keeping careful records of who they bought dope from and when. Then after five or six months they take their records into the prosecutor's office and get bench warrants for the arrest of everyone who has sold them dope.

This means that undercover narcs are almost always strangers who show up on the scene and immediately start pestering everybody they meet to sell them dope. This is a pattern that isn't quite the same as a regular dope fiend's. Normally, a man is out to establish the best contacts he can, which means that he connects from only a few people, although he wants to have reserve connections to use if necessary. But when he gets good dope at a fair price from a connection, he keeps coming back.

But once an undercover agent has bought dope from somebody, he isn't interested in that dealer any longer, except to maybe meet his supplier. Another way to make an undercover narc, is that they are always interested in names—real names. Throughout most of the dope scene, people go by nicknames. It's not that real names are kept a secret—when people have grown up together it would be pretty hard to hide real names —but nicknames just seem to stick in the streets. So when some dude casually asks around about so-and-so's name, people are inclined to be more than a little suspicious. And, of course, undercover agents don't get the same treatment from the police that street junkies get. If a party gets busted and eight or ten people are taken downtown and one person is out on the streets in two hours while all the others are held in lockup until the next day, that dude had better have a pretty good story because a lot of people are going to have questions.

The point is that undercover narcs can be made and beaten.

They are the lowest kind of impostors and backstabbers, but they can be neutralized. The only problem is that because of undercover narcs, the dope scene is riddled with suspicion and paranoia.

Ronny, Ellie, and I were sitting around their room one night waiting for the Fox to come by for some dope he has asked about. There was a knock on the door.

"Who's there?" asked Ronny.

"Is Ronny there?" came the reply from the other side of the door.

"No, he's out of town for a while. Who is that?"

"Billy the bartender at Fat Charlie's told me to come by."

Ronny moved into the closet, and Ellie opened the door. On the other side was a white kid in his early twenties.

"I just come up from Endfield 'cause there's a warrant out for me. I'm sick as a dog, but I've got money. Can you help me?"

"Shit man, I'd like to, but I just got on a methadone program, so I'm clean. Did you know a dude named Ripple in Endfield?"

"Yeah sure, he's in the joint now behind a weapons bust, isn't he?"

"I hadn't heard, but then it's been a while since I been in Endfield. What about a big black dude with orange hair named Floyd—you ever run into him?"

"Sure, I was in lockup with him last winter. He got his woman to help me make bail."

"Yeah, he's that kind of a guy. Well listen, I'd like to help, but I can't even let you stay here, because they'd throw me off the program if they heard I had a dope fiend staying with me. Sorry. Go over to the Night Owl and ask for Wishbone; maybe he'll help."

After he left I asked Ellie why she hadn't sold to the guy.

"I damn near did, but he was jiving. There's no spade going under the name of Floyd in Endfield. That fucker was probably the heat!"

Later on, it came out that there is also no Wishbone!

Because of undercover narcs, one of the most important rules in the dope scene is to know who you're dealing with. This rule makes good sense, and most people who observe it stay out of trouble, at least as far as undercover narcs are concerned. But the trouble is that the rule makes narcotics users suspicious and distrustful of strangers. And so it's hard for a dope fiend to move into different circles, or make new connections when his regular cop man is too hot or goes dry.

In the long run, undercover agents are nothing but a nuisance to the street community. They are usually so lame that most of the people they bust are kids who sell them a nickel bag of grass or a couple of grams of hash. An experienced dealer should be able to make an undercover narc in a crowd just as a matter of course. But their mere existence makes the streets a more uptight place.

One of the first things a newcomer to heroin learns is that the police are a constant threat that must be dealt with. The best way to beat the Man is to never let him become suspicious in the first place. This means being a nobody—just another college kid, hippy, or guy who happens to be out of work and is doing the best he can. But to pull this off, the user has to be very careful who knows that he is doing stuff. Buying and selling has to be done very quietly, and even dope talk has to be restricted to a small circle of close friends.

Being a nobody is a good strategy, perhaps the best, but it's hard to keep up for very long. Other dope fiends will say it's paranoid to be so secretive, and slowly the word spreads that so-and-so is messing around these days. Sometimes, this doesn't mean much, but usually there comes a time when the user starts to feel that his number is due to be called soon. Maybe a friend tells him that the narcs were casually asking about him, or three or four people in his circle get busted. However it happens, there usually comes a time when a dope fiend realizes that too many people know what he is into, and he has to do something. Some users respond by holing up—pulling back and not spending any time on the street. Others quit using stuff for a while. But when the heat is really on, the easiest answer is to run. Cops are not organized regionally at all, so a dope fiend can move to another town and start all over with a clean slate. Even if the police should hear that a guy they are interested in has moved to another city, they would never notify the police in that city. So by moving to a new location, a dope fiend can become just another face in a new crowd.

There are many narcotics users who are always on the move. They never seem to spend more than a couple of months in town before moving out for another city down the coast. But the problem with running as a strategy is that many people simply find it hard to keep moving. For a young dope fiend it is easy and exciting, but as he grows older and works out good connections and living arrangements in one place, it gets hard to chuck it all and start out again someplace new.

So, many dope fiends eventually find themselves in a position where the narcs know about them and are putting some pressure on, but they don't want to just cut out. For a while you can bluff the Man—tell him you don't know what he's talking about and you'll call a lawyer if he doesn't stop bugging you. But this kind of bluff is pure jive, and won't work more than once or twice (if that), and then some kind of an arrangement is going to have to be made, or else you're going to find yourself behind bars. The police, especially narcs, are more than happy to make deals, because more than anything else, they need information. So they'll be the ones who offer the deal.

Hey Kevin, I heard you got picked up the other night. What happened?

Shit, it was one of those things that I knew was going to happen. I was walking home from Fatty's when Farrell and some other narc stopped me. At first he was nice, but then he searched me and "found" a bag of dope in my pocket.

You mean the fucker planted it on you?

Sure. So he threw me in the back of his car and told me the word was that I was dealing, so he was going to send me to Wintergate [Prison]. Then the other cop asked me if I had been copping from Sonny. I didn't say anything, and Farrell started the car and headed downtown. By the time we got to the station I thought I was in the middle of a bad dream. We went to the Vice Squad's office to fill out forms, and the other cop started telling me that it was a pain in the ass doing the paperwork on a small-time bust. I knew it was a setup, but what are you gonna do? I told them that Sonny had been dealing some, but I hadn't seen him in a while. They said they had seen me with him at the Horseshoe the day before, and Farrell got really mad, so I told him that Sonny sometimes had some stuff with him there in the afternoon. Farrell wanted to throw me in lockup, but the other cop told me to beat it. And I was out of the door before he was finished.

Shit, they sure know how to squeeze a guy!

Ain't that the truth. Look don't tell anybody, OK? I already told Sonny the heat is on.

In this situation, nine out of ten dope fiends will give up the information and then beat it. It's a tight situation to be in because there is no good way out. The best way to deal with the narcs is to stay out of their reach because once they have you they can make life miserable.

There are, by all accounts, some towns where a dope fiend can buy off the heat, but not around here. The only thing like this that goes on in Riverdale is that the really big guys, the ones at the top of the dealing racket, must have some kind of protection. How else do they continually avoid harassment, even when everybody knows who they are?

Unless a dope fiend has sold his body and soul to the police, he eventually takes a bust, and then he finds himself involved in a whole new series of hassles. From the lockup he first has to raise bail money, which means finding a bondsman and paying him anywhere from $30 to $750. Having a bail bondsman who is willing to go bail is a really important thing. Normally, bondsmen are reluctant to pay up for someone busted on a dope charge since so many dope fiends just split town once they make bail, so it is often necessary to talk one of them into it. If the addict can't get up the money to pay the bondsman's fee, or if no bondsman will put up a bond for him, then he has to stay in jail until his trial or until his lawyer can work some kind of an arrangement to get him out. And waiting in jail for a court appearance is the worst kind of situation. Being behind bars makes it hard to take care of other business. And although they give out token methadone, it's never enough, so the user has to deal with dope sickness while he is trying to take care of expenses.

Once a dope fiend has been busted, the best he can hope for is some kind of deal. Sometimes the narcs will offer to have the charge dismissed if he is willing to have a nice long chat with them, but more often he has to plead guilty to something and get some kind of sentence. What he has to cop to, and what his sentence will be, depends on how his record looks and what kind of lawyer he has.

As long as he hasn't had too many drug busts, the most important thing is his lawyer. But there are a lot of different kinds of lawyers. Public defenders are the worst kind, and it is only the most naive stoned-out junkie who would go into court behind a public defender. They are on the state payroll and they won't go to bat for anybody. They tell everyone to cop a plea and they will talk to the judge, but they just want their clients to plead guilty so the case will be easy for them to handle.

Legal Aid lawyers are a different matter. They don't have to rely on the court to pay them, so they are willing to fight for their clients. They are usually young and inexperienced as lawyers go, so sometimes they don't get the best deal possible. Also, when you ask for a Legal Aid lawyer you have to take the one who is assigned to you, and some are a lot better than others. And they are all really busy, so sometimes they can't put in the time to make a really good case for their clients. But even given these drawbacks, Legal Aid really does try to help addicts when they get into trouble.

The best bet, though, is to hire a private lawyer. Now admittedly there are good street lawyers and bad street lawyers, but when the dope fiend is paying the bill, at least he knows that his lawyer is working for him. You see, the whole legal thing revolves around making deals. The lawyer gets together with the prosecutor and the police, and in return for a better deal they work out an arrangement where the addict agrees to plead guilty and go along without making trouble. The way they work it is something like this:

> Me and Shirley had gone down to the poolhall to cop, and we was driving down the Avenue when we seen Smith and Seely in a car behind us. They pull us over, and Bull tells us to get out, cause he wants to see what we're up to. He finds eight bags under the seat, so they takes us downtown. I find out later that they charging us with sales. Set bail so high it was three days before I got the scratch together to get out, and me sick as a dog all the time.
>
> I got a Legal Aid lawyer and he came back saying that the pros-

ecutor was talking about giving me three to five at Wintergate, but he thought if I copped a plea he could get the charge reduced to possession and I could get a suspended sentence. You know I didn't want to hear no three to five for a couple of bags, so I told him he could do what he liked, but to keep me out of the joint. So I came back in a couple of days, and this lawyer tells me the Man doesn't like it because I had a couple of other busts, but if I get on a program he's pretty sure the Man would go along with the deal. So I said OK, and when we went to court I just sat there and didn't do nothing and before I knew it I was down in the probation office.

The lawyer is at the center of the whole thing; he is the guy who is doing all the dealing. There really is not much that a stone junkie can do in dealing with courts. All he can hope is that his lawyer will take care of him as well as possible.

Usually a dope fiend knows that if his case hasn't been dropped before going to court he will have to go to prison, on probation, or on a drug program. Once in a great while the prosecutor will nolle a case because his lawyer has been able to pull some technical trick, but by and large the addict is going to wind up copping to something, and then it's only a matter of what the sentence will be.

With good luck, a good lawyer, and not much of a record, a dope fiend will just end up on probation for a year or two. And probation isn't really too bad. He gets assigned to a probation officer he has to go see every now and then—once a week at the beginning, tapering off to once every five or six weeks toward the end. Going to see a PO is just petty hassle. He tells you to see him, say, Thursday afternoons, and you put it off until 4:30 and then his waiting room is crowded with people. After about twenty minutes he calls you in and asks you how things are going and if things are OK on the job and how you're doing in the treatment program and whether you've thought about getting your equivalency diploma. And you tell him everything is OK and ask him if you can go down to D.C. to visit your aunt, and that sort of thing. That's all there is to it. It's a hassle having to stop by his office all the time and also to have to get permission to leave the state, but by and large PO's don't make much trouble. The big problem with probation is that if you get busted again they can revoke your probation, even if the bust won't hold up in court. The PO always has the option of revoking it, which means you have to serve the sentence that was suspended when they put you on probation.

So probation is no simple matter; it involves a good deal of hassle to make appointments, and constant worry about being revoked. But prison is a lot worse. There was a time, ten or fifteen years ago, when practically all dope fiends did at least one bit in the joint. In those days, and even today among older addicts, going to prison was an inevitable part of being a junkie, and any narcotics user who had not been to prison was considered wet behind the ears or suspect. But today, most heroin users have never even seen the inside of a prison (that's a *prison* we're talking about, not jail). Now that is not to say that addicts aren't being sentenced to prison any more—it happens every day. But the importance of prison contacts in street life has diminished. It used to be, say back in the early '60s, that a guy would never be really trusted on the streets until he had done a bit in prison. Now there are so many people involved in dope who have never been inside that the old standards have broken down.

Prison is just about the worst thing the Man can do to a junkie. The first couple of months are totally unreal, colored by an uncontrollable rage at the Man for stealing time. But after a while a prisoner learns how to take care of most of his needs, and in a weird way it isn't so bad getting three square meals a day and a cell of your own. The bad part is being out of touch with the real world; not knowing what your old lady (or old man) is doing, not knowing about your buddies, and generally losing track of business deals and other arrangements. When a guy gets out of the slammer, he doesn't know where he stands any more. He doesn't know if his old lady is waiting for him; he doesn't know where to get dope, who to trust (and, more important, who not to trust), and who will help him get his feet back on the ground. A lot of times, when a guy gets out, he has literally nothing to come home to, so he more or less naturally falls in with the guys he knew in prison. And that is usually a dead-end situation.

TREATMENT

The most likely result of court cases is being sent to a treatment program. Usually this means going to one of two places: the state hospital or the Narcotics Addict Unit of the Riverdale Mental Health Center.

The Central State Hospital maintains two wards for detoxifying alcoholics and narcotics addicts. It may seem a bit strange to have winos and dope fiends sharing a ward, but to the staff, both groups are simply detoxifying and have the same needs. Actually, it's not too bad because the winos—especially when they dry out—like to talk, so they relieve the boredom. Of the two wards, one is locked and is for people who are under court orders, and the other is open and filled with voluntary admissions. But both wards are essentially the same. When an addict is admitted, they give him methadone in decreasing doses for about a week. Then they give him tranquilizers for another couple of weeks and then release him. Treatment isn't very complicated. They do have therapy groups and that sort of thing, but it's all optional, and most people aren't very interested.

Detoxing at CSH is not such a bad experience. To be sure, withdrawal is never a pleasant experience, but after the first three or four days are over, you can lay up, eat fairly well, and meet all kinds of other dope fiends and swap stories. Sometimes there is some dope to be had on the ward, so it is possible to get off once in a while. When people are withdrawing, it's usually very hard to sleep, so the rap sessions may go on until late at night. CSH is a good place to learn new places to cop dope, new ways to beat the heat, new hustles, and new places to go.

It's not that CSH is a country club. It is a state hospital and any state hospital is a drag. When the ward is filled with a bunch of junkies all withdrawing at the same time, it can be a miserable place. Sometimes when drugs are found on the ward they have a crackdown, which means that nobody can have visitors and the staff gets strict. So detoxing at CSH isn't exactly like vacationing on the Riviera. But on the other hand it can be a tolerable change of pace from life on the streets.

Central State provides only treatment for withdrawal from narcotics or alcohol. The people they take in are all addicts or alcoholics, and the hospital's only concern is to detoxify them and then send them back out into the streets (or to prison if the addict is under a court order). They have no control over a person after he leaves the hospital, and although they always try to hammer it into your head not to do any more drugs, they really don't care what happens after you leave.

The other treatment program is the Addiction Unit of the Mental Health Center in town. The unit is a complicated place that is changing a lot, but it seems to be basically a methadone program which has some sort of ties with some other kinds of rehabilitation programs. Their programs are not like CSH in that they really expect the people on their programs to stop using drugs. So instead of spending a couple of weeks detoxifying, they expect people to sign into programs for at least a couple of years!

As a drug, methadone has been around for a long time. It's something like heroin but is synthetic. Ever since the '50s some doctors have given it in tablets (called dollies) to addicts who say they want to quit. Those addicts would turn around and sell them on the streets for a dollar apiece, so they were always around. There were always dope fiends who would crush up the tablet, cook up and strain the powder, and then shoot it. They said you could get high from it that way, but that it didn't have the same rush as street heroin. But most dope fiends weren't into getting high off dollies. They would keep a supply around because dollies keep an addict from getting sick when he can't get any heroin. So if a guy couldn't connect, for whatever reason, he could take a couple of dollies even if he wouldn't get high. A lot of times when an addict was going to quit or get his habit down to a manageable size, he would take dollies for a week or so instead of going cold turkey.

Then a couple of years ago, they started using methadone in

rehabilitation programs. They said that if they gave an addict enough methadone it would produce a "blockade" which would keep him from feeling the effects of any heroin he shot for the next day or so. So now they have these programs where they give addicts enough methadone to keep them from getting sick, as well as to blockade the effects of stuff. The doctors who ran these programs say that addicts can be maintained on methadone and won't need (or want) to shoot any more heroin.

But methadone is even more addicting than heroin, so the people who are in methadone programs are still strung out. The only difference is that now they are addicted to clinic methadone instead of heroin. They have to pick up their methadone every day or they will be dope-sick, just like with heroin. If their dose is too low, they get sick waiting for the next day's medication, and if it's too high, they spend the whole day nodded out.

Still, methadone programs look good to many addicts. Their attraction lies in the fact that the addict doesn't have to rely on some psychiatrist or social worker who tells him he can quit if he just has enough will power. Instead, he gets a drug that makes him able to keep saying no to heroin. If you want to quit, it's easy to say no once or twice, but it's pretty hard to say it every day without any help. A user who is trying to quit doesn't want to be told that he can do it if he really wants to, or that he has to learn to live like the straight Johns he already despises. He knows there is a physical thing about heroin, and it's this physical thing that he needs help in beating. And methadone is a drug that can provide physical help, not just words of encouragement.

So for many addicts, when they find themselves in a position where they have to get their lives a little more together, the first stop is at the Mental Health Center to get on methadone. But then they find it isn't going to be that easy. It turns out that they have this special committee at the Center, made up of doctors and ex-addicts who give everybody who goes in to sign up a workover. So it's the addict who ends up having to run some line to convince this committee that *they* should accept *him!* It's kind of turnaround, because before he went over there he was

expecting them to try to convince him that he should sign up.
Actually, the scene is pretty funny. There are about a dozen junkies sitting around, nodding off because they took a big hit just before coming in, and about half a dozen staff people trying to run interviews. And these junkies, at least those who have never been there before, are all shook up because not only do they have to convince the program to take them, but they find out that the Mental Health Center has some other programs besides Methadone Maintenance which they are more liable to be stuck on.

One of these programs is a live-in place like Phoenix House or Synanon. It's called Zap House or something catchy like that. They have all ex-junkies running the place, and they live in this one house with two or three dozen other dope fiends for a couple of years and learn how to be honest and have some self-discipline.

Actually, there isn't much of a line on the streets about Zap House because not too many people sign up for it, and of those who do, the ones who split usually are less than anxious to talk about the place, and those who succeed in making it through never seem to reappear on the streets. They're around, just not on the streets. Sometimes they become rehabilitation counselors or work with some mayor's council on drug abuse, but they never show up on the doorstep to tell the street people what they've been doing.

The other program that is tied in with the Addiction Unit is a special clinic they have for kids who aren't old enough or strung out enough to get methadone. This clinic seems to be a pretty confused place, but it involves kids going to the clinic all day long for group therapy. After about three or four months they don't have to go in the daytime any more but go to therapy groups at night. But nobody ever gets through the whole program. The kids get their court cases cleared up, or con their probation officer, or just get tired of playing the game and split after a couple of months.

Because this clinic is mostly for kids, they don't use any methadone, but they do make the kids take cyclazocine, which is something like methadone, in that it produces a blockade which keeps a person from feeling the effects of heroin if he should shoot any. But unlike methadone, it does not deal with physical craving for stuff, and if a kid has any heroin in his system when he takes the cyclazocine it brings on cold turkey withdrawal. This means, of course, that if the kid does any fooling around with heroin while he is taking it, not only will he not get off on the heroin, but he will also get deathly sick the next day when he takes his cyclazocine. The funny thing is that the kids keep trying it to see if it really works that way.

So that is the lineup at the Addiction Unit. It is pretty complicated. They have screening committees, and social workers, and secretaries, and rehabilitation counselors, and more programs than any stone junkie can ever hope to figure out. But there is one important thing about the place. If you can play their game the way they think you should, they will take care of almost all the hassles that continually torment dope fiends. Being a patient at the Mental Health Center seems to work wonders with the courts, probation officers, family, and other problems. It even helps with the police. The cops don't believe that an addict ever cleans up, but they seem to stay off the backs of program members. So the Mental Health Center is never in need of patients. Addicts fall by, for one reason or another. Some never get past the first interview; others really become involved in that whole social set and fade out of the streets. By and large, the doctors and counselors don't like the patients to hang around on the streets, so the people on the program have their own social thing for just themselves.

Getting out of It

Getting out of dope is a lot like getting into dope: different people do it in different ways for different reasons. Some people overdose, but the actual number of OD's is very small. Most people finally just give it up. It's not easy, but when a guy finally stops doing heroin, it's not as hard, or spectacular, as he expected.

> Yeah, I was on the methadone program for almost a year.
> Were you cheating while you were on it?
> At first I was—I was doing a lot of cocaine—that and speedballs. Then one day I asked myself why I was doing this and I

couldn't think of any good reason, so I quit. That was in the winter. Then last spring I got thrown off the program for not coming to meetings, but that didn't mean much, because once I had quit using drugs I didn't need the program at all.

This guy happened to quit when he was on a methadone program. But not everybody has to get on a program to quit. A chipper who doesn't have any kind of a real jones can just give it up because it's too expensive. Some people quit when they get busted, or they move away, or they get a job. Most addicts who have got over their love affair with dope always seem to be trying to quit. Sometimes they go cold turkey, sometimes they get into other pills, downers mostly but sometimes even acid, and sometimes they cop clinic methadone on the streets for a couple of weeks at $20 a day. When they fail, they are right back on the streets and everybody knows they didn't make it. But when they succeed, they just kind of fade away.

Hey Spider, you seen Little Willie? He owes me a deuce.

I wouldn't count on it. I ain't seen him. Blind Al said he had gone to Boston.

And he didn't tell anybody?

I don't know. He told me he was gonna clean up. You never know.

If and when a guy cleans up, there's not much point in his spending much time on the streets. The streets are geared to suit the needs of dope fiends, hustlers, and other outlaws, so the guy who has cleaned up generally feels pretty uncomfortable there. In addition, he usually finds there are a lot of people he had been tight with that he can't relate to once he is straight.

So it doesn't happen very often that a person quits dope and then remains on the street where all his dope friends can ask him about how he did it and how he feels. Instead he usually doesn't make it, and there he is, back on the street, copping dope so everybody knows he's back. It's usually only when a person drops out of sight that he *might* be staying clean, but then practically nobody notices.

3 A Cop's View of Narcotics Work

The following two chapters are about the Vice Squad of the Riverdale Police Department. They rely largely on observations made by the author in the summer of 1968 and to a lesser extent on continuing talks with the same detectives over the years that followed.

Official Riverdale is quite proud of its police department. The Chief of Police is prominent among law enforcement officers. The department is well organized and employs many modern techniques of police management. While the amount of corruption is always relative, even the Vice Squad's opponents never claimed that they took bribes.

These chapters, however, are not about the police department as an organization but about the day-to-day world of Vice Squad work. The first chapter is a first-person account, as though written by a detective. It was not, but the style allows the reader to appreciate the flavor of discourse the detectives used. Almost the entire chapter is made up of quotes from various detectives taken directly from the observer's field notes. Some modifications have been made in order to make the monologue flow smoothly but it is hoped that the fundamental meanings have not been changed.

The Riverdale Vice Squad has changed a great deal in the last two years. Departmental scandals, a declining narcotics problem, and new leadership have all had their effect. The following chapters might have to be quite different if the current squad was being described. Whether an account of the present Vice Squad would better represent other vice squads in the United States cannot be known for certain. This description tries to represent the Vice Squad detectives as they saw themselves and their work at the height of the drug crisis in Riverdale.

I WANT to try to give you a fair and objective view of the drug problem and the problems we have, as cops, trying to deal with it. I know that about nine out of ten people who read this will not believe that a cop can give a fair view of the situation. It's kind of funny, we're supposed to be the guardians of public order and the citizens are supposed to support us, yet most people would rather believe a junkie than a cop when it comes to describing what the situation is really like.

What I want to talk about is the sort of work I do. Before I do that though, I have to give you some sort of an understanding of the drug problem as a whole, particularly about the role the police have to play in it. I know there are people, maybe even most people, who think the reason cops bust junkies is that we enjoy it. They also think we beat up on them and stomp on their heads for no good reason and that we're all sadists. It's all our fault. But the police don't make the laws, the legislature does. All we do is enforce them. Besides, if we didn't pick junkies up for drugs we'd have to arrest them for something else. The burglary squad spends half its time chasing around after junkies. All we do is to shorten the process. We try to pick addicts up before they've beaten up some innocent citizen. I had a professor, at the state college where I took a criminology course last year, who said that at least half the major crimes in this city are committed by drug addicts. Myself, I think he underestimates it. Still, whatever the percentage, it's awfully high. The only way we're going to stop the rising crime rate is to try to do something about addiction.

The thing that must be understood is that heroin causes crime. Junkies get themselves addicted and then they've got to get money in order to pay for their habit. If you think about it, a guy with a ten-bag a day habit, at $6 a bag, has got to steal $60 a day in order to keep from getting sick. If you multiply that by the 1500 addicts we have in Riverdale you get an awful lot of crime. Hell, if we could put just half the addicts behind bars we'd stop $45,000 worth of crime each day.

There are people around who say that the problem is just that drugs are illegal, that the only reason addicts steal is because drugs are so expensive; if drugs were free or cheap they wouldn't steal. I guess there is some truth in that, but I don't think those people really know what they're talking about. They haven't seen this thing close up the way I have. These junkies become so degenerate, it is sad. They live in such filth. You should see the apartments I've been in. What's more, junkies have no consideration for their families and their friends. When you've seen what I've seen, it's hard to believe that somehow everything would be all right if heroin were legal. I think the drug does something basic to a person. I don't know what it is, I'm not an expert on that sort of thing, but it seems as if drug users just don't have any morals left after a while.

The problem is this thing has gotten out of hand. We, the police, can't deal with it. We're just a small bunch of men against a whole floodtide. Five years ago when I first went to work for the Vice Squad, most of our business was gambling and prostitution. We thought we had a lot of drug addicts then but we only arrested 200 of them and most of those arrests were for pot. Last year the Vice Squad arrested 650 people for drug crimes and most of those arrests were for heroin. What's more, drug addicts used to be all colored. Now we get nice little white girls from the suburbs who come in here to shoot up heroin with their seventeen-year-old boyfriends. There are a lot of people around who will tell you that marijuana doesn't lead to heroin but every one of these kids I've ever arrested started smoking pot.

I don't know what we're going to do about the problem. A few years ago I used to think that we could stop it by getting tough but nothing we do seems to make much difference. Maybe in the end we're going to have to give heroin to them free just because we can't fit them all in the jails and prisons. I've got to admit I really don't understand junkies. You would think that sending them or their friends away to jail for five years would do something. You would think it would keep them away from that stuff. But it doesn't. It must be one hell of a kick. Why else would they go through what they go through for it? I never had much faith in treatment. Addicts are too crazy for that. At any rate I know treatment isn't working any better then what we're doing. Even the addicts they've got on the program, the ones who don't leave as soon as the law is off their backs, are using dope. I think they sell more cocaine over at the Mental Health Center than they do anywhere else in the city. What's more, the methadone they give out there is getting sold in the streets. The one thing I think might work is trying to get at the supply. If the Feds could stop it from coming into the country, maybe that would work. They seem to be trying and they don't seem to be getting anywhere. No matter how big a haul they make, there always seems to be enough coming in to keep the addicts supplied. Still, it seems to me that stopping the supply is the best chance we have. I used to think the best chance was to get the pushers in town, but now we've busted so many of them and that doesn't seem to have any impact at all. Like I said, maybe we'll have to give it to them free, but I sure would hate to see it. But that's not what I want to talk about. Figuring out what to do about addicts isn't my job. My job is to arrest them.

This game is 90 percent information. If you've got good information, you're going to be a good cop. If you don't have good information, you're not a good cop. That's not all there is to the job, but most of the other things you can mess up on a bit and it doesn't hurt. You may notice that all the busts you read about in the newspapers are made by the same guys. They're always the narcotics detectives. Nobody else on the force really makes any busts because they don't have any informants. Of course, the guys up in burglary or over in robbery have informants, but they use them for arresting burglary and robbery suspects. Likewise, I don't use my informants to solve burglary problems. It may be selfish, but my job is to arrest addicts and not burglars. But the guys in the patrol division, they just don't have informants like that. The only time they ever make drug busts is when they stumble across them.

There are a lot of ways of getting informants. If you talk to the junkies on the street about it, they'll probably tell you that we have enormous sums of money to pay people with. Well, we do have some money, but not all that much. I mean, I'll pay some money from time to time to get some interesting information but basically it isn't the best way to get what I need. Another thing you'll hear is that we give heroin to informers for information. That's just not true at all. There might be some departments where they do that, but not in this one. After all, that's defeating the purpose. We're here to try to get these guys off heroin, not to get them on it. I suppose that some of them use the money we pay them to buy heroin, but we just don't pay them that much. If a junkie were to keep his habit going from what money he could get from the police department he would have to turn in every other junkie in town. For example, I might pay somebody $25 if he sets up an arrest where I catch somebody with fifteen or twenty bags. If I'm going to catch somebody with a piece, I might pay him 45 or 50 bucks. But that just isn't very much money to a junkie.

Besides, that's not the way we do most of our work. The primary way of getting information is by arresting people. Let me give you an example. Last week we picked up a kid who was running for one of the bigger dealers in town. He'd just come back from selling all his stuff but he had a set of works on him and they were probably dirty, so we picked him up and took him down to the station. Now in this particular instance the kid probably isn't strung out. It didn't do any good to threaten him with a high bond, so we told him that if he would play along with us we'd play along with him and let the charges drop. We were lucky with this one. This kid ratted out the whole organization. We busted them with five half loads as they were walking out the door to distribute it. It was a good bust. Usually we're not that lucky. But usually you bust somebody that you've known for quite a while and bargaining is tougher. For example, this guy might clean up. I hope he does, but he probably won't. In that case we'll see him again in another month or two and by that time he'll probably be addicted. So now he has a habit and we agree to let him out ROR and he gives us some information. If he doesn't give us any information we lock him up with a $10,000 bond. Then he has to sit in jail for four days until his lawyer can get the bail reduced. Given that sort of choice most of them will decide it's easier to rat on one of their friends. Then a few months later his case is going to come up in court and he's got two choices. Either he can go over to the drug center and get into treatment and try that dodge or he can call me up and give me some more information and I'll talk to the prosecutor for him.

The whole thing is a pretty dirty game. But what are we going to do? There is no other way to do it. It's like these kids who spend all their time objecting to Vietnam. They seem to expect the government to fight a war without using bullets. It's the same sort of thing. We can't always do it the way we want to because that's the way the junkies play the game. They play dirty, so we've got to play dirty too.

The problem is that nobody else has any good information except addicts. The only real exception to this is prostitutes, who are out on the streets at all times and really know what's going on. But then again, most prostitutes are addicts anyway. That's why most of them are prostitutes to begin with. The drugs drive them into it. But prostitutes are really good sources of information because we've got them over a barrel. They've got to give us information or we won't let them keep operating. There may be some people who object to this, but it seems to be a pretty good trade. I figure that prostitution is going to go on anyway, no matter what we do, and we might as well make good use of it. It's not that we don't bust prostitutes sometimes, but we know we can't ever stop prostitution. If one of them robs her trick and he complains, we'll arrest her, but I can't help feeling that the guy was asking for it. If he's going to leave the wife and kids at home and come down here and hustle one of those broads, he deserves what he gets. So a lot of the time we let the broads operate and use them as sources of information. Hell, half the broads out on the streets of the city are informants of mine.

Prostitutes are not the only ones who give us information. We have mothers calling up all the time to tell us that so and so is dealing drugs to their kids. If the mother calls us up we feel an obligation to do something about whatever she called us about. I go out and try to bust the guy who's dealing to her kid, but her information isn't much help. It's never enough to know who's dealing. You've got to know when he has it, where he has it, what it is he has, and how we can catch him with it. You just can't get a search warrant for a guy's house on the basis of some mother calling up and saying that he's selling dope to her kid.

I guess this gets us into the whole topic of what's good information and what's bad information. Being able to tell the difference between them is important. Good information leads to a good bust, bad information is a waste of your time and makes you look like a fool. This is a good squad, we get a lot of information. We don't use two-thirds of the information we get; we couldn't possibly use it. So if we want to be efficient we've got to be sure to use the best information we get. But more important than that, we don't want to make fools of ourselves. Every time we bust into somebody's house and it turns out that there isn't anything there, whether or not they're using junk, we end up looking like fools. It's not simply that it's embarrassing—we've got to maintain a reputation in this town. If we're to have any chance of controlling this thing the addicts have got to think we're good. We've got to keep the pressure up and the only way we can do that is if the junkies are scared of us.

Even if the information looks good on the surface, even if we know exactly when and where somebody is going to have the dope, and even if it looks as if there is going to be enough dope there to make it a good bust, still you can't be sure. You have to know your informants and you have to be able to calculate what's going on in his head. Every once in a while we get one of those guys who just makes up the information. He knows somebody is using so he decides that he'll give us a whole mess of information about how to get him when he really doesn't know.

Another problem is having an informant who wants to get even with somebody else and informs on him for revenge. Now as far as my job goes, that's all right. I don't care what private motives my informants have for picking one addict or another to inform on, but the odds are that the informant doesn't know very much about his enemy. He usually has to make it up. The trick is to get yourself a few good informants and to work them hard. That, of course, isn't easy. For one thing, you've got to have somebody else busting them all the time. You've got to have both bail and a sentence hanging over an informant's head if he's going to give up a lot of information. Protecting an informant also presents a real problem. It's a problem under any circumstances but it's worse if you're going to use an informant for a long time. If you don't let informants take the rap sooner or later, someone's going to get suspicious. Addicts have been known to do pretty ugly things to informers in this city. One of John's informants had "fink" carved on his forehead with a knife.

Of course there are other ways of learning what's going on. The most important way is just going out and cruising around and seeing what you can find. This doesn't take the place of having informers, but it supplements what informers can give you. You can't really find anything out unless you already know something to begin with. I don't know how to explain this. Somehow you've got to develop an eye for narcotics. It's a special sort of alertness which takes time to develop. You've got to know all the people. You simply have to learn who is an addict and who isn't; it's impossible to watch everyone in the city for narcotics. Another thing you have to learn is where the addicts hang out. If you spend enough time cruising by their hangouts you soon learn who the addicts are.

This, of course, is what we spend most of our time doing. You can't sit in the office all day just waiting for informants to call you up. So you get in the car and drive around and see what you can find. By and large, the addicts give themselves away. All you have to do is look at them crosseyed and they'll either run or try to swallow what they're holding. Sometimes they'll try to be subtle and throw it away. That's one time when you've got to have a good eye because you've got to notice the slightest motion. We do things like drive the car past them a little bit on the street and then stop and back up. Almost any addict in the city, if he's holding, will run if you do that. Then all you have to do is catch him. Sometimes we just pull up to the curb and talk to addicts and if they look suspicious we search them.

But that isn't the way to make very good busts. Usually all you do is get somebody with a bag or two that he was going to use himself. The top men don't usually carry their stashes around with them. Some of them don't even use the stuff. Most of the big busts you make are with warrants. Warrants aren't hard to get, but you've got to fill out the warrant in the right way or the judge won't sign it. It's simply no use going to a judge with an improper warrant. So either you get the proper information or, if you don't have it and you really think you need to have the warrant, you fill it out as if you did have the right information. Generally, what it takes to get a warrant is the word of a "known and reliable informant" who has told you where and when and what you will find. Then you have to do some surveillance to corroborate the information. The surveillance doesn't have to be much. All you have to do is find out, for instance, that the two people who are supposed to have the dope do know each other and that one of them lives at the address you have. That will usually do. Frankly, warrants are a pain. For one thing, they take a lot of time to write up and even more time to get signed. Furthermore, you feel a bit hesitant about waking the judge up at 12:30 on Saturday night. But a case in which you have a warrant is much more likely to stand up in court than one in which you don't. It's really a question of quantity versus quality. If you don't have a warrant you can be pretty sure that the district attorney either isn't going to take the case or isn't going to push it as hard as you'd like. On the other hand, you can waste an awful lot of time with warrants. I guess that most of the arrests we make are without warrants. There are a lot of reasons for this. Suppose an informant tells me that so-and-so is dealing and he's over at his house now putting the stuff in bags and he's going to go out to deliver it later this evening. If I go back down to the office and make out a warrant and then go out to try to find a judge to sign it, the dealer will probably have left by the time I get there. In that sort of case it doesn't seem worth the risk of losing the bust just to get the warrant. Under these circumstances we use the doctrine of "speedy information" which allows us to enter a house when there isn't enough time for us to get a warrant.

    Now at this point some smart-ass defense attorney is going to tell you that what I've just said proves that the cops have no concern for the constitutional rights of defendants because we're not concerned about having warrants to enter houses. I'm not sure I can express how really stupid that argument is. It's not that I'm against having warrants. I don't think that police should be allowed to enter people's homes without warrants. What's more, I believe that people should be considered innocent until proven guilty. But that's simply absurd when it comes to the junkies that I bust. It's not as if there is any question about their guilt. Most of them have told me that they're addicted and I've seen the track marks on the arms of most of the others. When I run up to a guy and he swallows something and smiles and says: "Ha, I beat you," should I believe that he's just another innocent citizen? You don't spend your time hanging around with junkies unless you're into junk. It's as simple as that. It's true that when you bust them they might not have the stuff on them, but that's really just a technicality. They are chronic criminals and there is no way of getting around that. If they don't play the game by the legal rules, why should they expect us to?

Most of our arrests are made in apartments or hotel rooms. The key thing is to get in as quickly as possible. The addict always tries to get rid of his stuff as fast as he can. It usually ends up in a race for the bathroom where he's trying to flush the dope down the toilet and you're trying to stop him. The big problem is that he knows where the dope is and you don't. Otherwise, they'll just try to swallow the dope. That's even harder to stop. All you can do is grab the guy by the neck and try to keep him from swallowing. At any rate, you can see pretty quickly that this sort of a thing doesn't look much like it looks on *Mod Squad*. You don't bang on the door and say: "Open up, this is the cops." They'll open up all right, but before they do they'll have flushed everything down the john. So you get subtle and try to get them to open the door without knowing who it is. Half the time when they open the door there will be a chain lock on the other side. Now I'm pretty good at opening those locks, but not with somebody standing on the other side trying to close the door on my hand. So often we have to kick the door in. They don't like that, but what can we do? You've got to be tough about it. If you hear a lot of movement on the other side of the door you don't wait until somebody comes and opens the door, you've got to kick it in. Once you get in you've got to stop them quick. If you tackle them and have them on the floor fast, you may not have an all-out fight on your hands.

As a general rule I don't worry very much about whether or not I have a warrant when I go into a house. Sometimes you take a little flack from the people in the house about not having a warrant but usually not much. If you find something, they can't argue that you weren't justified in going in. If you don't find anything they're so relieved that they're usually willing to forget about the whole incident. Besides, addicts are not very likely to complain about that sort of thing. They know they're guilty and what they want most is to stay out of the limelight. What good does it do for them to have a big stink made about one cop and then have the rest of the squad out trying to bust them?

Usually, once I find something, I'll arrest everybody I think might be involved. You can always let some go later. You've got to assert your authority. You can't let them go and change your mind later. Besides, the courts give people more than an even break, and if they're innocent they'll be let off. Sometimes, with other types of arrests like for gambling, I might let somebody go if everyone there bitches about it. But by and large I don't think it's really my job to decide which of several people might be innocent or guilty. That's up to the judge. Maybe I'm giving the wrong impression. If we go into somebody's house and it turns out that the eighteen-year-old kid there has a bunch of heroin in his back pocket, we don't arrest his mother. You've got to use common sense. But if we go into a house and we find four people there and one of them has heroin on him and somebody else has works on him, we're likely to arrest all of them. Addicts usually hang around together, so it is a good bet that the other two are addicts also. Besides, the law simply states that you are guilty if you are present when heroin is found. My job is enforcing that law.

The same thing goes for the charges that get filed; generally

I'll book addicts on everything I can. If I find somebody with thirty bags of heroin I'll book him on both possession of heroin and possession with intent to sell. Now I know, in this state, it's impossible to convict him on intent. There is no way of proving it. Nonetheless, it seems worthwhile charging him with it. It's something the DA can use when he bargains with the defense attorney.

My long-run strategy is to make a few busts of users and then try to get them to inform on the people who deal. Then I'll try to get those people to inform on the people who are dealing for the whole city. I'm really not very interested in arresting the little guys, the users, or even the small-time pushers unless I can use them for something bigger. The only real use we have for addicts is as informants to get to the big-time dealers. Besides, putting pressure on the dealers is the only way you can keep the pressure on the little guys. It's only by making dope hard to get and expensive that anybody's ever going to get off the stuff. I don't care how good the treatment programs are or how tough the jails are. Until it gets unpleasant enough, junkies aren't going to quit.

There are lots of times when I don't think we're doing a damn bit of good. For the last four years I've been working on narcotics in this city and I've been working at it hard. So have all the other guys on the squad and yet I think there is more dope now than there ever was. It's eight men against a tidal wave. We just can't stop it at all. Sometimes I think it might work if it weren't for the courts. If the courts would only do their job properly maybe we could make it work. But as fast as we arrest people the courts let them go. Last week I arrested a guy for possession and brought him down to the lockup. Half an hour later I drove by his house again and there he was sitting on the stoop. They let them out on bail so fast these days that it doesn't seem worthwhile to arrest them. Hell, we've got to arrest somebody three times before he goes to jail. The first time he gets arrested the court sends him over to the Mental Health Center. When he busts out of that they send him over to the State Hospital for inpatient treatment. Any fool can bust out of that place. They don't even have guards. All the addicts have to do is walk out. It's just that a lot of them don't want to. One of the junkies told me that he'd never in his life been in a place he liked so much. There is more booze, drugs, and women up there than most of them can handle. The third time an addict's arrested, he'll probably only go away for a year or so. We may arrest him for robbery, possession, sale, and two counts of breaking and entering, but he ends up pleading to one count of possession and the DA nolles all the rest.

I guess there are a lot of frustrating jobs in this world, but there aren't many in which everybody hates you as much as they do when you're a cop. I don't mind it from the kids or the colored people. I expect it from them. It's the people who are supposed to be your friends, the ones that come up and pat you on the back and tell you what a fine job you're doing but who really hate your guts for being a cop. That's one of the reasons I don't go to parties much any more. When I used to go out, everything would be fine for the first couple of hours. People would come up and tell me that I'm doing a fine job, except maybe to ask why did so and so have to bust his relative last week. After a few hours when everybody would get drunk, there would be a fight; everybody against the dirty cop. Now I won't go to a party unless there are going to be other cops there. That's why I spend most of my off-duty time with cops. Hell, except at home I never take off my gun. One of the things about being a cop is that every time you turn a corner you expect somebody to be there ready to jump you.

Another thing I should talk about is the dirty part of being a cop. Every addict in this city will tell you about how he's been beaten up by the cops at some point or another and of course that's not true. But it is true that sometimes we have to beat people up. It comes down to this. When I have a choice of whether I'm going to punch somebody in the nose or wait for him to punch me, I hit him. I'm a family man. I've got a wife and three kids to support. I don't care what anybody says about police restraint and not using violence. Only a fool would sit there and let himself be hit. I've got to support those kids and I can't do that if I'm dead or crippled. What's more, if some guy takes a swing at me, I'm not going to let it drop when I hit him back. I've got to teach him a lesson. People have got to learn that they can't hit cops. Three weeks ago I arrested some guy and he tried to hit me over the head with a chair. We beat the living hell out of him. I don't apologize for that, I think we had to do it. Three days later, the guy's lawyer got up in court and started talking about what a brutal beating this bastard had gotten from the cops. It's true, we stomped him, but he deserved it. He started it. If we don't do that, every two-bit punk is going to think that he can get away with hitting a cop.

There is one thing that some guys on the force do which I won't defend. Some guys plant dope on addicts when they think they have to, but I won't do it. I think there are some limits to every game you play and that's one of the limits in this one. A guy has got to have some integrity in the way he does his job, I simply don't think it's right to plant something on somebody who doesn't have dope on him. That isn't to say that I haven't wanted to sometimes. A couple of years ago we had this one guy we kept getting reports on that he was selling to high school kids. No matter how hard we tried we just couldn't catch him with anything on him. It turned out later that he never carried it. Anyway, in a case like that, I often think we ought to plant it. How else are you going to get him off the streets? How many addicts is he going to create out of those high school kids before we get him? We're bound to get him sooner or later, it's only a question of time. But in the meantime he can do an awful lot of damage. The problem is, addicts can do whatever they want. They don't have to play by any rules at all, but we're expected to play as if we just got through reading Hoyle. I guess part of the temptation to plant the dope is that it's so easy. One can do it without ever getting caught. It can even be done so that one of the other cops gets the flack for it. For instance, when you go through a junkie's pockets you can drop a bag in and then a few minutes later one of the other guys goes through the pockets again and he finds the bag. The junkie probably doesn't even realize for sure that he didn't have the bag in his pocket anyway, so there's no problem. But even if he did, he isn't going to blame you for it. If you're in an apartment you can drop a bag someplace on the floor and feel pretty sure that one of the other guys is going to find it later. If no one else does, you can always find it yourself. I've thought about doing that a lot of times. It isn't hard, and some cops do it, but it seems to me that it's going a little too far. I can't really say why, given that the world would probably be a lot better off if I did, but I just can't bring myself to do it.

One of the biggest problems we have in trying to get anything done is the stuff that goes on over in court. Ten years ago, when we wrote up our police reports, we wrote down what actually happened. Now we can't do that any more. The courts have set up a series of rules that make it impossible to arrest anybody. For example, according to one of the decisions of the Supreme Court, when entering an apartment you've got to identify yourself as a police officer. Now maybe that might make sense to a Supreme Court justice, but it sure doesn't make sense if you're responsible for making arrests. If everytime I banged on the door I identified myself as a police officer I'd never find anything because everything would be flushed down the john. So instead, I identify myself as a bellboy, or one of their friends, or something like that, and I hope they'll let me in without my having to kick the door down. But when it comes to writing up the police report, I've got to write down that I identified myself as a police officer or they throw the case out of court.

Another example is this business of having to inform a suspect of his rights. These guys don't have to be informed of their rights; they know their rights better than their lawyers do. You'd think every one of them had been through three years of law school. Besides, if you go into that long speech about their rights, they start thinking they're lawyers and you can't get any cooperation out of them at all. That would be a hell of a way to run a police department. We exist on information and you can't get information if the suspect won't talk to you. But again, when I write up my statement for court, even when I give my testimony in court, I've got to pretend that I informed them of their rights. Hell, everybody in court knows I didn't do it. The judge knows it, the prosecutor knows it, the defense attorney knows it, but they don't care. They know it's as silly as I do.

But they've got to have it down on the record that I did or the case would get overturned on appeal. The problem is that you can't pay any attention to those formal requirements and get anything done. What really annoys me is the courts acting as if we're the criminals instead of the junkies. Some place along the line the courts seem to have got the idea that police are dangerous. I don't want to live in a police state any more than the next man, but this isn't a police state. We don't bother anybody who isn't breaking the law. It's just that you can't expect to have effective law enforcement if you don't give the police the power to do anything. You've got to give the police the power to enforce the laws.

4 A Hell of a Night

This chapter is different from all the others in this volume because it involves the observer as a character in the events being portrayed and allows the reader to watch the data-gathering process as a very practical accomplishment. Despite the fact that the "I" in this account is the observer, not the detective, the primary purpose of the chapter is to allow the reader to understand the detective's world as he himself understands it. The only difference is that the observer has not been edited out.

Whereas the last chapter concentrated on the attitudes and beliefs of the Vice Squad detective, this one concentrates on his activities and the ways in which concrete situations present themselves to the detective. Despite the fact that the night described here was one that ended in the largest heroin bust the Riverdale Vice Squad had ever made, it was in many ways a very ordinary night. The characters involved and the way time was spent were hardly unusual. Other nights might involve more time with prostitution and gambling and less time with heroin, but not necessarily so. What made this night exceptional was that the bust was so large and the dealer had such an awesome reputation as a dangerous person. Yet the reader may be surprised that this big bust did not involve Holmes-like detective work or the elaborate drama of The French Connection. *Unfortunately, the high drama of real-life detective work in Riverdale simply does not have as much excitement as movies about New York City.*

IT WAS five minutes before eight and I was walking up the grimy stairs that lead to the office of the Riverdale Vice Squad.

"Hey Chuck!" came a voice from the bottom of the stairs. I turned around to see Rick Winters, 210 pounds, six foot four, a black cop I had been riding around with for the past two weeks.

"What's up?" I asked as he bounded up the stairs. We walked into the office.

"Nothing much, but we'll see if we can't turn up something before the night's over." I knew he would. Friday nights with the Vice Squad are rarely dull. Rick and I sat around talking, as we waited for his partner, about a bust the squad had made on Wednesday.

The phone rang. Someone in the other office yelled for Rick to pick it up. It was an informant telling Rick that Ted Brown, one of the larger dealers, was driving around Southville making deliveries in his girl friend's Pontiac. He also wanted Rick to do something about a case he had in a neighboring town. Rick told him that he would call the DA over there when the informant came up with some information worth something. Everyone knew that Brown was making deliveries in that car. Rick was telling the truth. Only four days before, Rick's partner had pointed out the car and made the same comment.

Rick's partner, Wilson Smith, walked in during the call and went into another office to talk with the other detectives. Smith, like Winters, was black. Unlike Winters, he was small, angular, and handsome.

Rick put down the phone and yelled, "Hey, Will, let's go. Chuck here is impatient to make a few bust." Rick laughed and I felt embarrassed. The three of us walked downstairs and Wilson, who was usually the leader of the team and the driver of the car, said, "You drive Rick, I'm sicker than a dog," but instantly changed his mind when Rick showed little enthusiasm. "All right, you can drive in an hour," Wilson said.

One thing about Wilson, he never lacked enthusiasm for his job. He drove the old Chevy out of the police garage fast enough to make me cringe and headed for Southville, the poorest black section of Riverdale. Riverdale does not have one black ghetto but several. Only Southville has been untouched by the Redevelopment Corporation. Whatever Wilson was looking for, he didn't find it in Southville, so he drove over to Western Avenue.

"See that bastard, Chuck," Wilson said, pointing to a well-dressed man on the sidewalk. "We busted him three weeks ago for policy selling. Want to bet on what he's got under his hatband?"

"He's still doing it?" I asked.

"Pinky will be selling numbers at his own funeral," Rick said with a smile.

We kept driving and pulled in behind a housing project where there was usually a game of craps. There wasn't one tonight but Rick saw someone who spotted us, and we drove through an alley after him only to almost hit a drunk lying against the wall. The man got away.

We drove around some more while Smith and Winters traded gossip and information about who was using what drugs, what was happening in the numbers racket, and what was happening to various pimps and whores they both knew. Suddenly Rick said:

"Hey, that's him. It's Snooper."

Wilson drove the car up alongside Snooper, who was walking peacefully along the sidewalk.

"Come on Snooper, get in," said Rick, pulling the front seat forward to let the guy get in back with me and squashing his own large frame in the process. "Empty out your pockets," he said as if he were a doctor asking a patient to undress for a physical. Snooper had nothing in his pockets or his shoes, but his wallet contained $300 in cash.

"Hey man, give that back, that's mine."

Rick ignored the implication that he was intending to keep it and said, "You've been dealing, Snooper, and we know who you're working for."

"No, not me, I'm working for Manpower," Snooper said as if he were telling a self-evident truth.

"You can't make it that way; you're dealing. You beat us this time but we'll get you next time," said Wilson confidently.

"Nah, Will, I told you, I'm working for Manpower," said Snooper sullenly.

"Come on, if you want to play; you've got to play by the rules." Wilson tossed his wallet back to him so that it hit him on the cheek.

"Come on, don't give us trouble," said Rick soothingly as Snooper glared at Wilson. Rick opened the door and Snooper walked slowly away.

"Don't worry, Rick, we'll get him next time," said Wilson as he slammed his foot on the accelerator of the Chevy and the car spurted ahead.

"You drive like hell," I said as he hit 45 on one of the city's busiest streets. Wilson smiled and said:

"Hell, Chuck, you ain't seen nothing yet."

Wilson pulled the car over and got out to talk to a middle-aged man. Rick told me that his nephew was involved in a dope ring. All Wilson said when he got back was, "There are a lot of kids involved in that ring."

We made our way back to Southville by an indirect route. Wilson seemed to be cruising rather than heading anywhere in particular. We passed an elaborately endowed female and Rick said:

"Mmmm, mother! Do I want some of that."

"Give me two," I said.

"You like that?"

"Twice on Sundays."

Rick laughed, probably as much at me as with me.

Wilson pulled the car over in front of a poolroom that I had never seen before. All three of us got out of the car and went in. The place was dark and no one was playing pool. Four men, perhaps in their late thirties, were standing around. The man behind the counter looked at Wilson and said with exaggerated imitation of fear:

"Oh, Mr. Smith, sir! Ain't nobody been doing nothing bad here." He looked like he was doing an exaggerated imitation of Stepinfetchit—if that's possible. Then he smiled at Wilson and Rick. "What can we do for you guys?" However, by the time he got the sentence out the other three people in the room were talking and yelling at the two detectives. Mostly the hubbub focused around Wilson.

"Aw, Wilson, I'm surprised at you. You're in the wrong place. There hasn't been a game here in three months."

"Just stopped in to see my old friends," said Wilson as he exchanged hand slaps with another man.

"Hey, Wilson!" said the third man, "when are you going to take a vacation?"

"I've just come back. You missed me?" Wilson had the pleased smile he always had when he outsmarted someone.

The joking went on for a few minutes. I noticed that Rick was off in a corner talking intently with the proprietor. Their conversation was punctuated with a laugh or joke in just the manner I had learned to expect when he was talking with someone who was giving him information and he wanted to make it look like casual talk.

As we walked out I asked Wilson:

"What did you expect to get there?"

"Nah, there wasn't a game. They're all straight guys; they take their pinch and don't bitch." Wilson was never very good at giving straight answers.

We got back in the car just in time to get a call over the radio for Wilson to call Sergeant Daley, who nominally runs the Vice Squad. We drove to the nearest police phone and Wilson called the office. Daley wanted to talk to him about hitting a game on the corner of Edgehill and Simon that we had hit twice in the last three weeks with little success. DeMatteo, Watson, and Daley would come from one direction and we would come from another. Rick was pleased. He said that the owner of the bar on that corner had it coming, ever since he called up the chief to complain that Wilson and Rick were harassing him. "He's been serving teenagers in there for years and Moscow sells numbers in there, but I never hassle him because he keeps the kids out of trouble. But this pisses me off."

To get to Edgehill we had to practically drive past the office and right next to the new mall we saw two white kids hitching. One of them flashed a V "peace" sign and yelled a greeting to Wilson. We stopped.

"Hey, Wilson." the kid said. "Can you give us a ride down to New York Avenue?"

"No, but I'll get you to that bus that's going there. Hop in."

They got in the back seat and one of them looked me over very carefully as if to remember the face of this new "narc." I cringed and thought "I'll probably meet him at a party next week."

"How are things?" the other kid asked.

"Fine. How long did it take you to make bond?"

"Eight fucking days; ain't that a bitch?"

"Sure is."

As they got out and caught the bus Wilson said, "Eight fucking days! The bastard really got his. I guess he'll beat it, though. Fucking junkie."

The raid on the game was a flop. Daley got there too early and scared the players away. Of about twenty guys in the game, they got only four. We left Daley and his car waiting for the police van to take the four down for booking.

We dropped by Wilson's house for a minute so that he could pick up his gun, which he had left home. "I don't do that often," he said in a tone that meant almost never. "You never know when you're going to need it."

Five minutes later there was another call from Daley so Wilson called the office again. This time we were to meet Daley in a parking lot behind some building on Columbia Avenue which the Vice Squad generally used as a place from which to watch the broads on Columbia picking up their tricks. It's a good place for that because the way the streets are set up the trick has to drive his car a block with the girl in it before he comes to the driveway out of the parking lot. This gives the detectives plenty of time to get into their cars and follow the trick's car without losing him.

When we got to the rendezvous, Daley and Wilson did most of the talking. Rick loitered in the background talking to the other detectives. If Daley didn't have "Sergeant" before his name, one would think that Wilson ran the squad. DiMatteo had a key to one of the buildings across the street. He and Watson proposed to go up there and watch, and radio down which cars should be followed. Daley wanted Wilson and Rick to follow the cars but Wilson managed to convince him that he had something important "on the line" and that he should take Watson and do the following.

Daley also told everyone, "Let Susie Clark operate for a few days."

Wilson responded, "Okay, she's a good kid and she's given us some information at times." Daley's comment meant, of course, that she had given him some good information about something, but the phrasing seemed peculiar to me. I wondered if he was trying to keep that from me. He was the only one who wasn't accustomed to my being around.

While I was pondering this Wilson said to Daley: "Hey, did you read in the paper about the guy who got 'held up' down here two days ago?"

"Yeah, boy, that's a laugh."

"Why?" I interrupted,

"Because the odds are ten to one that one of the whores ripped off his wallet and then he had to explain it to his wife so he screamed that he got held up."

Daley, DiMatteo, and Watson stayed there and we went back to cruising. We drove up to the poolhall on Western Avenue where all the junkies in that part of town hang out. We pulled up to the curb and Wilson got out, directly but slowly, and walked in with Rick and me following. Inside the poorly lighted room were about a dozen black men, none of whom I knew or recognized. Wilson nodded to several but then he simply walked out. Rick talked to one guy for a minute about nothing at all and then we both walked out. Rick said to me:

"That's really strange. Not a fucking one of them here. I wonder where they've all gone?"

Rick and Wilson seemed discouraged. They had not done much so far. We drove down the street and Wilson saw a guy who looked suspicious. He backed the car down the street toward him but the guy didn't seem to notice us. Wilson sighed and drove on.

"That's the test; if he don't run he ain't got nothing on him." The comment struck me as funny because only two days before DiMatteo had said to me, "you can't always tell, a cool guy will just stand there and talk and smile while he's holding."

We drove around some more. Wilson looked really down; when Rick noticed it he started telling stories to cheer him up. It turns out that both Rick and Wilson had played minor league baseball. Rick was in a class B league and had a brief tryout with the Braves. Wilson said that he played AA ball and spent six weeks with the Orioles. However Wilson is a bullshitter and

I don't really believe him. The talk seemed to cheer Wilson because suddenly he slammed the accelerator down on the floor and said:

"Come on, let's see if we can't get something before the night is over."

We headed for the main street in Southville and then turned down Athens Street and stopped about three doors from the end of it. We got out. Both Rick and Wilson seemed to know where they were going. It took me a few moments to realize that we were headed for a house I had seen them look at and comment on previously. Wilson did not head for the house but went down the driveway toward the garage. An area that looked like a small back yard was enclosed by a six-foot fence.

"There is supposed to be a fair amount of stuff buried back here," said Rick in a tone indicating that Wilson already knew it and he was just bringing me up to date.

We peered over the fence into a yard of ragweed three feet high. There were several trails in the ragweed but no obvious place where any stuff was buried. Wilson seemed to decide very quickly that he didn't have much chance of finding it because he kept looking at the house. As we walked back to the car he said:

"There's supposed to be thirty-five half loads taped to the back of the dresser in the kid's room. What do you think?"

"We probably ought to get a warrant on something that big," Rick said.

"Yeah," Wilson replied, "but we'd have to get Judge Royce out of bed; it's almost 10:30." I could see that Wilson didn't relish the idea of an hour in the office writing out a warrant. He started the car and we headed down the street. Wilson had apparently decided not to bust in without a warrant. Suddenly Rick said:

"There he is," and Wilson jammed on the brakes and they both dashed out of the car toward a young black kid wearing matching electric green shirt and pants. The kid didn't run.

"Okay, up against the car," Wilson said.

"What's going on? I didn't do nothing", the kid said, looking somewhat scared. Rick pushed him over to the car and proceeded to pat him down. In the left rear pocket he found something that looked as if it was used to carry a small screwdriver set but instead contained a set of works. Rick looked them over closely and handed them to Wilson who examined them while Rick finished the search. They put him in the back seat with me and we headed for his house.

Wilson said, "We're gonna search your house, Jack."

"Oh come on Will, you don't have to do that; that's not fair."

"If you're gonna play this game kid, you gotta take what's coming to you," Rick replied.

We got out of the car and went into the house, which must have once been a spacious home for a wealthy family. Now it was cut up into three flats and looked dirty and depressing. As we approached the door Jack said:

"Hey, Ma, . . ."

"Shut up kid," Rick said.

"Hey, Ma, get dressed."

"Come on," Wilson said.

"Jesus Christ, my mother's in bed sick. At least you can let me tell her to get dressed."

Rick nodded hesitantly.

"Mom, can you get dressed? Some people want to come in."

After a few minutes a rather tired-looking woman appeared at the door in a dressing gown. Wilson started talking.

"Sorry to get you up ma'am. I'm Detective Smith from the police department. We have reason to believe that there are narcotics hidden here in the house and we would like to get them out of here if it's all right with you. I know you don't want them around and we'll be sure to dispose of them properly for you."

The woman looked a bit puzzled and then said;

"Narcotics? I don't know nothing about them. I never had nothing to do with them."

"I know you don't ma'am. But we have information that some have been hidden here without your knowledge and we'd like to get them out of the house for you."

"Well, I guess so; so long as you don't tear up everything."

We all walked in and looked around. The place looked like a sick room; the curtains were drawn and there was a bed behind the curtain in what was meant to be the living room. Rick took Jack back into the kitchen and searched him more thoroughly. He found eleven bags of heroin on him but he was clearly more interested in the thirty-five half loads that were supposed to be behind the dresser. He gave the eleven bags to Wilson and started searching the apartment. He made a perfunctory search of the kitchen and then headed for the kid's bedroom. He looked under the bed, in the drawer of the side table, checked the drawers of the dresser and finally looked behind the dresser. There was nothing there. Rick's face dropped but he continued searching.

Meanwhile Wilson was explaining to Jack's mother that he believed Jack was being used by some of the big dealers in town to peddle their drugs for them. Jack's mother suddenly seemed to become aware for the first time that they were accusing her son of having narcotics.

"Jack is a good boy. He wouldn't do that."

"I know that. I've given him several breaks because I know he's basically a good boy but he's in with the wrong crowd and getting himself in for a lot of trouble." The conversation continued and Wilson said nothing when Rick brought the eleven bags in from the other room, but the woman noticed it. Wilson tried to get her to understand the situation as one where her son was being led astray by others. When Jack returned from watching Rick, his mother hit on him.

"Jack, I want you to tell these men the truth. I don't want you to cover up for anybody else. Tell them the truth."

"She's right, Jack," Wilson said, "heroin is no joke. Straight business. You're only upsetting your mother by all of this stuff and getting yourself into trouble. You ought to clean up and show us where the rest of the stuff is." Wilson continued like this while the woman got more and more upset. Jack kept looking at his mother and he seemed concerned about her agitation.

"Don't worry, Mom," he said, "these guys are nothing but three clowns." One glimpse at Wilson's face showed that he didn't feel very comic. However, Wilson seemed to have decided that further talk would get him nowhere so he explained to the woman that he was going to have to take her son downtown for further questioning. She wanted to know whether or not she should come also and Wilson said that Jack could call her later if he needed her.

We walked outside and as soon as the door slammed Wilson's face changed from the polite deferential expression he used when talking to respectable outsiders to a look of hard anger.

"You little mother-fucking bastard," he said, giving the kid a swift kick in the seat, "three clowns, huh?" He shoved the kid toward the car. "Get the fuck in." The kid got in the back seat behind the driver and I got in on the other side behind Rick.

"Listen to me, you lousy fucking pipsqueak junkie. You're in way over your little nigger head. I'm gonna tell you one thing and I want you to get this through that thick fucking skull of yours. Don't you ever, ever, call me or any of my friends names again. You understand?"

The kid nodded. He looked very scared.

"Good. Because if you ever do anything like that again you're going to be in really big trouble. I'll take you down to the station where they can't see me and I'll beat the living hell out of you. Hell, I'd do it in your own goddam backyard. I'll beat that little pea-sized brain of yours to a pulp and I'll do it with one hand tied behind my back."

Wilson went on like that and I looked at Rick hoping maybe he would do something that would relieve my anxiety about Wilson's anger. Rick just sat and watched. I knew he didn't like it much more than I did. Rick admired many things in Wilson but his use of threats and violence wasn't one of them. He preferred to con and negotiate.

However, Wilson's tirade had clearly scared the kid because he said: "OK, OK, I take it all back. Hell, if you hadn't run your mouth off like that about the heroin in front of my mother I would have told you where the stuff is that you were looking for."

"Run my mouth off, did I? You little cock-sucker . . ." Wilson continued angrily.

"Wait a minute, Will," said Rick, picking up on what the kid had said. "Look, if you'll tell us where that stuff is we'll let you go right now and forget about the whole thing."

"No, I can't do that. They'd find out about it and then I'd be in real trouble."

"Don't worry about that. If you want we'll just let you out right here and no one will be the wiser. Or if you don't want to talk here we can go down to the station and let you out on minimal bond and we'll take care of it when it comes up in court. Just don't worry about it, we'll take care of it."

"But it will get in the papers."

"We'll lose the arrest card, don't worry about it."

"Well, I don't know, if I do that you guys will think I'm a fink and you won't respect me."

"Oh shit," Rick said, "You can't really believe that."

We were almost downtown at this point and it was clear that they weren't going to let him out near his house, but take him instead to the station and book him.

"Now let's get some preliminary information, just to make sure you are really going to cooperate with us and that you're not just gaming on us. OK?" Wilson asked. The kid nodded. "How much stuff does this guy have?"

"A piece." Wilson's eyes lit up.

"What's his name and where's he from?"

"I don't know his name. They call him William and he's from out of state. The Midwest. Iowa, I think. At least he's mentioned being there at times."

We got out of the car and Wilson and Rick walked on either side of him as if to conceal him from strangers. They joked with him as we headed up the stairs to the office. When we got to the office, they took him back into the bathroom and closed the door to the hall from which the approach to the bathroom could be seen. I had never before seen them so careful about hiding an informant, but neither had I ever before seen them have a lead on that much heroin.

I couldn't fit into the space near the bathroom so I sat on the radiator a few feet away. Rick did most of the questioning in such low tones that I could hear only about half of it. From the talk, and what Wilson told me when he stepped back from the questioning, it became clear that the kid was still very worried. William not only had a shotgun in his car at all times but various small arms in the house. The kid said that William was a hit man for the Syndicate and worked on contracts. This seemed to add to the excitement.

I asked Rick if he planned to get a warrant. He said, "No; hell, we can always go in on 'speedy information.'"

"Yeah, but it might not hold up in court," I said.

"Well, we can search him and the room he's in and we'll probably find something. If not, we can still pick up the dope and that's all that counts."

In the meantime, however, Daley had come back and decided that he wanted to have a warrant, "just in case anybody gets hurt." McDowell, the desk officer, sat down and wrote up the application for the warrant. When he was finished both he and Rick signed it and I decided to go with them to get the thing signed. They called a few judges and found that Judge Costanzo, who lives in East Riverdale, was home and would look at it.

We got in a car and Rick drove. It was an interesting drive because McDowell had never liked Rick. McDowell, a nice, somewhat plump family man, couldn't stand "colored people." He makes an exception for Wilson because he is "the best cop I've ever known," but not for Rick, whose special sin is that he whistles at white girls. Still, he was such a nice guy that even a hard-core liberal like me couldn't really dislike him.

"Nice piece of work you guys did," McDowell said.

"Not me; Wilson. I never saw the kid before."

"Hell," I said, "Wilson would have still been fighting with him if you hadn't shut him up."

"No, you just don't know Wilson. He would have gotten it another way."

"Best cop I ever met," put in McDowell.

"Will Costanzo sign it?" I asked.

"He'd better. It's a perfectly written warrant," said McDowell proudly, passing the paper back to me. We were driving on the freeway and I could just make out what it said by the overhead lights. It contained all the usual junk about the "known and reliable informant" and the surveillance of the house showing that the suspect lived there, etc.

Costanzo, they told me, was a good judge for getting warrants signed, although he didn't like being gotten out of bed. McDowell, however, felt that this was a big enough thing so that he would not mind. When we finally found his house they told me to wait in the car and the two of them went up to the house. A short bald man in a bathrobe greeted them somewhat grumpily. Three minutes later they reappeared and the judge was smiling and wishing them good luck.

Rick called the office on the car radio.

"V6 to V1, V6 to V1. Out."

"V1 to V6, go ahead. Out."

"We've got it, Will, see you at intersection at 24 hundred. Out."

"Good! Out."

They had arranged to meet at an intersection two blocks from William's house. We got there at ten minutes before midnight and Daley, Smith, DeMatteo, and another detective from robbery were already waiting.

Daley said, "Wilson, you and Roger take the back door. Take Chuck with you and keep him out of trouble. Rick and I will take the front and Walt and George will watch the sides. We'll go in at five of exactly."

They set their watches and we went around back. The house was in one of the black working-class neighborhoods and, although easily sixty years old, it was still pleasant. The back had a small yard with a low fence over which we climbed and a screened-in porch which was not locked. We waited. DeMatteo seemed nervous and kept fidgeting. I was scared. Wilson wasn't. He had a large black shotgun with both barrel and stock sawed short.

Suddenly, we heard the others bang on the front door. DeMatteo banged on the back door and yelled, "Open up." Without waiting for a reply he kicked his heel hard into the door where the lock was. The door sprung open. DeMatteo dived for the right side and I suddenly realized I was right in the line of any fire that might come from the other side of the door. I dived after him and hit the floor hard. I turned and saw that Wilson was hugging the left side of the door with the shotgun pointed around it into the hall. There was no one there.

"Come on Rog," Wilson said. They moved into the hall and I, still shaken by my great confrontation with a nonexistent danger, followed them slowly. We walked down the hall and into the living room where Daley and Rick stood with guns pointed at two young men and a woman. Roger ran up and searched one man while Rick searched the other. They found a few bags on each of them. Roger patted the girl down for weapons and tried not to look embarrassed. No weapons were found.

"Where's William?" said Wilson, guessing that neither of the two teenagers looked much like a syndicate "hit man."

"He's out," said one of the men.

"Where?"

"I don't know; he didn't say," came the sullen reply.

"When's he gonna be back?"

"I don't know; pretty soon I guess."

"Well, we'll just have to wait for him," said Daley. "Sit down over there," pointing to the couch.

Everyone put away his gun except for Rick who stood near the window waiting for a blue Chrysler that William supposedly would return in. McDowell watched the three on the couch and the others began to search the house. It didn't take long. Wilson called Daley into the kitchen and everyone else came too. Lying on the kitchen table was a clothes hanger bent into a circle with a nylon stocking stretched over it. Next to it in a plastic bag was perhaps three cubic inches of white powder. Wilson explained in an authoritative voice that they must have just finished crushing the piece and straining it through the stocking and the next thing they would do was cut it and put it into the bags.

The next half hour was spent waiting and searching. McDowell and DiMatteo searched clothes, chairs, every drawer, under mattresses, in cupboards, and everywhere else they could think of. After a while I joined in out of boredom and searched a chest of drawers. I found nothing. Then McDowell decided that he had better recheck it, "just to make sure." He found two ten-dollar bags, one stuffed in a baby's shoe and another in a blouse pocket.

Bags seemed to have been stashed all over the house in one place or another. After half an hour of searching they had collected about two dozen regular bags and half a dozen dime bags. It would have been a good bust even without the piece.

Rick stood by the window hiding behind the curtain. Occasionally he would turn and listen to Wilson and Daley talking about how to handle William's return. Suddenly he said in a quiet voice;

"I think this is them."

DeMatteo moved the three prisoners into a back room after warning them to keep quiet unless they wanted their heads shot off. His gun was drawn again. I thought he looked scared. Wilson put himself behind a wall with his shotgun poked around the corner. Daley took cover behind the couch; Rick stayed behind the curtain and others covered the door from various angles. I hid behind a wall so I could not see William's entry. I heard the latch click and William and his girl took a few steps into the hallway when Wilson yelled at him not to move. I waited for the gunfire but none came. I peered around the edge of the wall to see Wilson searching William and Daley searching the girl. They had no guns on them but Daley found six bags in the girl's pocketbook.

William certainly did not seem as impressive as I had expected. A short dark man with a sheepish grin, he certainly wasn't type-cast as a Mafia hit man. Daley must have gotten impatient waiting because he barely said a word to the archvillain and escorted him out to his car. Wilson and Daley took William and his girl, and Daley and McDowell took the other two. Rick, the robbery detective, and I were left standing around.

"Well, Chuck, what do you think of that?" Rick asked when we got into the car.

"Oh, I don't know, run of the mill," I said jokingly. "I bet they paid $750 for that stuff, maybe more. God knows what it'd bring on the street."

"That's the most dope I've ever gotten in one bust."

"Yup, not bad," I observed.

"Sure has been a hell of a night," Rick said lighting a cigarette and taking a deep drag.

5   O. Ryan's Day in Court

The District Court is a very confusing place for an outsider. Until one knows the routines and the personnel of the court, it is difficult to tell what is going on. Even when this basic knowledge is available, just what is happening at any moment is not a simple matter, if only because conversations between the prosecutors and the defense attorneys leave a great deal tacitly assumed. Despite the legal background of one of the two observers, it took much of the combined total of five months of going to court every day and taking extensive notes before we felt we had an adequate grasp of the way court personnel do drug work. Even so, we had to spend endless hours rereading notes and analyzing conversations.

The following chapter depicts the prosecutor's handling of the problems of drug work and something of the way court work transpires. No single day can ever completely represent the totality of court work, nor could we, even though the events depicted in this "day" actually occurred on several different days. On this particular day the prosecutor is having a lot of trouble with the judge. On a "typical" day he does not. Yet his problems with the judge are "typical" of a more general problem that prosecutors in Riverdale are never free from—the problem of managing the docket so as to get through it relatively efficiently.

ORSON RYAN ambled into court, a basket of files under his arm. His stooped form and shuffling gait did not detract from his enormous body. O. Ryan, as he was called, was painfully aware that his night school law education did not make him an adequate match as a prosecutor for the better-trained defense lawyers he had to deal with, at least on the fine points of law. Nevertheless, O. Ryan was sharp, in ways that only his opponents fully realized. What's more, he was both gentle and just, qualities which earned him respect from everyone in court, a respect which many of the legally sharper prosecutors could never gain.

O. Ryan was a little late this morning. As he entered the courtroom he was besieged by defense attorneys wanting to deal with their cases in the District Court so that they could get over to Superior Court when it opened at ten o'clock.

"Everyone out; one at a time! You know how I do things. You, Paul, what have you got?" Paul had been around a long time. Ryan liked his direct humor. The other attorneys went into the courtroom.

"Well, number 44 is a breach with the guy's wife. I think she'll drop it; give me two weeks, will you?" Paul began. Ryan nodded and marked a date two weeks hence on the file. "I'm gonna file for a bill of particulars in the Wilson case, number 21. You remember that one, marijuana and pills on the floor at the party. The girl is mine." Ryan looked at the motion. It was the usual shit. They granted these routinely. He just nodded, meaning that he would not oppose the motion when it came up. Paul continued: "I think we can have them all plead to marijuana if you nolle the pills. Is $25 or $50 all right?" Again Ryan nodded. Paul was easy to work with. He didn't fuss and try to get unreasonable dispositions. There was no trouble with this one since it would be hard to prove to whom the drugs belonged anyway.

"The Malone case is a tough one. I'm gonna have to file a motion on it. It's a bad case. Only a fool would give a cop forty-eight bags of heroin," Paul commented. "Malone is no fool; that's a bad bust and you know it." Ryan said nothing, but he knew that Paul was right. Still, Paul would have to do better than that before the judge. No judge was going to drop a case on the grounds that a cop was obviously lying even if he thought he was.

"I'm not going to nolle it," O. Ryan said.

"The last one I've got," Paul went on without contesting Ryan's decision, "is 72, Juan Sanchez. He's been in this country for five years. No trouble. He got a little drunk and busted a guy in the chops. They've got it down as aggravated assault. Do me a favor and reduce it to a breach. He's been trying to get his citizenship. A felony would ruin it." The prosecutor looked at the police report. It appeared to be just another barroom fight. He'd probably reduce it anyway. "Sure," he said. "Hell, let's make it drunk and disorderly if you think he's all right." Ryan began writing out a new charge. "Thanks a lot, O., I appreciate it." Paul walked out, satisfied.

The next lawyer to enter was Roger Johnson—handsome, pleasant, and out of Chicago Law. Ryan could not stand him, but he hid his feelings well.

"Well, what do you have today?"

"Wilkins, 88, a heroin bust, two bags." Ryan read the police report. The arrest was done with a warrant and it looked pretty good. Johnson would probably get him into treatment.

"Does he have a record?"

"No."

"What else you got?"

There was a shoplifting case in which Johnson was going to file a motion to dismiss on dubious grounds. Ryan shrugged. Let him file. The next case was for breach of peace and ignoring an overhead signal. The breach of peace came from yelling at the cop. Ryan nolled it in return for a guilty plea to the other charge.

John Renfort, a Legal Aid lawyer, followed Johnson. Renfort had two heroin cases. It looked like quite a day for heroin. Piatelli, Chief Prosecutor, had been talking about trying all the drug cases on the same day each week. Maybe he had started this without telling anyone.

Renfort tried to talk Ryan into keeping jurisdiction and not binding it over to Superior Court on one of the possession cases.

"How many bags did he have?"

"Just a couple. Small-time shit."

"What about his habit. Does he have one?"

"No, he just started. It takes them a while you know."

Ryan figured that Renfort was lying. He probably hadn't the faintest idea what sort of habit the kid had. Ryan had caught Renfort lying before and he didn't trust him. Nonetheless, the kid had only a few bags and no record. He might as well keep the case. They'd only put him on probation if he bound it over.

"Will you plead him today?"

"Give me two weeks. I've got to get him a job and, you know, build up something to work with."

"OK." O. Ryan had seen Renfort work before. By the time the judge got around to sentencing the punk he would have a job, be in a treatment program, and look sweeter than candy. Still, it wouldn't hurt the kid any.

Renfort wanted a continuance in the next case too. Fannie Perkins, a long-time prostitute Ryan had seen many times, was trying to get a letter from the Mental Health Center stating that she was on the Methadone Program. She hadn't been in the program long enough, however. Renfort asked Ryan to put the case off for three weeks until he could get the letter.

The next case involved two lawyers, one private and one from Legal Aid. Two men had been arrested for breach of peace. One had come home and found the other in bed with his wife. Now their lawyers wanted the charges dropped. Ryan agreed; it was none of his business anyway, the cop had only arrested them to stop the fight. Both were pretty banged up so they got what they gave.

Roger Clark, a full-time prosecutor (O. Ryan served only part time) finished doing the arraignments and Ryan could start calling cases. Clark also mentioned that three lawyers asked him to put off their cases until they got back from Superior Court; Ryan nodded. It was all right provided they got back before he ran out of cases to call.

Ryan stepped from the back room into the courtroom and looked around. It was raining. The normally grubby courtroom was even drearier than usual with its fluorescent lights and gray rain-soaked light coming in through windows that hadn't been washed in twenty years. The court was packed as usual with blacks and some hippies. A well-groomed middle-class man sat in the middle of the sea of faces looking very uncomfortable. Ryan wondered why he was there. Did he have a kid on drugs? No, there was no son or daughter next to him. It would be interesting, he thought, but he never did find out why the man was there.

Ryan walked over to the long gray table that he worked on and put down his basket of files. The table was situated five feet from the "bench" behind which the judge would sit. The prosecutor and the defense attorney stood on the far side of the table facing the judge. On the other side of the table, with their backs to the judge, sat the court reporter and the clerk, whose joint business it was to keep a record of what happened.

Judge Fineberg entered to the cry of "Everybody stand." O. Ryan was already standing.

"Good morning, Your Honor."

"Good morning, Mr. Ryan," the judge said with a stern pomposity that Ryan hated. "A soft judge, but very sticky," was Piatelli's verdict on this guy. It was going to be a pain dealing with him. He was pretty soft in sentencing, which was helpful because the defendants would plead in front of him. Although once in a while Fineberg let someone off with a ridiculously small sentence, the real problem was that Fineberg was sticky; he always tried to run the court his own way. Sure enough, he began immediately.

"Well, Mr. Ryan, I trust that you are ready to move things right along today."

"Yes, Your Honor."

"Good. When I was here the last time it was taking five months to get cases settled. Now you know that I believe that we should have all cases settled in ninety days, except in exceptional circumstances. So let's get cracking."

"Yes, Your Honor. The first case is number 22." Ryan was already annoyed. Fineberg was at his worst. It was his first day in this court this year and he obviously intended to make an impression. If he was going to try to speed things up, he would probably make a fuss about continuances. Ryan had, in other circumstances, been known to complain about the same thing. The court was jammed and cases dragged on from one continuance to another. But, as prosecutor, there was little he could do about it. He could get the defense to go forward with their cases, but the odds were that they could talk the judge into a continuance anyway. Besides, defense attorneys got angry when one tried to push them.

At least Fineberg was not like Adams, who had been on the bench the last two weeks. Adams didn't care how much time it took, and since he used to be a prosecutor, he never wanted anyone to get off too easily. That was one reason why there were 130 cases today; every defense attorney had had a good reason why he needed a continuance during those two weeks.

The first few cases had gone all right and Ryan began calling Paul's cases. He always tried to call the private lawyers first, since their time was money.

"Sarah Ann Wilson, number 21, represented by Attorney Dudley." Paul Dudley had an impressive courtroom manner. Despite the fact that he always looked as if he had been on a binge the night before, he could crack a gentle joke and then get away with something outrageous. But this wasn't his day.

"Your Honor, good to have you back."

"Thank you, Mr. Dudley."

"Your Honor, in this case I wish to file a motion for a bill of particulars."

"Fine, we'll set that down for tomorrow afternoon." A shocked look ran around the table. "Oh well," thought Ryan, "at least it's not a motion that matters." It was pretty much routine to give two weeks to prepare arguments on such motions.

"But Your Honor, I'd like at least a week to prepare the argument."

"Come, come, Mr. Dudley, if you've filed the motion surely you know what it is you're asking."

Paul didn't say anything, but turned to go. Ryan caught him by the arm and said: "The next case is Juan Sanchez, number 72, also represented by Attorney Dudley." Paul turned and smiled weakly.

"I'm going to file a substitute information in this case, Your Honor," said Ryan. "I think the charge of assault is not based on the facts in this case. It was a simple barroom fight and I'm not at all sure that Mr. Sanchez was responsible. So, based on Mr. Sanchez's fine record in Riverdale, I am filing a substitute information for a charge of drunk and disorderly."

"Is that all right with you, Mr. Dudley?"

"Yes, Your Honor."

"All right, will you enter a plea to that charge, Mr. Dudley."

"Yes, Your Honor. My client wishes to plea guilty." Dudley was pleased with the $35 fine. The judge disposed of the case. Ryan couldn't have cared less.

Ryan called Johnson's cases and Fineberg gave him a week to file a motion to dismiss. This raised the hope that maybe Fineberg would be more reasonable, but that hope was crushed when Renfort came up.

"Your Honor," O. Ryan began, "the next case is number 104, Richard Sametz, charged with possession of heroin. I'd like to have it put down for a plea in two weeks."

"You're going to keep jurisdiction, Mr. Ryan?"

"Yes, Your Honor."

"Why can't he plea today, Mr. Renfort? Surely he knows whether or not he is guilty."

"Uh, yes, uh, Your Honor, uh, it's just that we have not yet had time to consult in detail."

"Well, plead him now and we'll consider a change next week."

"Yes, Your Honor, we will plead not guilty." The defense lawyer gave Ryan a helpless look. The prosecutor knew that this procedure was a pain. He had to remember to mark down the agreement on the folder so that the next guy to get it didn't start preparing for a jury trial. Renfort wanted time, of course, which is what the old fathead didn't want to give him. The whole thing was stupid because Renfort would get his time anyway and there was nothing anyone could do about it.

Ryan continued to call cases he could do something with. He nolled the charges in the breach of peace over the man found in bed with the other man's wife and got pleas in a couple of cases. Ryan was now almost ready to ask for a recess to deal with the petty cases where there was no lawyer and talk to the public defender and the one or two lawyers who had shown up late, but he still had one of Johnson's cases and a dozen continuances which were going to be a problem. He called Johnson's case and a pretty black girl stood up and asked that the case be passed because Johnson was in Superior Court.

Ryan took a deep breath: "Your Honor, I would like to request that in cases 16, 42, 8, 13, 94, 17, 85, 111, and 109 continuances be granted for two weeks." Any other judge would have agreed, but Fineberg leaned back and said, "Let's take them one by one."

The prosecutor had been afraid that would happen. He had, of course, routinely granted many continuances that morning to lawyers who were out of town, to lawyers with phony excuses which meant their clients hadn't shown, and so forth. It was just the way it was done. Now he was just going to have to fight and lie about these cases.

"Well, Your Honor, cases 42, 8, 17, and 109 are new cases and we have always granted two weeks to the defense to prepare the case."

"They could have put in a plea, couldn't they?"

"Yes, Your Honor."

"Mr. Clerk, put a note in those files saying that there are to be no more continuances until there is a plea on record."

"Yes, Your Honor."

"Mr. Ryan?"

"Well, with number 16, Mr. Ritoli is out of town at the ABA meeting in Cincinnati."

"OK, one-week continuance." That was a surprise; someone else could have been sent from Ritoli's office.

"Numbers 13 and 111 are Attorney Wilson's cases and he is on trial in Superior Court."

"One week."

"The Reed case, number 85, is still waiting for a drug-dependence exam."

"Two weeks."

"Number 109 is Attorney Robertson's and perhaps he can explain why his client isn't here." Ryan turned to the short stocky Legal Aid lawyer. He hoped Robertson could do it, but Ryan couldn't see any reason why he should catch hell for Robertson's clients failing to show. Robertson couldn't be blamed either, though; junkies just can't be counted on.

"If Your Honor please, I am afraid that is my fault. My secretary usually calls clients the day before, but she was sick yesterday and I was too busy to call." His secretary had probably been trying to get the guy all week.

"Have there been any other continuances?"

"Yes, Your Honor, the last two times the case came up it was continued," said the clerk.

"Call the bond and order a re-arrest." Ryan was not surprised. It was bound to happen at some point and this was as good a case as any.

Ryan then explained that in the one remaining case the lawyer had simply left a note. But Fineberg seemed placated and granted a one-week continuance; he may have thought he was helping to speed things up by doing this, but really he wasn't. What would speed things up, Ryan didn't know. Maybe if it weren't for all the technicalities the Supreme Court had set up in the last ten years, the defense attorneys wouldn't take up so much time with trivial motions. Anyway, it wasn't Fineberg's business to try to do Ryan's job for him. He gave no more continuances than anyone else; only when there was a good reason!

It was now 11:30, court had been in session for a hour and a half, and Ryan had run out of cases on which he could act. He asked for a recess. The judge left and Ryan turned around to face the spectators and the defendants. As if on cue, about twenty people from the audience rushed toward him forming a rough line. The negotiations here were mostly trivial. One man had been arrested for breach of the peace and wanted to know if it could be settled today. Would he plead guilty? "Well, you see it was like this . . ." A brief story followed on how he was a little drunk and so-and-so had started an argument. Ryan read the account. Would he plead to drunk and disorderly? Sure. What would the fine be? Probably fifteen days suspended. That would be okay. Someone else wanted to know what to do; his lawyer wasn't there. Who was his lawyer? The guy didn't know. Ryan looked it up; his lawyer was standing ten feet away. Another defendant said he couldn't afford a lawyer and was told to wait until his name was called and they would assign the public defender. Then came somebody's mother. She wanted her son to plead guilty to a marijuana charge. Ryan said he'd give her the public defender. No, she could pay for a lawyer but did not want one; she just wanted her son to be properly punished. Ryan told her to take it up with the judge.

After fifteen minutes Ryan caught sight of Arthur White, the public defender. He motioned to him and they went into the back room and closed the door. Art White was about five feet six, thin, and stoop-shouldered. He carried himself in a way that said quite distinctly that he did not want to offend anyone. His face was usually sad, and at forty he looked fifty-five. Nevertheless, White was the best PD the court had had in the past five years. Ryan liked him. At least Art knew some law and saw his job as more than a way of getting paid.

"Boy, it's a real bitch of a day," Ryan said.

"Aren't they all?" White replied.

"Yeah, but have you seen Fineberg? He wants to run the court himself."

"That's what they're supposed to do, you know. It's the judge's court."

"Bullshit. Nobody runs this court, it's chaos, but it's up to me to see that it's orderly chaos." Ryan laughed at his own joke. "Well," he continued, "what have you got?"

"Half the damn docket, as usual."

"Let's just throw them out the window."

"Great," said the PD, motioning to get up and then sitting down with the smile gone from his lips. "We've got two breaches that are almost identical. Saturday night drunks. Shall we plead them to drunk and disorderly?"

Ryan nodded.

"We've got the Antonelli case again, the stickup on Grand Street. He just won't plead to theft, so I guess you'll have to bind it over."

"You gonna waive?" asked Ryan. White could go through the formality of a probable-cause hearing before the case got bound over to Superior Court, but he knew that White would waive it; he always did. The only use for such hearings was for each side to see what the other side's witnesses would say and how they might stand up under cross-examination. White wouldn't waste his time on this when the case was going over to Superior Court where another PD would be assigned. The defendant was a fool. He should have agreed to plead to theft; he would get more time in Superior Court. The case was open and shut; there was no chance of his winning on a motion or at trial.

White continued to take cases. "Give me another two weeks," White asked, "before we plea on the Walters case. He's trying to get some treatment at RMHC, and I can't see why he should have to plea before then."

"I'll do my best, but remember who's out there," Ryan said, referring to the judge's desire to curtail continuances.

"Well, hell, if you have to put it on the jury list go ahead." White pulled another file and said, "I've got a problem with this one. My kid admits that it was his stuff, but it was a bad search. I mean, if someone got ahold of this and found that I'd pleaded it, it wouldn't look good. Besides, he's twenty-six and doesn't have a record. It's the sort of thing that you could nolle on the grounds of the search."

Ryan looked at the file. White was right; it was a lousy search. But Ryan didn't like to nolle heroin cases. Heroin is too dangerous to just let a junkie go outright. "Why don't you file a motion? Fineberg will go along and I won't fight it."

"I'll file to suppress and then you can nolle it."

"OK."

"I can't do anything with Mary Mullins' case now. The medical exam isn't back. Put it over for two more weeks."

"I think I can get that by."

"Now I have this guy Schwartz, he's an alkie and he's charged with forgery. I figured that we'd plead him to it, but this woman comes to me, I guess it's his wife, and says that he isn't guilty of forgery; maybe obtaining, but not forgery. Well, you know, I think she's right."

"What did she look like?" Ryan smiled at the PD's naiveté.

"The woman? I don't know, white hair, short, maybe fifty-five."

"Yeah, I guess you haven't been around long enough. That's Patricia McConaghy, and she's seventy if she's a day. Old Harry Grady told me that his father was arrested in a brawl in her whorehouse when he was ten. She's been around a long time. Now she just has some drunks who do a little shit for her now and again."

"So that's it, it all fits together. Will you keep jurisdiction?"

"Sure."

"Shall we plead him to obtaining?"

"Yeah." Ryan was barely listening. He was musing about Patricia McConaghy still hustling at seventy. He wondered how many other prosecutors had had to deal with her. He had to admire her.

"And this guy, I think I can plead to indecent behavior. He's crazy, but he's been to CSH several times and there's no sense in sending him back again. He doesn't know what's going on; just like his attorney." White laughed; "He'll do what I tell him."

"OK," Ryan said. "Anything else?"

"Just this thing. It's another rotten bust of Smith's. My guy walked in during the raid and they busted him too. The search is no good."

"The report says he had it in his hand."

"Yeah, but he didn't. It was in his pocket. They put him up against the wall and searched him."

"Well, file a motion."

"To suppress?"

"Yeah."

They walked out into the courtroom, White to tell his clients what was going to happen and O. Ryan to reconvene the court. He almost bumped into Paul Dudley.

"That bastard," Dudley said. "He really screwed me up."

"Why, it's not so bad."

"The hell it isn't; her old man owes me 5 C's and I want him to pay me before we settle this."

"We'll get you two weeks tomorrow when Fineberg is in a better mood."

At this moment Ryan noticed a policeman approaching and he turned toward him.

"Excuse me, Mr. Ryan, but could you explain to me what this motion is all about?"

"What's the case?"

"Elijah Thomas."

"That's Renfort's heroin case."

"I don't understand the motion. It says that I did not have the right to search other rooms of the apartment, but there was only one room in the apartment."

"They have the right to file whatever motions they want to file."

"Yes, yes, I know, but I don't understand what the motion is all about, that's all."

"Look," Ryan said with a somewhat too dramatic air, "he's just busting balls, that's all there is to it. Don't worry about it."

A few more lawyers were discussing their cases with him when he noticed Leslie Parker come into the room and head toward him. Leslie was a rather pretty young girl whom Ryan liked because, unlike some other female lawyers, she never seemed to use her sex as a means of winning cases. She did not try to seduce him into giving her nolles. Nevertheless, Leslie was probably a Communist. She defended every long-haired radical in town; she also had a habit of trying to dig up all the muck in the police department and the city administration and smearing it all over the headlines. Ryan liked Leslie personally even though he couldn't stand her politics.

"Good morning, Mrs. Parker," he said with a smile knowing what would come next.

"Ms. Parker, if you please," Leslie responded with mock indignation. She laughed and went on. "I have a political case again and I want it nolled; Richardson, number 124."

Ryan read the police report and said, "A political case, eh? It looks as if that means what it always does; you don't have a defense." It was a simple breach of peace at a demonstration, but Leslie Parker always fought these. "The last time anyone challenged the breach of peace statute on political grounds, it went all the way to the Supreme Court and lost."

"Yeah, but that was before yesterday's decision," she replied, referring to a new decision about vagrancy statutes being too general for the court.

Ryan looked at the file and noticed that Leslie was filing a demurrer. "Well, if you want to break stones, I'll see that your guy goes away for six months. For Christ's sake, Leslie, it's a lousy little breach. Why don't we plead him to some lousy little ordinance and we'll both be rid of it?"

"Why don't you nolle it, and we'll both be rid of it? You know it's a bad bust."

"See you this afternoon," said Ryan. They would argue the motion then. "It's OK with me if he goes away."

Leslie just smiled and said, "It's OK with me too. You know the story about the guy given a year in jail who turned to his lawyer and said, 'Well, what do we do now?' and the attorney answered 'Well, I don't know about you, but I'm going home.' See you after lunch." Ryan told the bailiff to get the judge to reopen the court.

"Your Honor, before we deal with any more business, we have several more arraignments to do."

"Can you bring them all in so I can explain their rights to them all at once?"

"They are right here, Your Honor." The bailiff motioned to the defendants. Four men and a woman got up. Fineberg recited their rights to them with all the enthusiasm of a race-car driver explaining the importance of speed limits. The defendants did not look much more interested, but the law required this formality.

Ryan called the first case: "Mr. William Kilkowski. Charged with breach of the peace and operating a motor vehicle without a license."

"Mr. Kilkowski, can you afford an attorney? If not, the state will assign the public defender to your case."

"I will get my own lawyer."

"OK; Mr. Prosecutor, do you want bail?"

"No, Your Honor, I think he can be released in his own recognizance."

"Is two weeks enough time for you to get an attorney, Mr. Kilkowski?"

"Yes sir."

"Set it down for two weeks."

Ryan proceeded to arraign a young lady for shoplifting and a drunk for breach of peace. The drunk had called the cop a motherfucker, which O. Ryan described as "referring in an improper manner to the arresting officer's Oedipal complex." In neither case did he ask for bond to be posted. Both would probably show up, at least assuming the drunk was sober. The drunk looked as if he worked, so Ryan had little worry. The public defender was appointed for the drunk and Art White took the man off to talk to him.

The final arraignment was a truck driver named Anatoli arrested for running cigarettes into the state from North Carolina to get around the high cigarette tax. Mr. Anatoli felt sure he would have a lawyer and so did Ryan; the mob would certainly supply him with a good one. Ryan did not ask for bail. The police had confiscated his truck and 5000 cartons of cigarettes. The truck driver would be back.

Next Ryan disposed of Art White's cases which they had previously agreed upon. Perhaps Fineberg was getting tired, because he agreed to all of White's continuances.

Finally Ryan began calling all the cases in which he had no agreement or in which there was no attorney. In many of these it was simply a matter of having the judge appoint the public defender. Ryan would ask the defendants if they could afford an attorney and when they said they couldn't, the clerk would give them an application to fill out and Art would take these forms to his desk. The judge almost never denied an application if the defendant was making less than ten grand a year. Anyone who wanted Art White as his lawyer could have him. Not that Art wasn't a good lawyer, but with eighty cases a month it is pretty hard to do it well.

During the morning when he had called a case and neither the attorney nor the defendant was there, he had placed the case in the back of his file. The odds were pretty good that the clerk's office had messed it up when neither of them appeared, so the Court tended not to do much except continue the cases, but Fineberg might be different.

"Your Honor, the next case is number 4, Walter Moscow. Neither Mr. Moscow nor Attorney Kilpatrick is in court."

"What's the charge?" Fineberg asked.

"Rape, Your Honor, the case is down for a probable-cause

hearing today. However, Your Honor, to my knowledge that is the first time this has happened. Mr. Kilpatrick is usually quite reliable."

"Rape is a serious charge, Mr. Ryan, but if you feel that this is an administrative mix-up, I'll go along with you. One week's continuance. Mark it this time, notice to counsel."

"Thank you, Your Honor," said O. Ryan. Max Kilpatrick owed him one for that. "Number 22, Ilya Roscovitch, represented by Attorney McDougall. Mr. Roscovitch says he has not seen Mr. McDougall and neither have I."

"Do you know where your attorney is, Mr. Roscovitch?" the Judge asked.

"No, Your Honor, he told me to be here and here I am."

"Two weeks, notice to counsel."

So it went through three more cases. Then he had three cases where the lawyers could not find their clients despite their earlier promises to do so. Ryan let them try to wriggle out of it themselves. Fineberg called the bond in one case where the client had been missing for two weeks in a row, but he gave continuances in the two cases where the bond had been posted by a professional bondsman. There was no reason the bondsman should pay for his client not showing.

Ryan's final problem was to deal with three black addicts who had been sent to CSH for treatment. This was a rather simple procedure. The hospital sent the court individually typed form letters stating that the defendants had received "maximum benefit from the treatment environment." Since the original agreement was that if the hospital thought the defendants did acceptably well, they could go on probation for two years, this deal had to be formally carried out. Fineberg made a show of being hesitant to agree to put them on probation, but it was only a show to make the defense attorneys look persuasive. All of them were given two years probation with the stipulation that they get outpatient treatment at the Mental Health Center.

The only real problem arose on the last case. Along with the robbery and possession charge that the other two had, this defendant had a nonsupport charge against him. Fineberg wanted to make payment of support to his wife a condition of probation, but Robertson, the defense attorney, argued strenuously that payment should be left to the discretion of the probation office. He said it would not be possible for the defendant to work if he was in a treatment program all day and he would probably have to be on welfare himself. Art White stepped in to help Robertson argue the point. Ryan considered pointing out that some people work nights, but decided that it didn't matter much. Fineberg finally gave in.

Three motions remained, but they would be taken up after lunch. If O. Ryan was lucky he would then have a few hours left before dinner to finish his preparation for a divorce case that he was working on in his private practice.

6 Defending Drug Cases

The chapter that follows describes the drug world from the defense attorney's perspective. It is the product of nearly five months with the criminal staff of a Legal Aid organization located in Riverdale. The two most experienced attorneys in the organization were the most closely followed, but the remaining staff of five were also observed. Through the cooperation of this organization, and the prosecutor's office, little that was meaningful, however informal, went unobserved.

Any attempt to observe and understand the defense in drug cases must be reconciled with the great diversity of cases and practicing attorneys appearing in criminal court every day. Drug cases in Riverdale are handled by public defenders, Legal Aid attorneys, and private attorneys alike, and the same attorneys who handle drug cases also represent clients on all kinds of criminal charges. In the course of our field work, we observed both private attorneys and public defenders representing clients on drug cases and other criminal matters. Thus this chapter includes our observations of private attorneys and public defenders as well as Legal Aid attorneys.

As we stated in the introduction, the goal of our work has been to present the phenomenon as it appears to itself. Yet this poses a dilemma. All that can be described is an observer's informed approximation of the actor's understanding of the phenomenon—in short, the phenomenon as it appears to us that it appears to itself. This dilemma is explicitly recognized in chapter 4 where the narrative style retains the observer's presence. It is implicitly recognized in other chapters where a third-person narrative is employed, not in the language of the observer but in that of the observed.

This chapter is an experiment in the presentation of our observations in a traditional scholarly style. It is explicitly written by the observer, not the observed. However, we have been careful to use only the language and concepts familiar to the world of defense attorneys. And, in an effort to bring the reader even closer to that world, the chapter begins with our notes on one defense attorney's day. Nonetheless, the reader should not conclude from the didactic style of presentation that this chapter contains anything more or less objective than an observer's account of defense perspectives on drugs, drug users, and drug cases.

FRIDAY, FEBRUARY 13.

Met Tony, the senior man on Legal Aid's criminal staff, in Superior Court. First case was Karen Joyce . . . violation of parole, possession of heroin. Tony: "It looks like a bad search. She was picked up for parole violation and searched on the street." Police found thirty bags in her purse. If she pleas to possession, State has offered 1½ to 3 concurrent with the parole violation. Tony told her she could get more than that if they lost a motion to suppress. He implied that they would lose. She agreed to plea. Tony asked for a continuance in the Alvarado case. Said he needed to talk to his client again. It was his first; the state has had three. (Tony: "They're uneasy about this one.") Later, Tony said he wanted the delay to get it before Judge Palko.

Next case was in District Court. Three clients, possession of marijuana. Two others were busted at the same time. They're represented by two private attorneys. All at university; live in duplex on 3rd St. Vice Squad had search warrant. (Tony: "It's a damn good thing O. Ryan doesn't have time to look at the warrants on file in the clerk's office. He'd see that one of my clients is supposed to deal heroin and that would screw everything up.")

Tony to O. Ryan: Why don't you continue Greenwalt—it was his stuff—and nolle the other four? None of them have a record and they're going to graduate in three months anyway.
O. Ryan: "No chance. I'll nolle the other four, but I'll have to have a change of plea out of Greenwalt first. Otherwise you'll come back in a couple of weeks and tell me the stuff belonged to one of the four I nolled."

Tony went to Kellerman and suggested the same disposition. Kellerman agreed and transferred the cases to his courtroom. Result: four nolles and a six-month continuance. If Greenwalt isn't arrested again, the charge will be dismissed.

Sentencing in Superior Court. LeRoy Williams on two counts: heroin possession and breaking and entering. Williams has been in jail for nine months already. Couldn't make bail. Tony has an "agreed rec." for a suspended sentence. But Williams' parents want him to get treatment. Tony and prosecutor, David Ambrose, talked it over and agreed the best thing to do was to put it before the judge.

Tony: Your Honor, I feel obliged to inform the court that Mr. Williams' parents think he should be treated for his drug problem.
Judge Ullman: Has he had treatment for this problem before?
Tony: His parents tell me he was on the Methadone Program, but it didn't help him much. He only got high.
Ullman: I don't understand that.
Tony: Neither do I, Your Honor.
Ullman: Well, he could commit himself to CSH, I suppose. Shall we make it a condition of his probation?
Tony: That may be the best answer, Your Honor. I have to see some clients there on Tuesday, so I could drive him up.
Ullman: All right. Any objections, Mr. Ambrose?
Ambrose: No, Your Honor.

Another sentencing, Richie Smith. Two counts, robbery and breaking and entering. An early NAU program member. The agreement: three to eight at Wintergate. To get the plea, Ambrose nolled a sales and a possession charge.

A comment by Tony: "You know, CSH seems to have improved. I had a long talk with Dr. Katz last week, and he's making progress up there. There isn't as much stuff getting onto the wards as there used to be. And my clients are staying up there, not running away. In fact, I've got some clients who were discharged five or six months ago and still haven't gotten into any trouble."

District Court. Tony's last case today. Margaret Howard. Kellerman dismissed the possession charge (three bags). Tony explained to me: "Last spring Kellerman agreed to defer her prosecution if she stayed out of trouble. She was just experimenting and didn't have any kind of record. She stayed straight, and now she's going to get married. You might call it a wedding present."

The defense attorney lives in a world of clients, cases, and courtrooms. His workday alternates hectic moments spent juggling too many cases with long periods of passing time while waiting for a motion or a case to be reached in the order of court business. He is constantly pressured by the needs of his clients, the negotiating positions of prosecutors, and innumerable deadlines in seemingly countless cases. The defense attorney must cope with the law, human needs, and bureaucracy, while managing to provide his client with an effective defense against a criminal charge.

The concept of an effective defense should not be confused with that of victory. If a jury returns a not-guilty verdict or a judge dismisses the criminal charge, the defense has unquestionably achieved a victory. But such clear-cut success is rare. More often, an effective defense involves building little victories and concessions into a total result which is acceptable in light of the client, his needs, and the peculiarities of the case at hand.

To provide an effective defense, then, the attorney does not ordinarily concentrate on building a case for resolution by a judge or jury, but rather for a negotiated settlement with the prosecutor. Before such a settlement can be reached, some issues, legal or otherwise, may have to be resolved by a judge, but ultimately the defense attorney directs his efforts toward influencing the prosecutor.

In preparing his case, the defense attorney will pose a number of questions. A picture of the defendant is essential to the negotiations. Does he have a record? Does he work or is he in school? What is his family like and how will they come across in court? Who does he hang around with? Has he had any counseling or treatment in the past? If he has been on probation before, what will his probation officer say about him? Is there anyone, like a coach, teacher, or minister, who will speak up for him?

Of nearly equal importance is the criminal behavior with which the client is charged. Was there a weapon involved or anyone injured? Does the client have a record of this kind of conduct? Has he had run-ins with the arresting officer before? Was anyone else the motivating force behind the crime? Did the client realize what he was doing at the time? What made him do it?

Also, there are questions relative to the possibilities for a negotiated solution to the case. Can there be restitution? Can the arresting officer be persuaded to drop the resisting charge, or would it be better to bring in evidence of the client's injuries? Will the prosecutor accept some counseling as part of the recommendation, or will he hold out for inpatient treatment? What will the probation officer say in his pre-sentence report? What has the client received on similar charges in the past? If he has to do time, what is the best way to get him eligible for an early parole? What judge can we get this before?

After a while, certain cases take on a pattern. Some assaults turn out to be family problems, auto thefts often are found to be tampering cases, and burglaries turn into drug cases. When a case is referred to in this manner, it fits into a familiar class for which there are established patterns of definition, procedure, and disposition.

Heroin Defendants

The type of drug in a drug case bears on the defense attorney's concern for his client. For marijuana and pills (which include hallucinogens, barbiturates, and amphetamines), he worries primarily about the impact of a conviction. What will a criminal record mean for this client's life? Will he be able to get a job? Can he get into college? Will it affect child-custody rights? The attorney worries about the social, legal, and economic consequences of a criminal conviction.

While the possession of a controlled drug other than heroin presents the defense attorney with problems, the problems are not qualitatively different from those of other criminal cases.

The presence of heroin, however, brings the defendant's health and welfare into the picture. In a sense, the presence of heroin makes it a *drug* case, as opposed to an ordinary *criminal* case.

The drug. What is so peculiar about heroin that it causes the defense attorney to worry not only about the normal consequences of a conviction but also about the individual's well-being? The answer partially lies in heroin's apparently captivating high and in the significant problems it creates in the individual's life. But, primarily, the concern of defense attorneys stems from the belief that heroin addiction is likely to be a permanent condition.

Heroin use is intrinsically pleasurable, but it is also exceptionally attractive to its users as a means for avoiding the cares and frustrations of a normal existence. As one attorney explained it:

> We have a different kind of kid coming in now. Two or three years ago the addicts were older and they said they were pretty much at the end of their string. Then we could get them into some kind of treatment and do something for them. Now you have seventeen- or eighteen-year-olds who are really into the whole drug thing and don't regret it. They like what they are doing and only want to know how you can get them off.

Or as a public defender once commented: "The clients I have now don't want to go straight. I know they'll be back out in the street shooting heroin as soon as they are out of CSH." Thus the defense attorney expects to find that heroin is the most important thing in his clients' lives.

Heroin may be a pleasant and convenient means for escape, but it also creates problems in the life of the user. In approaching his cases, the defense attorney expects to see evidence of such problems. His clients may be on welfare as the result of absences or poor performance at work. Their family life is usually breaking down into squabbles and separations. If the client is young, he is probably performing poorly in school and running with the wrong crowd. Heroin users are generally in poor health and they are devious and unreliable clients. In short, the defense attorney credits heroin with a capacity to degenerate his clients' bodies and lives. He does not expect to be defending individuals who have a good family life, are in good health, and perform well at work or in school.

Perhaps the most striking truth about heroin which defense attorneys learn from their clients is its capacity to addict:

> I've defended Tommy Green at least five different times before, and now he's got a robbery and a B&E. He has a really severe drug problem. He's been in treatment several times; this last time he was on the methadone program. In the past I've helped him get out of trouble and he's always slipped back into drugs. This time, he's going to get some time at Wintergate. I only hope he cleans up there.

The client who cannot be rehabilitated no matter how many programs he enters, the addict who returns to heroin as soon as he is out of jail, and the former client who dies of an overdose all tell the defense attorney something about the permanence of heroin addiction. His association with his clients also gives him a chance to categorize heroin users. In their negotiations with prosecutors, in their statements at sentencing hearing, and in their informal comments, defense attorneys consistently use several descriptions of their heroin-using clients.

Experimenters. An experimenter is an irregular user of heroin who has not yet become addicted. He may simply have sampled heroin to see what it was like, or he may have fully experienced heroin's pleasures. As an experimenter, he lacks any of the symptoms indicating that heroin has begun to cause problems in his life. A clean record is clear evidence of experimenter status, as is a regular job, continued education, or a good family situation.

Defense attorneys consistently apply two assumptions to those of their clients whom they describe as experimenters. The first is that they can get out of heroin fairly easily: experimenters are not committed to heroin use, and heroin has not, as yet, begun to create problems in their lives. The second is that even though some experimenters may fully understand heroin's pleasures, no experimenter can realize the inevitable consequences of a heroin career. So an experimenter is anyone who is just getting into drugs and trouble.

Drug problems. When a client has used heroin long enough for some of the ultimate consequences of a heroin career to be evident, he is said to have a drug problem. A sufficient criminal record may have been accumulated to indicate the kind of criminality that is needed to finance an expensive habit. Expulsion from school, the loss of a job, or significant family problems would strongly suggest that the client has gone beyond mere experimentation with heroin. Allegations of drug selling, the possession of more than a small quantity of heroin, and physical signs such as needle marks also are evidence that heroin has become a problem for him.

Heroin-using clients may have drug problems or serious drug problems. The difference lies not only in the degree of the client's addiction but also in the extent to which his case shows complications. A serious drug problem is evident when the prosecutor will not agree to a disposition which does not include an incarceration period.

One defense attorney represented a client who was charged with possessing fifteen bags of heroin, and described him to the court as having a "serious drug problem." He argued for a reduction of bail from $2000 to $500 and later explained that he was trying to get his client released so that the client could apply to the NAU: "Since he had more than five bags, it'll be bound over to Superior Court, where I may have a hard time with it. If I can get him into the NAU, I may be able to get the prosecutor to leave him there."

A client also has a serious drug problem when his record shows one or more treatment failures, or when he gets into trouble while he is out on bail awaiting trial on prior charges. If the defense attorney suspects that the prosecutor will require some time off the streets, the client may be described as in need of intensive inpatient care. Such clients are assumed to have some potential for rehabilitation, but the defense attorney has reason to fear that they are approaching a point of no return.

Hard-core addicts. There are some clients for whom the defense attorney holds no hope of rehabilitation. When speaking to his colleagues, he will refer to them as hard-core addicts. In his negotiations with the prosecutor, however, he will assert that they have serious drug problems. The hard-core addict is an incorrigible who has been in and out of treatment programs and jails. He will not, or can not, stop using heroin, and the defense attorney knows that the prosecutor will want such a client confined.

Heroin Cases

Drug cases have some unique features, and some problems that only infrequently appear in other criminal cases. The client's physical condition makes the prospect of pretrial confinment particularly troublesome. Then there is the certainty that a trial would simply come down to an issue of police credibility. The high level of public concern about drugs limits the prosecutor's discretion and lends a special air of gravity to drug cases. The belief that addiction is like a sickness, and that the disposition should help alleviate the client's condition, puts the defense attorney in the uncomfortable position of having to negotiate a disposition that is appropriate for the client's needs as well as his criminal behavior.

The picture, however, is not totally bleak. Drug cases do have some useful peculiarities. One is the availability of a variety of dispositional alternatives for drug-using clients. These range from conditional release to imprisonment and include an array of treatment opportunities. Drug cases inevitably involve an official seizure of an illegal drug and, consequently, it is the rare drug case that fails to present an opportunity to contest the constitutionality of the search and seizure. But the opportunities for effective defense work lie primarily in the ambiguities of drug cases.

The five-bag rule. Possession of heroin, as a crime carrying a maximum sentence of five years, resides in that gray area of concurrent jurisdiction that permits prosecution in either the District or the Superior Court. To locate the proper jurisdiction for particular cases, a practice eventually developed that requires the bind-over to Superior Court of any case that involves the possession of more than five bags of heroin. But the rule is subject to negotiation depending on the defendant's record, the probability that an illegal search and seizure claim can be won, and the likelihood that the defendant is a heroin user, rather than a dealer. To persuade the District Court prosecutor to retain jurisdiction over a case with more than five bags, the defense attorney might argue that his client has a serious drug problem needing treatment, and that the client is not a criminal (a dealer), but really a victim (a user). He might imply that his search and seizure claim has some merit, but is not strong enough to warrant the time involved in preparing briefs and conducting hearings. When he has a client with a record, the defense attorney might work very hard to avoid the consequences of the five-bag rule. On the other hand, if the client has little or no record, the attorney might just let the case go over to Superior Court. There the possession of seven bags of heroin would be one of the least serious charges on the docket and would call for a light sentence in relation to other cases.

Works. Another peculiarity of drug cases in Riverdale is the crime of possession of paraphernalia. One attorney commented about this charge:

> You're right. Technically, possession of works is not against the law here. But, then, the possession of heroin is, and if those works had traces of heroin in them, my client could have been charged with that. If I let the charge stay at "works," the case looks a lot different to the judge than it would if the charge sheet stated possession of heroin.

In Riverdale the possession of any quantity of heroin, however minute, is a criminal offense, so in some cases it is advantageous for the client to plead guilty to a nonexistent crime.

Accommodation sales. The sale of heroin is normally a serious charge. But the defense attorney may try to portray the sale as a transaction his client entered into reluctantly for the benefit of a friend, and not for profit. If he succeeds, it will be called an accommodation sale, and he will have achieved a significant victory in his negotiations with the prosecutor.

Addiction and responsibility. When the accommodation argument is unavailable, the attorney will often describe his client as a "little man," who sometimes buys and sometimes sells. He is a user, not a dealer. In fact, the attorney expects most of his heroin-using clients to do some selling. So when he represents a user in a sales case, he emphasizes the fact that the client is a user who is selling only because of his need to have heroin: "If he wasn't dealing a little, he'd have to be stealing."

Evidence of heroin use is also important to the defense attorney representing a client on a property-crime charge. If the charge is shoplifting, burglary, breaking and entering, or obtaining money under false pretenses, and if the defendant is a heroin user, then it will be argued that the crime was committed by someone who had to steal to finance a habit. The clear message is that the client is not a willful, malicious person deserving punishment, but rather an unfortunate who is trapped by something beyond his control and is in need of help.

Evidence of heroin use, however, is not always an advantage. If the client cannot control his behavior because of his need for money to finance a habit, he can be expected to continue his criminal behavior if he is allowed to go free pending the disposition of his case. This makes bail a difficult issue. The defense attorney cannot advance his client's drug problems too persuasively, for if he does, he may find the bail commissioner, the prosecutor, and the judge unwilling to set bail at a level the defendent can afford.

The defendant's drug problem also turns into a double-edged sword when the case is one that the defense attorney is convinced should not be prosecuted. This is referred to as a "bad case," where an arrest or search appears unconstitutional, or even unfair. A prosecution which is unworthy of the state, such as an accommodation sale, is also bad. When the defense attorney attempts to persude the prosecutor to agree to a low bond or to nolle the bad case, the client's drug use becomes a problem. Any kind of release means returning a heroin user to the community, and defense attorneys often find prosecutors reluctant to go along with such a result.

Handling Heroin Cases

The defense attorney's role in a drug case normally begins soon after the defendant's arrest, often at the time of arraignment when the defendant is informed of his rights and bail is set. Later, a plea to the charge must be entered, motions filed and argued, and, if the case is not nolled or dismissed by the prosecutor, a resolution to the defendant's guilt or innocence must be accomplished by plea or trial, and a disposition arrived at.

Pretrial release. The attorney's initial concern is for his client's liberty during the life of the case, and anything other than pretrial detention in the county jail will be acceptable. If the attorney learns that there is a warrant out for a client (usually when a client calls to say he has heard a rumor to that effect), he will try to persuade the client to turn himself in, thereby laying the groundwork for a claim that the client is reliable and can be expected to appear when required. If it looks as though bail will be set at a level beyond his client's means, the attorney may try to have him ordered to CSH for a drug-dependence exam and medical treatment. Or he may attempt to get his client released to the custody of the local store-front ARCH (Addiction, Referral, and Community Health agency).

Obtaining pretrial release for the client marks the end of the first stage of the drug case. The outcome that is achieved, whether release on bond, transfer to CSH for examination and care, or release to ARCH, is important not only because it is an alternative to indefinite detention at the country jail, but also because it contributes to the achievement of an acceptable final disposition to the case itself. A failure to get his client out of the county jail will pressure the attorney into negotiating from weakness, and often it may pressure his client into accepting any disposition, even one that will lead to time at Wintergate.

Once the client's pretrial status is resolved, the defense attorney turns to the possibilities for winning the case. If he can win, he knows he will not have to negotiate, but the prospects for winning are usually very poor. Winning the case may involve demonstrating that the substance seized was not an illegal drug or that the defendant was not the proper person to be charged with the crime. But it is the rare case that will offer these opportunities, and then it is mostly a question of luck, as when the substance sent off to the state labs turns out to be quinine rather than heroin.

There are, however, some opportunities with respect to the legal meaning of possession or sale. If two people are stopped in an automobile and heroin is found in the back seat, who is the proper defendant? Did both possess it? If an apartment shared by several people is searched, who is charged with the heroin found in the living room? If heroin is found hidden in the cellar of a building, who is charged—the only known user who lives there? What should be the charge against a third party who, unaware of the agent's status, leads an undercover agent to a dealer—sale, conspiracy, or being an accessory before the fact? There is always room for interpretation and argument in the application of the broad language of the drug statutes to the defendant's behavior, and this room can be the grounds for a successful challenge to the charge.

Search and seizure. In possession cases, the most important legal issue involves the manner in which the police found the defendant in possession of heroin. If a judge concludes that the search and seizure was unconstitutional, he will order the evidence suppressed, and the case will invariably be dismissed for lack of any other incriminating evidence.

If there is any doubt about the constitutionality of the search and seizure, the defense attorney, shortly after his client's arraignment, will usually file a motion to suppress and ask for a hearing. There will be little or no need for this if the police applied for a warrant, and if the warrant looks proper on its face. But more often than not, the search will have been made without a warrant. Then the state will have to justify its seizure of the heroin.

Perhaps the police will claim they did not make a search: "The suspect threw something away as we approached him." Or maybe there was a crime taking place in the officer's presence: "When I approached the defendant's car to examine his license and registration, I smelled burning marijuana." There may not have been time to get a warrant: "We had speedy information that the defendant was breaking up a piece just brought in from the City." Or perhaps a search made to protect themselves led the police to the evidence: "As we approached the suspect to question him, he made some quick movements which raised a suspicion that he might be armed; so we patted him down, and touched something that felt like a knife, but turned out to be works." These accounts, and others like them, are sufficient to justify a warrantless search.

The defense attorney may adopt one of a variety of approaches to challenge the search. He may try to portray the search as a novel situation, for which there is only ambiguous precedent. He may try to show that the police made a mistake by searching his client. Or he may try to show that the police are lying. The first approach asks the District Court judge to expand existing search and seizure law for the defendant's benefit. The other approaches rely on the defendant's ability to credibly contradict the testimony of the police.

Defense attorneys expect to lose most search and seizure challenges. The police make good witnesses and heroin users do not. The police generally know the law and know what it takes to justify warrantless searches. The defense attorney may believe that the police frequently lie about their searches, but there is little he can do about it. Often, when the search seems to be a blatant violation of his client's rights, the attorney will approach the prosecutor:

> John, you know the search was bad in the Malloy case. If they had taken him to the station and searched him there, it might have been OK. But stopping him on the street for a violation of probation and searching him for narcotics is out of the question. Why don't you nolle the heroin charge and we'll go before the judge on the violation?

Even though he may expect to lose most of his search and seizure claims, the attorney sees this as one of his few opportunities to win the case for his client.

Trial. He sees even less hope for a victory if he goes to trial. All he can visualize is a white, middle-class jury hostile to drug users, and competent and persuasive witnesses testifying for the state. But a trial may be necessary if the client continues to maintain his innocence. As one attorney explained it to a prosecutor:

> I'm sorry John. I'd like to plead him to a trespassing, but he says he didn't do it. Sure, someone committed that B&E, but Jones says he was just in the neighorhood and ran when he saw the cars coming. I think the trespass would be the appropriate disposition for this one, but he says it wasn't him, so I guess we'll have to go to trial.

Going to trial, under these circumstances, is nearly hopeless. Presumptions of innocence notwithstanding, the defense attorney knows he has to cope not only with the criminal charge but also with the jury. A comment to a colleague:

> That jury is going to kill us. How are we going to make them believe those cops made a mistake? The only way would be to show who really did it, but that only happens on TV. I'll have to put Jones on the stand, John will ask him about his record, and it'll be all over.

So the prospects for winning a trial are bleak. Furthermore, the defense attorney knows the defendant will pay a high price for going to trial. "You don't waste everybody's time with a trial, and then walk your man out the door. He's going to have to do some time."

Appropriate dispositions. In most cases an acceptable result can be achieved not by going to trial, or winning motions, but by negotiating with the prosecutor. During these negotiations, the attorney usually has an appropriate disposition in mind, that is, one which seems to fit his client and which is acceptable in light of the usual dispositions for cases similar to his client's.

His efforts to arrive at such a solution include negotiations with his client. The attorney might refuse to represent a potential client unless the client promises to participate in a treatment program. Or he might try to portray the client's case as particularly difficult in order to pressure him into taking the first step towward rehabilitation:

Tony: Have you been to the NAU yet?
Client: No, I'm going to go next week.
Tony: Look, Tommy, they've got you this time, and you have two other possessions, plus a B&E, on your record. Its a tough case, especially with Chester on the bench; so you better get down there soon, or it's going to be Wintergate.

If Tommy does get to the NAU before his sentencing, then Tony will use this as evidence of his desire to be rehabilitated. In such negotiations defense attorneys see themselves as promoting their clients' long-run interests and at the same time enhancing the immediate prospects for an appropriate disposition.

The crucial issues in negotiations with prosecutors often are determined by the circumstances surrounding the criminal charge. The client may have complicated the case by resisting arrest. Perhaps a large quantity of heroin was in the client's possession when he was arrested. The client may have carried a weapon with him while he was committing a breaking and entering. Anything indicating that the client is either dangerous or a drug dealer severely complicates the defense attorney's negotiating position. A client may have a serious drug problem, in which case the appropriate disposition would include treatment. If the client stole at gunpoint, however, or if the arresting officer was assaulted, the prosecutor will probably entertain only a treatment disposition which gets the client off the streets and into a secure setting, and he may even insist on time at Wintergate.

When he is faced with a case with these kinds of complications, the defense attorney will try to make the best of a bad situation. By requesting continuances, he may be able to get the case handled by a different, more flexible prosecutor or have the client sentenced by a more sympathetic judge. Sometimes, when the docket is clogged in one courtroom, the case can be transferred to another where a different judge and prosecutor are conducting business. Perhaps the attorney can negotiate a reduction in the charge in return for agreeing to go before a judge for sentencing without an agreed-upon disposition.

The defense attorney's most prized advantage in these negotiations is the prosecutor's lack of time:

If I were to file every motion that I was allowed to in every case I have, and if everyone else were to do the same, the prosecutor could never get his job done. So he has to give a little too. If he were ever to say, "No more bargaining," business would stop. Some of my clients would get hurt, but in the long run, he would have to start negotiating again.

The threat of motions, hearings, and an occasional trial gives the defense attorney some leverage when he is defending a client on a difficult case. When the case shows no complications, however, agreement on an appropriate disposition can be reached without much delay.

Dispositions in drug cases depend heavily on where the client appears to be in his drug career. The experimenter will normally receive a sentence consistent with his tentative, misguided use of heroin. The intent, apparently, is to let him know what will happen if he continues in his drug career. He is ordered to participate in a drug program, which will show him the danger of his ways, keep him busy, and help him avoid temptation. Outpatient programs are most appropriate for experimenters, as there is not enough need to protect the community to warrant taking them off the streets. Thus the experimenter is generally given a suspended sentence (two or three years), with probation for several years, conditional on participation in a treatment program.

In some cases, experimenters receive a continuance for a period of time (six months normally), with the understanding that the case will be dismissed if the defendant is not arrested during that time. Such continuances without a finding occur in those unusual cases where the defense attorney can persuade the prosecutor that any record of a conviction would be unduly harmful to the defendant, either because he is from a prominent family or because he is exceptionally young or capable, and a record would damage his future beyond the importance of the offense.

For those with drug problems, treatment is in order. This usually means that the disposition will involve a suspended sentence, probation, and an order to engage in whatever program is deemed appropriate by the NAU. Often the defense attorney will encounter a strong prosecutorial bias against outpatient treatment for his client with a drug problem. But generally, clients who have no serious complications with their drug problems will be expected to end up in outpatient treatment. Those with serious problems will probably be required to undergo inpatient treatment at CSH or Zeta House.

For hard-core addicts, incarceration is the appropriate disposition. Since such defendants usually have extensive criminal records, together with a pattern of treatment failures, prosecutors normally insist that the defendant has had enough chances and should be isolated for the community's protection. In these cases, defense attorneys aim for a disposition with the minimum possible time in prison and try to persuade their clients to seriously pursue a rehabilitation program while they are there.

Finally, if the attorney is representing a client in a sales case, he will try to get a disposition appropriate for a user. But he must cope with a statute which requires a minimum sentence of five years for a sales conviction. If treatment can be agreed upon as a disposition, then the client will normally get five to ten years suspended, and a stipulation for inpatient treatment. If time must be served, the attorney will often try to get a possession count added to the sales charge. Then he will negotiate for a suspended sentence on the sales charge, with the prison time, generally two to four years, attached to the possession charge.

Heroin and the Law

Representing clients in drug cases is often a frustrating experience for defense attorneys. Possibilities for a traditional legal defense do exist in some cases, but more frequently the attorney finds that the best he can do for his client is to be a good negotiator.

This might be enough if the attorney's clients in drug cases resembled his other clients. But those in drug cases are different and they have different problems. As one attorney remarked:

You know, we just can't do too much for them in our job. What we need is an addiction counselor to work for us and keep track of all our drug clients, to try to get them into programs and stay with them during the treatment process. Otherwise, they'll just be back here on other charges and it will start all over again.

So even the successfully negotiated appropriate disposition often appears to be only a temporary victory.

If heroin users could be counted on to seek help of their own accord, these problems would be less troublesome. But most defense attorneys believe that their heroin-using clients will avail themselves of treatment opportunities only under pressure. On the other hand, attorneys often find themselves agreeing with dispositions which force their clients into treatment even though they are less than confident that the treatment will be successful:

I've got to agree to sending him back to Zeta House, but I don't like it. He was there before and left after three months. I think they were pushing him too hard and too fast. He wants to get into the Methadone Program and it probably would be good for him. But the prosecutor says it has to be inpatient, and I've got to go along with him.

It appears to attorneys that legal pressure is necessary to get their clients into treatment. Yet by the time they are involved in the case, they may not be able to get the program that is right for the client.

Any program, however, is better than no program, because treatment appears to be the only alternative to prison. The possibility of legalization as an alternative to the current system is sometimes discussed:

These people shouldn't be brought in on possession cases. They're not really criminals, you know, and what crime they do commit is because they have to support their habits. Besides, it's a waste of everybody's time. I don't have time any more for anything but drug cases. I'm not really for legalization, but I can't see how any of this is doing any good.

Many defense attorneys thus hope for a time when they won't have to defend drug cases and send their clients to treatment or to prison.

7 All in a Morning's Work

Probation work is a peculiar mixture of bureaucracy, threats, and efforts to help people who often don't seem to want to be helped. Most of the probation officers in Riverdale were intensely aware of these and other conflicts in their jobs. A few of the probation officers responded to these conflicts with passive acceptance. Others used the paradoxes and the frustrations as reasons to work harder.

The following chapter tries to show the frustrations of the job and the illusiveness of the rewards. Drugs posed a special problem for the probation officers since, at the beginning of the drug crisis, most were completely untrained and unfamiliar with the problem. Furthermore, many of the conflicts between helping and being part of a punitive system seemed particularly intense when dealing with addiction.

Alexis Kyriakos, the protagonist of this chapter, is a composite of several officers. He is a man caught in the middle of those conflicts. The chapter does not show the resolution of the conflicts in the form of intensive cooperation with treatment agencies which evolved in Riverdale by 1972.

The research for this chapter consisted of six weeks of observation of probation officers who worked in both the Superior and District Courts. Although most of the time was spent with only three probation officers, there was plenty of opportunity to talk with and observe other officers in their work.

ALEXIS KYRIAKOS is a tall man whose deadpan, tired face seems to be in constant conflict with a strong gait and stylish clothes for domination of his soul. He walked slowly this morning as he crossed the park and went into a large sand-colored building. He climbed the thirteen steps to the probation department, walked down the hall and into his office in time to pick up the ringing phone, ready for any one of the usual series of calls that he routinely got in this job.

On the other end of the line was Roger Brewster, one of Riverdale's young defense attorneys. "Hi Alexis; Roger here!"

"Hi Roger, what do you want?" said Alexis with an exaggerated mock boredom.

"Oh come on, what would I want from you? It's just a friendly social call."

"Yeah, right. It's just a coincidence that Lester Greene is your client."

"Oh, now that you mention it," said the lawyer, obviously enjoying the subtle game they were playing, "I just wanted to make sure you know that he's been over at RMHC every day for the past week. I think he's gonna make it. Seriously!" Brewster's tone had become serious.

"Yeah, Roger, I'll remember that," said Alexis, trying to hide a bored cynicism.

"I think he's really a pretty good kid. Got in with the wrong crowd but he'll straighten out."

"Um."

"Think it over. He's basically all right."

"OK, I'll send you the report next week."

"Yeah, OK, see yah."

"Bye, Roger."

Alexis hung up and smiled, partly at Roger Brewster, whose manner he enjoyed, and partly at the silliness of the conversation. Defense attorneys often called him before he did a presentence investigation on one of their clients. They never said anything of much consequence. It was just a way of conveying that they would appreciate it if Alexis would not be too harsh on their clients. Alexis suspected that Brewster would probably be pleased in the end. Alexis wasn't a very tough guy. Like most of the other probation officers, he sometimes felt the addicts were walking all over him, but this didn't particularly change him. After all, it wasn't his job to be a cop.

Alexis leaned back in his chair and looked up at the high ceiling of his small square office. Even the walls seemed to be sweating. It was eighty-five degrees out at 9:30 in the morning and the air conditioning had broken down permanently two weeks before. They couldn't get it replaced yet because the governor had put a freeze on all new department expenditures because of the tax situation. Alexis wondered how many manhours were being wasted because they couldn't get the new equipment approved. His mind wandered back to the phone call. Another junkie! That's the third pre on a junkie in as many weeks. The drug problem seemed to be getting worse and worse all the time.

Six weeks ago Alexis had gone through a week's special training program at the Mental Health Center on the drug problem. He had rather mixed feelings about it. They had spent a lot of time in groups that were interesting and fun, but he wasn't sure what the groups had to do with the drug problem. However, he had been very impressed by some of the doctors from the treatment unit who insisted that probation officers should be tougher. They had said that the clinics were badly in need of somebody to motivate the junkies and that the clinicians alone couldn't do it. The doctors seemed to want Alexis to put the junkies in jail as often as possible. It seemed a bit ironic, but it made some sense. "The goddam doctors," Alexis thought, "they sound like Joe Matthews." Matthews was the chief probation officer for Riverdale and head of the old guard. Susan Antonelli, one of Alexis' closer friends in the office, and the office radical, once said that he hadn't had a new idea in fifty years, which was unintentionally funny since Matthews was fifty-one. Matthews was an ex-cop who got the job when he retired from the force and in Alexis' opinion he never really understood that he had changed jobs.

Yet Alexis knew that Matthews was right in some ways. It was no use kidding oneself that this was some sort of clinic. Despite all of Susan's idealistic talk, Alexis couldn't see how he could do therapy or counsel people when he had never had any training. In the eleven years that Alexis had been in the office, nobody had ever bothered to explain to him how he was supposed to supervise people. There was a lot of talk about treatment, but everything Alex knew about that came from reading he did on his own time. Besides, he had 120 cases to supervise. How do you see 120 people once a week or even once every other week, let alone say anything to them? Of course most of the cases he had were not hardened criminals. Mostly they were just kids or young addicts. What Alexis usually did was pretty simple. He'd see them all once a week for the first couple of months while they were on probation, and if everything seemed to be all right, he would stretch it out to once every other week and then finally to once every three weeks or once a month. At the end, most probationers would just stop in, say hello, smile, exchange pleasantries, and walk out the door again. That allowed him to spend more time with the new ones and to work intensively with one or two kids. He liked the young ones particularly. Somehow there seemed more hope for them.

Often he worried about how he could get through to these kids. Most of them thought of him as some sort of cop anyway. It took so long to get them to trust him and by that time there would be another hundred cases waiting. So most of the time Alexis gave them a fairly tough talk and maybe some of them would get a bit scared. He must be doing something right, he thought, because he had to violate fewer people's probations last year than anybody else in the office. Since most officers violated their probationers only when they were arrested on a new charge, it must mean that he was doing a fairly good job with them.

The drug addicts were the biggest problem. They were hard to get through to because often they would come in high on something or other. Sometimes he couldn't tell whether it was heroin or the methadone they were getting over at the clinic, but when they were high they were too dazed to talk to. It made him angry that they came in to see him while they were high. It seemed vaguely insulting. But then, junkies don't seem to have much respect for anything. He hoped the guy who was going to come in later for the pre wouldn't be high. It was always hard doing one on somebody who was stoned; all he would do was give one-word answers. Treating these drug addicts was another story entirely. There was something so persistent about the addict's need for drugs that it defied understanding. They did the most foolish things in order to keep up their habits. You couldn't count on them to keep an appointment because they'd get high and just forget about it entirely. Maybe they did remember the appointment and just didn't think it was worth coming in. There really was no way to tell. Whatever it was, he couldn't count on them to show up. The guys down at court had the same problem with them. Just this Monday, which was report day, five people had failed to show up. Four of them were junkies, or at least they had been junkies.

On the other hand, Alexis couldn't understand how he was supposed to treat these guys. What did he know about treating addicts? Even the people at the Mental Health Center couldn't keep them off dope. He sent almost all the addicts he saw over to RMHC. After all, there wasn't much else he could do. Throwing them in jail didn't do them any good. They never stayed clean after they came out, at least not very often. Maybe that was because there was so much dope in the jail itself. Last week one of Lou Schwartz's probationers told Alexis about the time he had spent in jail. He said he had managed to keep a habit of between a bag and two bags a day going all during the six-month sentence. So sending them to RMHC seemed like the best bet. But Alexis had to admit that he wasn't very satisfied. Of all the people he sent over there he didn't think that more than half ever even got into a program, much less succeeded if they did get into one. It was true that the junkies didn't really want to get in but it didn't seem like the Mental Health Center wanted to take them very much either. Alexis had sent a kid over there a few weeks ago who really wanted to clean up. The kid came back three days later saying that he was going to have to go over to the state hospital because they wouldn't take him at RMHC. That was too bad. Central State was hardly an ideal treatment environment. One of his probationers described it as "a six-week-long party, all the dope, booze, and girls one could want and free bed and board besides." The Mental Health Center definitely was the best place to send addicts, but even that didn't work very well.

He wondered when he was going to see Bill Richards again. Richards was a funny little guy all the probation officers met with every second or third week to talk about the problems that they were having with the Mental Health Center.

They were supposed to meet yesterday but Richards had to go to Washington. Alexis had learned something from Richards. He used to think that treating people meant that one should be kind and permissive. Richards kept saying that this wasn't true with junkies. The junkie had to be treated tough, particularly by the probation officers. As Richards spelled it out, and most of them had come to agree, the role the probation office had in treatment was primarily to force the junkie to stay in treatment. That meant that he had to violate the probation of anybody who dropped out of a program without permission, which would seem to make Alexis a tough guy. The Mental Health Center would say to the junkie, "OK, you can leave the program, but we're going to have to report you to your probation officer." Since almost all of them had two- or three-year sentences hanging over their heads, that threat was a pretty good deterrent.

Unfortunately, there was a communication problem. Half the time Alexis never heard if the guys he sent over to RMHC were rejected or thrown out. Even when he did know, it was hard to tell whether it was the addict's fault or the clinic's fault. Indeed, he was beginning to be skeptical of the stories the clinic told him. After all, why should he believe the clinic people and not the addicts? Alexis didn't like violating probationers who had been in treatment for six months and had not been arrested for anything. It was his job to keep them out of trouble, not to keep them in treatment. Probationers have some rights too. The other big problem was sending addicts to RMHC for drug-dependence evaluations. They had to go over there if they were going to be certified as drug dependent, but somehow the forms kept getting lost in the office and didn't get over to court in time. Then the judge would get angry and blame the probation officer. Actually, Alexis thought, that hadn't happened for a month or two, but you could never tell.

Alexis got up and stretched. He thought to himself, "I sure am in a bum mood this morning; they're not really all that bad. After all, the Mental Health Center does cure some of them and that's better than any other way I know." Besides, what was the alternative? All that he could do was the sort of supervision that Joe Matthews did. Matthews would go out and drive around and try to see all his probationers hanging out on the Avenue so that he could hassle them with some kind of information he'd gathered about what they were doing. He hoped that they felt he knew everything they were doing because he knew one lousy piece of information. That technique did work somewhat, but it almost never stopped the addicts from using heroin. It frightened them and it made them more covert and tricky, but it didn't seem to get very far in the end. Matthews also used one probationer as an informer on another, so he could find out what they were doing. Alexis had to admit it had some appeal. At least he knew some of what was going on. But it ran against his grain.

"After all," he thought, "that's what the cops are supposed to be doing. They already think of me as a cop and how am I ever going to get to the things that are bothering them and caused them to become addicts if they think I'm a cop?" Alexis knew that Matthews' probationers didn't trust him at all; he had talked with some of them. Unlike Matthews' probationers, a fair number of Alexis' probationers seemed to enjoy coming in to talk to him, and they sometimes told him the truth about what they were doing. In some ways it wasn't very different, Alexis thought; the probationers are trying to hustle you either way. One way, they get you committed to not violating them if they tell you what they're doing, the other way they just don't ever let you know. The ultimate irony of it all was that the idea of probation was to allow people to stay out of jail in order not to crowd the jails too much. If he were to violate everybody who deserved it on the basis of his activities, Alexis would probably have to violate half his probationers. Besides, he couldn't violate them all or everybody would think that he was a lousy probation officer. Not that it mattered all that much. With civil service they wouldn't fire a probation officer unless he raped one of his probationers. Alexis wasn't worried about getting fired. He felt himself to be one of the better officers in the place and he knew that others thought so too. Besides, the people in the capital couldn't care less anyway.

Another silly frustration was that even when you violated a

probationer, it didn't really make any difference. The warrants just got stuck up in the detective bureau somewhere and the police never did anything with them. Alexis remembered a talk he had once had with Sal Petrocelli, a detective from the robbery division. Alexis had become angry and told him off about having five warrants out for months and not picking up any of these people.

Finally, Petrocelli had said, "Look Alexis, what can I say? I can't do anything about it. It just isn't a good pinch. We don't get any credit for it. If I see one of your guys, I'll pick him up, but I'm not gonna go out of my way. I've got a lot of other things to do."

"Yeah, but what sense does it make for me to violate someone if he doesn't get picked up?"

"Search me," and Petrocelli shrugged.

In practice, the only time probationers were ever brought to court was when they got arrested for something else. Somebody in the detective bureau would look in the files and find there was a warrant out for the guy. Then they'd tack that on at the end of the long list of charges and send it over to court. Once it got there the defense attorneys would always manage to get the prosecutor to ask Alexis if it was all right to nolle the violation of probation if he got such-and-such a sentence on one of the other charges. So the only good the violation did was that they couldn't legally put him on probation again. However, most of the violations Alexis had reported recently were really just pro forma. A guy would get arrested for something and the only thing Alexis could do was violate him for committing the crime he was charged with.

Still you do the best you can, Alexis thought, it wasn't all futile. Every year there were a few kids he seemed to have some effect on. Of course, it was hard to tell, but you get a feeling about that sort of thing. What's more, most of the people put on probation didn't get into trouble again. Whether it was because of the probation, heaven only knew, but at least they didn't have to go to jail. Probation not only was good for them but it also saved the state money. It costs a lot of money to keep somebody in jail for a year.

Alexis looked at his watch and realized it was ten o'clock. He hadn't done anything except shuffle a few pieces of paper around on his desk. He sighed and got up. Just then, Sue Antonelli and Walt Moscovitz appeared at the door suggesting that they get coffee. The number of coffee breaks the probation officers took seemed to Alexis to reflect the peculiarity of their job. They had either so much work they couldn't possibly do it or not enough work to keep them busy. If they tried to do all their supervision conscientiously, there was no way they could get through the work. If, on the other hand, they felt their main job was to do a pre and serve as a place for probationers to check in, they didn't have enough to do.

Sue and Walt chatted about the weekend as they walked to the coffee shop. It was air-conditioned and Alexis felt he would probably stay until a few minutes before eleven when his pre was due.

As they ordered their coffee, Sue commented to him, "This is the second week in a row that I've had three pre's to do. It's simply ridiculous. They ought to make it into a check list. That's what they do out in California, you know. I mean it's not like it does any good. Most of the time they don't even read them." Alexis realized that the question of pre's bothered Sue more than anybody else in the office. She was a probation officer for Superior Court where they had more pre's to do on average than they had in District Court. Alexis usually had one or two a week whereas Sue had two or three. However, what was particularly bothersome to her was not that she had so many but that they were almost completely worthless in Superior Court. Almost all the sentencing there was done according to predetermined recommendations agreed on by the prosecutor and the defense attorney, called an agreed rec. Thus, the presentence investigation was almost completely a formality. Not more than one in ten of these investigations ever affected the sentence in any way. Unless there was no agreed recommendation, the judge would probably pay no attention to the pre.

Only two weeks ago Walt had told him that he had had to spend two hours with Sue, holding her hand after an incident in Superior Court. Apparently she had been standing around when the judge came over to the prosecutor and asked him which of the cases coming up for sentence didn't have agreed recommendations. The prosecutor said he had just finished developing agreed recs with all the defense attorneys so that none was still undecided. The judge said, "Good, then I don't have to waste my time reading any of the PSI's for today." That had really upset Sue. Indeed, Alexis thought, it had upset Walt pretty badly too. Not that Walt didn't know what went on, but it still hurt to hear it. Sue had, of course, taken it rather hard. She was young and very idealistic. Of all the probation officers she was the only one who did real therapy. She had been taking counseling courses at night school and carefully scheduled her time so that she could see clients. "Clients"—the word sounds like social work jargon! Alexis admired her attitude but knew it was foolish. She wasn't the first who had tried to do stuff like that and he'd never seen it get anywhere. Still, it was probably better to try than not to try at all.

Sue was talking again about pre-sentence investigations, "I mean, what the hell are they for anyway? Three-quarters of the time the judges don't read them. Even if they do read them they aren't taken into account in any way, shape, or form, so why should we do them? Why not just make it into a check list?"

Alexis said to her, "I don't know. It seems to me if they do away with the pre you might as well do away with the probation office. After all, good pre's are what they respect us for."

Sue said, "That may be true over in District, but in the Superior Court they don't even read them. That's not just any incidental document, that's half of my goddamn time every week."

Walt butted in, "But somebody has to do an objective evaluation on the guy. I mean, after all, who's going to find out what's going on with the defendant? They sure as hell aren't going to do that in court. Sometimes we're the only way the judge can find out what the guy is like. And it's not only the judge. After all, they do use pre's over in the jail if the guy gets sent there for a while . . ."

"Yeah, and they're supposed to be confidential documents which nobody but the judge and the lawyers see," Sue interjected bitterly.

". . . and I use them in my work. Hell, if I didn't do them before the sentencing, I'd have to do them after when I got them back on probation," Walt continued.

Somewhat calmer now, Sue said, "You can't expect the prosecutor and the lawyers to be any different. After all, that's their job. But the judges! It's their fault. They're the ones who are supposed to be objective. They won't let us make recommendations because it would undercut their independent decision making, but then all they do is ratify the agreed recs."

"And Wilson [Director of the Probation Department]," said Walt, "it should be up to him to talk to Chief Judge O'Rourke about this business. What in hell do they talk about when they have those meetings anyway?"

The conversation drifted on in this manner but Alexis found himself losing interest. He'd heard it all before; it didn't do any good. One had to make do with what one had. The judges were not about to listen to the pre-sentence reports, and he wasn't about to get his case load reduced to fifteen or twenty so he could supervise them properly either.

The thought of the pre he had coming up in ten minutes did not excite him much. After ten years of doing PSI's he no longer got overly involved with what he had initially found to be the most interesting part of his job. The case itself wasn't even particularly unique. If he'd seen one black sixteen-year-old drug addict in the last six months he'd seen a dozen. He hadn't met the kid yet, but Walt, who had been in court the day the case had been given to the probation office, had taken down the standard information. The kid's address was in the middle of what Alexis had learned in the last few years to call the ghetto instead of the slums. Walt had not told him anything about the kid but the scribbled note stated that the kid had been charged with breaking and entering and possession of works. Nobody around the office had ever heard of a Lester Greene before and there was no previous file on him. Elias, one of the older probation officers, claimed he had seen a Walter Greene who lived around that area about ten years before and perhaps he was Lester's father. Alexis doubted it; the voice on the phone had the quiet southern drawl of one recently emigrated from the South.

Alexis got up, excused himself and walked back to his office to wait for Lester Greene. As he entered the office, he took off his coat and tie. Formalities were less important than comfort when it was ninety degrees outside. He barely had time to sit down and pull out the file he had started on Lester Greene when a small black youth appeared around the corner and asked without much excitement, "Are you Mr. Chyriakos?"

"Kyriakos! You're Lester Greene?"

"Yeah."

"Well come in, sit down. I suppose you understand that I'm here to do a fair and objective report about you. This isn't a criminal investigation; that was all settled on Friday when you pled guilty in court. I was asked to do this by Judge McFarling so he will have the sort of information on you that he needs in order to make a fair and just sentence next Friday when your case comes up for sentence. So I hope you'll cooperate with me in this because I think it's in your interest and everybody's interest that the facts come out correctly." Alexis said this with remarkable sincerity considering that he said it a hundred times before. The kid just nodded and Alexis went on, "Now let's see if I have some of this information right. You were born June 22, 1953, and you're sixteen years old, and you were born where?"

"South Carolina."

"Where in South Carolina?"

"Pottersville."

"OK. How tall are you? And how heavy?" The questions went on for a while until Alexis had finished getting the information he would need to fill out the face sheet. Then he began to get to the heart of the matter.

"Tell me about your family. How many brothers and sisters do you have?"

"I have an older brother who's name is Winfred, and he's eighteen, and an older sister, Janice, who is nineteen, and a younger brother, Horace, who is six."

"What about your mother?"

"What about her?"

"You know, how old is she, where does she work, and what kind of education did she have?"

"Well, I don't know about her education; I think she graduated from high school, but I'm not sure. She's forty-two, I think. She works over at United Candy, packing boxes."

"What's her name?"

"Agnes Greene."

"What about your father?"

"He's been dead for five years now. He died of cancer. His name was Roger and I don't know about his education and that stuff."

Alexis thought to himself that it was so often the case that these kids with no fathers got themselves into trouble. If this kid was going to go on probation, and he probably would because of the type of case this was, he would take some supervising. These kids need fathers. He asked, "When did your family move here from South Carolina?"

"Well, we only moved here last year but we've been here before. Before my father died."

"When did you leave the first time? The South that is."

"Well, we came here in '61, but then when my father died, my mother wanted to go back down and stay with her folks for a while. So we moved back there in '64. We only stayed two years."

The questioning went on like this for a while. Nothing very interesting developed. The kid's talk was pretty straightforward and matter of fact, but said nothing that was likely to affect the almost predetermined outcome. All that Alexis needed from this one was the information that was necessary to produce the report. He had to find out what sort of a work history the kid had. That was handled pretty fast when it turned out that he had never worked. His education was a little more complicated because Alexis had to record all the different schools he had been in. Marital history was no problem since he wasn't married. The kid had no money in the bank and no debts to speak of so that took care of "Economic Situation." And so it went, through "Habits and Recreation," "Health," "Religion," "Military Service," etc.

Finally Alexis got to the important question of the kid's previous criminal history. Alexis found out that the kid had once been to Juvenile Court, but he was too young to have much of an adult record. Lester said he had none.

"So, what about this case you got against you?" The answer would be quoted pretty close to verbatim, provided it was short enough, under the category of "Offender's Version of the Offense."

"Well, the cops found me inside the house all right, but I wasn't going to do anything. I mean I was just in there looking around. But I don't guess they'll believe me about that."

"Well, the charge was not just breaking and entering. What about the works?"

"Yeah, but I don't use any more. I was just into that for a while."

Alexis thought that was not likely to be true. Addicts were not noticeably reliable in what they said about their drug use, but there was really no way of knowing. The agreement on this kid would be to put him on probation and stipulate treatment, which meant that Alexis would have to make sure he stayed at RMHC.

"You mean you don't have a habit now?"

"That's right."

"But you chip a little? Why did you go to the Center?"

"No, I don't use any at all any more. They found that out and don't want me."

"A little grass?"

The kid smiled a bit, "Yeah, once in awhile."

The kid looked in pretty good shape, but who could tell? Later Alexis would handle this much as he handled other such situations, by writing in the report: "The offender claims to have stopped using heroin."

As the interview drifted to an end, Alexis had produced an official history of Lester Greene's life. It was not, of course, an intimate history. He did not know much about Lester Greene or what he was like. However, he knew how Lester had performed in school, at work, regarding the law, and what his family was like. Now the only other part of the investigation was to check out the information he had been given. Later, if he got Lester on probation, he might get to know him as a person.

It seemed to Alexis that it would be a good idea to call Mrs. Greene and ask some more about the family situation. There might still be more to learn. So many of these people had aspects of family history that the kids didn't know. Perhaps more important was to call the school and find out what his guidance counselor's record looked like. It might have his IQ in it, and some psychological tests as well as a rather important series of evaluations from his teachers and guidance counselors. They might not know him any better than Alexis did but still it would be another opinion. If the kid were older, they could check with his employer and find out what sort of work record he had. Alexis didn't like checking with employers though, because the employer was likely to be suspicious about an employee who was being investigated by the probation office; but sometimes one had to check out the probationer's version of his story.

It didn't look as if there would be much of a criminal history on this kid but still it made sense to go the Police Department and get their report from the FBI. The police sent in the name and the charges of every person they arrested and received from the FBI a compilation of any out-of-state or out-of-town arrests, the individual might have. In this case, the odds were pretty good that the FBI report wouldn't show anything, but you never could tell.

"Well," Alexis said, "I'm going to do some more investigating on your case and then I'm going to write up a report for the judge and I'll try to make it as objective as I possibly can. Is there anything else I should include in the report?"

"No, I don't think so."

"OK then, I guess that's it." Alexis got up and stretched. He looked at his watch; it was twelve o'clock. "I guess it's time for lunch."

8 Different Strokes for Different Folks

The Narcotics Addiction Unit of the Riverdale Mental Health Center is what is known in drug treatment parlance as a comprehensive or "multimodality" drug treatment center. It includes a methadone maintenance clinic, a residential therapeutic community (Zeta House), and an outpatient group therapy program (OPT). Each of these modalities is designed to treat different kinds of drug abusers—"different strokes for different folks." Screening and Evaluation is the NAU component that meets new applicants and then assigns them to one of the three treatment programs.

This chapter, which is divided into two parts, describes the screening and evaluation activities. The first part describes the applicants, why they are there, and how they present themselves to the treatment program; the second part describes how these applicants are received, how they are evaluated, and how they are moved along to one or another of the treatment modalities or, in some cases, back to the street.

Material for the chapter comes from several sources. Three members of the research staff served at various times during the four years covered by this account of the Screening and Evaluation Committee, which, together with a director and a secretary, make up the Screening and Evaluation component. Field notes from these sessions have provided all the direct quotes and dialogue (edited and adapted) in the following chapter. Narcotics Addiction Unit statistics have provided the demographic, drug-use, and legal background information on the applicant population, which determined the composition of the case load described in the following "typical" week. Personal interviews and notes from NAU staff meetings have provided information for describing how Screening and Evaluation staff relate to the NAU organization as a whole.

Stylistically, the chapter pursues two goals simultaneously: one, to describe a typical week (and the week is a unit of time that determines the structure and tempo of Screening and Evaluation affairs), and two, to present a representative sample of the kinds of cases seen and the kinds of decisions made during the first four years of Screening and Evaluation history. Any one actual week would have served to describe Screening and Evaluation activities, but it would not have been representative of such things as how many women, hard-core junkies, or Spanish-Americans came to the NAU. To have described the characteristics of applicants over four years, however, and how they have fared in the NAU, would have demanded tables and statistics in such profusion that it would be impossible to describe how Screening and Evaluation looks, sounds, and feels to those who have to run it and to those who have to come up against it. Therefore this chapter is stylized to the extent that cases, events, and dialogue have been picked from various times to construct a "typical" week.

Getting In

LORETTA THOMAS was in trouble. Wilson Smith, head of the Vice Squad of the Riverdale Police Department, had jammed her up. Loretta was a prostitute and a heroin addict, and Bull had caught her with dope. Loretta had had brushes with the police before, but this was her first bust. Now they had her on a narcotics charge. It was a bad bust, the police broke in without a warrant, but she did have heroin, a lot of it. Her man had just brought some stuff into town and Loretta was holding it for him. A few bags Loretta could probably have dealt with—but fifty bags would mean a sales charge which was going to be hard to beat. Her only hope was treatment. Although her lawyer couldn't guarantee anything, he thought he could probably get the charges reduced to possession with a stipulation to treatment if Loretta copped to the possession charge and got into the NAU.

It was thus that Loretta Thomas came to the Screening and Evaluation office. It was a Wednesday, and that was the day the Screening Committee met. She had come by on Monday but was told to come back on Wednesday: "Two o'clock sharp, and don't be late." Loretta was not late. In fact, she was ten minutes early, which was more by accident than plan, since she had had trouble finding someone to look after her children (she had two), and it was only because a neighbor had been driving downtown that she was able to cop a ride. But she made it, along with ten other people who were applying to the NAU that week for treatment.

The committee members had begun arriving at 1:30 and they were all there by 2:15. There were six members: one regular representative from each of the three treatment modalities (Methadone Maintenance, OPT, and Zeta House), one representative from the Addiction, Referral, and Community Health agency (ARCH), a NAU research observer, and the director of Screening and Evaluation, Bill Richards.

As each committee member arrived, he picked up an intake questionnaire (twenty-nine pages long) and an applicant to interview. Filling out the questionnaires took fifteen or twenty minutes per applicant, and sometimes longer. Most committee members felt that this part of the intake process was a big waste of time. Except for a few of the questions, the whole interview was pretty irrelevant. But all the questions had to be asked, Washington insisted on it, and the answers had to look correct.

Loretta Thomas found the interview confusing and somewhat humiliating. To talk about her family, her prostitution, and her involvement with drugs and the police in a room with sixteen other people, many of whom she did not even know, was embarrassing. To the Screening Committee members, however, there was nothing unusual or disconcerting about the process. The committee had been through hundreds of interviews and by now each story sounded much like a dozen others. Indeed, most of the committee members, now ex-addicts, had once been on the other side and they were familiar with the many lines applicants would run. In any event, a little humiliation was a price worth paying if one really wanted to get into treatment.

The eleven interviews kept the Screening Committee busy

until three o'clock. Then the meeting, with all applicants and all Screening Committee members participating, began. Bill Richards:

This is your first step into the NAU. Today we will begin to learn something about you and you will want to learn something about us and what we do here. There are no policemen here and everything you say will be kept confidential.

No decision will be made today about treatment, unless you need and are ready for detoxification in a hospital. *We do not dispense medication here.* Your next appointment, unless you are instructed otherwise, will be the day after tomorrow, Friday, at two o'clock—*prompt!*

The program we offer you will depend upon many things including your age, drug history, family and legal situation, and your interest in change. The three major treatment programs are: OPT, Methadone Maintenance, and Zeta House.

OPT is a drug-free program open to individuals who have been detoxified. It usually begins with three to five weeks in a day program, *full time,* and then is followed by outside employment or schooling and membership in a therapy group, meeting one to three evenings a week. Participation in activity groups and possible graduation to leadership training is based on an individual's readiness to help others.

The Methadone Maintenance Clinic, which uses methadone in high doses to blockade heroin abuse, is open only to hard-core addicts. Admission to the Methadone Clinic involves four to six weeks' membership in a day program or evening group for those currently employed and who have a successful work history. Graduation to methadone outpatient status and continuation on the program depends upon the member's keeping a job, staying away from drugs, and exhibiting responsible behavior.

Zeta House is a live-in therapeutic community run by ex-addicts. Residents are expected to stay from eighteen months to two years. Advanced status and responsibility within the House and eventually graduation come with personal growth and commitment to a new life style.

Are there any questions?

There were no questions, so the Screening and Evaluation director continued: "Who would like to be first?"

No one answered. Loretta Thomas thought about speaking

up, but she didn't know what to say. She had not listened to the director's opening remarks because she already knew about the NAU from friends who had been there before. She would get methadone, she assumed, so why listen to a description of all the other programs. She was too old (twenty-five) for OPT, which was for kids, and since she had children to care for they would not make her go to Zeta House. Besides, she probably had been using stuff long enough to qualify as hard-core. Actually, she had only been strung out for about a year, but she had been chipping on and off for several years before that and her habit was now close to five bags a day, although she used more than that, maybe as much as ten bags a day, when she could afford it. It took quite a bit of heroin now for Loretta to really get off. Since her man was dealing some, the two of them had been able to keep a pretty steady supply of drugs. Sometimes, when they couldn't get the money together to score enough to sell, they had to rely on her income from prostitution, but that was usually sufficient to see them through. She didn't know what her man was going to do now that she was jammed up, but she knew she was not going to go to Zeta House. Some addicts would take prison over that place and she thought she probably would too; at least she would take her chances on getting probation or a short sentence. This was her first bust and she was sure she could get probation, especially since she had children to care for. She was nevertheless relieved when the director passed over her to another applicant: "What's your name?"

Jones: LeRoy Jones.
Richards: How old are you?
Jones: Twenty-three.
Richards: What are you looking for?
Jones: I don't know, what programs you got?
Richards: What do you mean: I just described them to you.
Jones: I mean, I don't need any of them programs. What I need is to kick my habit.
OPT Rep: You mean detoxify?
Jones: Yeah.
OPT Rep: Detox is not a program. We don't even consider it treat-

ment. We can arrange for you to get detoxed, we have a detox program, but that would only be to get you ready for treatment.

Jones: But I don't need no treatment. I can take stuff or leave it. I went six years without getting no habit. I don't got no mental problems or nothin', so I don't see why I need a program.

Zeta House Rep: You may not know it but you got a problem; you need a program. You know you're playing Russian Roulette. You could get a bad bag of dope tonight and that would be curtains, or you might get busted and then where would you be? Do you have a job?

Jones: No, but I can get one.

Methadone Rep: Well, I doubt that. You got any cases?

Jones: Yeah.

Methadone Rep: Tell us about them.

Jones: B & E, weapons, tools, and possession.

ARCH Rep: You made a plea on these cases yet or are they still coming up?

Jones: The drug case has come up; I copped a plea. They had me on a sales rap but it was bad, I got it reduced to possession. The burglary case ain't come up yet.

ARCH Rept: Man, you're in trouble. You on probation or parole?

Jones: Probation. It was my probation officer said I should come here.

Richards: Did he tell you that you could get detox and that was all you needed?

Jones: No, not exactly. He just told me to come down here and get in the program. But I don't think I need treatment.

Richards: Well, that's your privilege, but we think you need treatment. You're strung out, you don't have a job. You married?

Jones: Yeah, but me and my wife ain't living together no more.

Richards: Then you're on your own. You have some heavy cases. If you don't get into treatment, you're going to prison.

Jones: I don't think so. I think I can beat it.

Richards: Maybe, but I sure would hate to stake my life on it. And that's exactly what you're doing. You can leave here and go back to the streets and take your chances. That's your decision. We can't make you come into treatment. Treatment wouldn't do you any good anyway unless you want it and know you need it. But take your time. You don't have to make your decision today. Come back on Friday, and we'll give you our treatment recommendation.

Maybe by then you'll have seen the seriousness of your situation. We think it is serious indeed. Now, who's next?

The next applicant, Carl Cofrancesco, was twenty-four years old, unmarried, unemployed, and what the Screening Committee sometimes referred to as a "garbage can." Although Carl had used heroin from time to time, it was not clear that he had ever been strung out. He used heroin mostly to come off speed runs. Amphetamines seemed to be his drug of choice, although he had been getting more into heroin lately and was also beginning to dig barbs. Carl had never used cocaine, had tripped on acid a couple of times, and smoked marijuana more or less routinely. His physical condition was poor; he was emaciated and had abscesses on his arms, and he seemed somewhat spaced out. Although he could talk coherently, he had trouble following the logic of the conversation and showed few signs of taking anything very seriously, even his legal condition, which included a number of new cases, some of them involving violence, as well as an almost certain probation violation.

Methadone Rep: Would you consider Zeta House?
Carl: Sure.
Zeta Rep: You said that pretty fast. You know what Zeta House entails?
Carl: Not exactly.
Zeta Rep: As we said, Zeta House involves a minimum of eighteen months commitment. Although our doors are not locked, you won't leave the House, unless it's on your own and for good, until you earn the privilege. That may be many months. You will have to face yourself; learn why you became a junkie and . . .
Carl: I'm no junkie. [General laughter]
Methadone Rep: You're not a junkie? Then what the hell are you?
Carl: I'm not using heroin. I never used it more than a few times. I have never been addicted.
Zeta Rep: And you're not addicted to speed and grass and barbs?
Carl: No. I can take them or leave them. [Laughter]
Zeta Rep: Then why haven't you left them? You body's a wreck, you mind's a wreck, your life's a wreck, and you want us to believe you can take drugs or leave them. As far as we're concerned, you are a junkie.

Carl: No, I'm not a junkie.
Richards: Well, we say you are and the sooner you come to accept that fact the closer you'll be to getting some help. Anyone who uses as many drugs as you do is dependent on them.
Carl: I'm dependent on drugs. That's valid. But I am not a junkie.
Richards: That's a fine distinction. Addict or junkie, you're still probably worse off than anyone else in this room. If you harbor any notions to the contrary, there is no hope for you. We are here to help people who have serious drug problems. If yours is not serious, then this is not the place for you.

The next applicant, who was well known to some of the committee members, having shot dope with them in years past, presented an easy case. Although Ernest Salter was somewhat older than most (twenty-eight), he accepted the fact that he was an addict and needed help. Black, and with his wife already on the program, he seemed a sure candidate for methadone maintenance. The only possible hitch was that he was not currently strung out, having just finished a two-year bit in prison a week earlier. But he spoke of getting strung out again and admitted to almost daily chipping since his release from prison. His wife had urged him to get on the program, even said she would leave him if he did not.

The committee members seemed to accept his story at face value, although Richards suspected that some members knew more about this case than they were letting on. The Zeta House representative pursued the idea of Salter's going on a drug-free program, either OPT or at Zeta House, but the candidate insisted he could not make it drug-free and everyone seemed to believe him.

The fourth applicant, Jerry Paulson, was something of an oddity. He was white, fourteen years old, from a suburban family, and he had never done anything more serious than smoke grass. His parents found out, however, from school authorities, and went bananas. Committee members and other applicants alike ridiculed his drug involvement and gave him a lecture about how they hoped this had taught him a lesson; drugs are serious business, not to be fooled around with. A private conference was scheduled for Jerry and his parents.

By now the applicants seemed to be getting a feel of how to "run their thing," and candidate number five started right off by reciting his name, Anthony Morelli, his age, twenty-one; his drug involvement, heroin for two years (ten bags a day now) following about three years of using nearly everything else; his legal status, on probation and new arrests for sales and B&E; his marital status, single; and vocational status, working as a gravedigger.

The interview was going too smoothly; it almost sounded rehearsed. Indeed it probably was, as it became clear that the applicant wanted to get into the Methadone Program.

OPT Rep: And why do you think the Methadone Maintenance Program would be good for you?
Tony: If I don't get in, my probation officer is going to violate me.

This was a mistake. The committee descended on him: "Then you came just because you wanted to clean up things with your probation officer and as soon as that's straight you will leave again?"

Tony: No, I came mostly for myself, because I wanted to.
Arch Rep: Don't give us that shit. You come because you had to. You're in love with drugs and nobody in love with drugs gives them up unless he has to.
Tony: No, I came because I want to give up drugs. [Laughter]
Zeta Rep: How serious are you about putting drugs behind you? Would you go to Zeta House if that was our recommendation?
Tony: I suppose. How long would I have to stay there?
Zeta Rep: Until you learn to take responsibility for yourself and quit bullshitting everybody like you've been bullshitting us and yourself.
ARCH Rep: Zeta takes form eighteen to twenty-four months.
Tony: That's a long time.
ARCH Rep: Zeta's got a valuable product; they don't just give it away. You've got to earn it. It's like you got a thousand dollars in your pocket—you don't give that away for nothing.
Tony: Couldn't I get on the Methadone Program?
Richards: We can't say today. We will discuss your case, everybody's case, tomorrow, and give you our decision Friday. You should be prepared, however, to take our recommendation seri-

ously. This meeting is not just an entrance to the Methadone Program; it's the portal of entry to the entire NAU. We have different programs and we are not here today to decide which is best for you. We'll consider that tomorrow. We can say this right now, though, you're in no condition to make that choice. Your drug involvement, your legal involvement, have demonstrated that you can't make wise decisions for yourself. Therefore, we will have to make that decision for you. We've had a lot of experience in making those decisions, including the experience of those like yourself who are here in this room today as staff members, who once used drugs.

Now, would you like to go next?

The applicant Richards spoke to, Sarah Cohen, was twenty-one years old and had a three-year history of heroin use but evidently had never been addicted. She had been busted once, breach of peace, but the case had been dismissed. When asked what brought her to the NAU, she indicated that she had been referred by the Riverdale Mental Health Center Emergency Unit, where she had wound up after a heroin overdose. The committee determined that the overdose was deliberate, an attempted suicide, and discussed the possibilities of a therapeutic community. Sarah indicated that she would go there if that was the decision of the committee.

Zeta Rep: Are you sure? You realize that any program you get into around here will involve a lot of group therapy? You will be required to take a very close look at yourself. Are you ready for that?

Sarah said she was and reiterated her willingness to accept whatever program the committee thought best for her.

It was four o'clock. There were five more applicants to go. Maybe they would actually get through by five o'clock today. That would be a treat; the meeting had not ended before six o'clock for months. Eleven applicants were somewhat less than the committee had been getting recently, and so far everything had been pretty routine. Then Joe Jarvis burst into the room.

Richards: Yes, may we help you?
Joe: I came to get into Methadone.

Richards: Well, we began our meeting two hours ago. You've been here before. Surely you know by now when screening begins. How did you get past the secretary anyway?
Joe: That bitch. I didn't even stop at her desk. Dr. Suber [the NAU director] said I could get onto Methadone and that's what I want.
Richards: Well, that's fine, but I'm sure Dr. Suber didn't tell you to come at four o'clock. Why don't you come with me and we can set up an appointment?

With this Bill eased Joe out of the room and the meeting continued. Bill knew Joe Jarvis very well. He was a perennial troublemaker and his mother, Ma Jarvis, as she was known in the community, was a legend. Ma Jarvis had three sons, all of them junkies and petty thieves. One was in the hospital with a bullet in his gut. Another was in Wintergate Prison where he would stay for quite a while, and then there was Joe. Joe had been in and out of the NAU many times. The only reason Joe got so much play was because his mother was an active black militant the NAU was a little bit afraid of. Although Ma Jarvis wasn't necessarily powerful in the community, she did have a big mouth that could prove troublesome if she unleashed it on the program.

Joe had been on methadone twice before and had been kicked out the second time after his fifth urine test showed illicit drug use (most patients are allowed only three dirty urines), and he split Zeta House on his first day there. NAU rules stated that a Zeta House splitee could not get into any other treatment modality for six months, although he could return to Zeta House at any time (if the House would readmit him). It has been six months since Joe left Zeta House and he had not gone back. He wanted methadone again. Ma Jarvis supported her son and claimed that the NAU was discriminating against him since they would not let him into the Methadone Program. Dr. Suber maintained that this was not true; that the six-months rule applied to everyone and had to be enforced to protect Zeta House. Without it, everyone would split, thinking he could just go to Methadone when that was not at all in their best interests. But now six months had passed and Joe was eligible for Methadone. Dr. Suber was sure that the Methadone Program would not accept Joe back, but there was no reason to tell Ma Jarvis this. He simply told her to send Joe to Screening. "I'm sure he knows where it is," Dr. Suber added sarcastically, as he ended the conversation.

Bill Richards knew all this and was angry because Suber did not tell such people that Zeta House, on clinical grounds alone, was the only possible alternative. Suber surely realized that Joe would come to Screening and demand methadone. This, Richards felt, was setting the committee up. Why did they always have to do the dirty work? But they did, and Richards could yell at Suber about it later. Right now he had to cool out Joe so that he would not interrupt the meeting. Richards considered it fortunate that he had gotten Joe out of the room as easily as he had. Now he had to think of something that would hold him until the committee staff could deal with him alone. What he did was to schedule a special hearing before the committee for the next day. This was contrary to usual procedures, Joe would know that, but would be flattered enough by the offer of special treatment not to figure out what was really going to happen. And that was all right with Bill Richards.

While Richards had been out, the committee interviewed the seventh applicant, Carlos Alverez, thirty years old. Carlos looked as though he had just come from a barroom fight. He had bandages on both arms and one of his legs and was using crutches. Furthermore, he could not speak coherent English, or so it seemed. The Screening secretary had had to round up a Spanish-speaking staff member to do the initial interview and fill out the questionnaire. It became evident that all this was an act, though, as soon as one of the committee members who knew Carlos from pre-NAU days called his game.

ARCH Rep: Look Carlos, talk English. I knows you can. I'se talked with you when you was high. I'se talked to you when you was drunk, and I doesn't know a word of Spanish. You must have been talking English then, so just drop the act and talk English now.

This ended the game and Carlos suddenly became coherent. Moreover, it was soon discovered that although he did have some abscesses, he really did not have anything warranting ten yards of gauze bandage and crutches. But the props did have an effect; no one thereafter even questioned Carlos' seriousness about getting into the program. Anyone who would go to those lengths just to convince the program that he was a junkie and needed treatment must be serious.

Carlos *was* serious. He had been using heroin for fifteen years and was in pretty bad shape. He had abscesses on his legs, he had run out of reliable veins on his arms years ago, and even the septum in his nose was perforated from snorting stuff when he couldn't find a vein to shoot into. Carlos was also now in trouble with the law, although it had taken all these years, during many of which he had dealt drugs, to catch up with him. Whereas the police didn't actually catch him making a sale (Spanish-American dealers never seemed to get caught selling to undercover agents), they did catch him with more than ten bags of dope on him and had charged him with possession with intent to sell. Carlos said that he had been lucky to make bail and stay out of jail while awaiting trial. Even at that, he had been picked up on a Friday night (the pigs probably did that on purpose) and was held all weekend before his brother could get bail money and a lawyer together to spring him. He reported that he had thought he was going to die in the lockup for a weekend without any drugs, but they did give him some methadone—10 mgs—Jesus Christ; it would have taken 50 mgs to hold his habit! Between that, and what his brother could smuggle in via one of the guards, he had survived. Now he knew that he had better do something about his habit. It was a big one, a dealer's habit, and Carlos had no intention of going cold turkey should he lose his case and be sent up. It looked to Carlos like the NAU was the only answer and he wasn't taking any chances. If it took bandages and crutches, so be it, but he wanted in and, from what he could gather, Spanish-Americans had a hard time getting into that place.

As it was, Carlos would not have had a hard time. The committee knew that. The NAU had always been conscious of the low percentage of Spanish-Americans in treatment and was sure that this was not due to a lack of suitable candidates in the Spanish-American community. For Carlos, an older, hard-core,

Spanish-American heroin addict, there would never have been a question. Indeed, he probably would have escaped the usual Screening Committee hazing altogether had he not come in that ridiculous costume. Carlos was not even told to come back Friday, as most applicants were. Instead, with full Screening Committee support, Richards told him that for "obvious medical reasons" he should go directly to CSH where he would receive methadone and proper care. When he finished his thirty days there, or earlier if the hospital arranged it, he could come back to Screening for final evaluation and placement in a program. No one doubted that that program would be Methadone Maintenance and it was the Methadone representative to Screening who saw Carlos after the meeting to arrange transportation to CSH.

The next case was routine—a nineteen-year old black youth who had been using heroin for a couple of years, had gotten strung out, had been in constant trouble with the law even though he never had developed a hustle more demanding of skill than selling dope to high school kids, and now he had hepatitis. His name was Norman Harris. He was a failure as a junkie; maybe he could make it as a patient. He was referred to the ambulatory detox program at Riverdale Hospital and told to report back for program assignment as soon as he finished detoxing.

After Norman came Patrick Shea, who was also nineteen, or at least he said he was. He looked younger. He was white and a senior in high school, where he ran around with a group that used quite a lot of drugs. Although the members of the gang had all tried heroin, only three were into it very seriously and none was really strung out, or so Pat contended, although the Screening Committee presumed that they were all as good as hooked. The association with a gang intrigued the OPT representative, who explored the possibilities of this applicant's bringing his friends into the program with him. Pat thought this a most unlikely prospect. Indeed, he acted worried that he had even mentioned the existence of drug-using friends, but the committee persisted in the notion that a drug user cannot hope to be successful in treatment so long as his friends continue to use drugs. Usually treatment entails making new friends, but the prospect of treating an already existing drug-using peer group, was something the OPT representative had often wanted to try. This might be his chance.

But Pat continued to evade the issue of his friends and by this time the committee had been too solicitous to suddenly turn on the tough act. Richards asked Pat to talk with his friends, to explore the idea of all of them getting into treatment before it was too late, and to come back Friday with his answer.

The tenth applicant, Raymond Pritchard, was sixteen, black, and very naive. He had been using heroin, so he said (and everyone believed him), for only a couple of months. He began during the summer grass famine when he could no longer get marijuana. He liked heroin and found himself using it more and more regularly, even every day. Grass had come back onto the streets, but he was no longer interested in it. What bothered him most was that he thought he was getting strung out on stuff.

OPT Rep: Then you like heroin; you prefer it to marijuana?
Ray: Yes.
OPT Rep: But you know it's not good for you and that you're headed for big trouble, and you want to quit?
Ray: Yes.
ARCH Rep: I doesn't believe a word you is saying. There ain't a man who's used heroin who wanted to quit if he didn't have to. You're no different. Man, you is in love with heroin. Ain't nothing we can do for people who is still in love with heroin.
Loretta Thomas: Can I say something? I've been listening to you talk to this boy, and others earlier, and you're saying that as long as people like drugs there ain't nothing you can do for them. Well, I bet there ain't nobody in this room who don't like drugs. Why do you think addicts take drugs anyway? Ain't there nothing you can do for people who like drugs?

Loretta was surprised at herself for speaking up, but she was confused. Here was a good-looking promising boy who had decided that he was getting into something he might regret. He needed help. Sure he liked heroin. If he didn't like it, he wouldn't be using it. But that wasn't the point. Here was someone who wanted to stop *before* he got strung out and into trouble, and these people were telling him they could not help him. Go back to the street, put on a jones, get a couple of busts, then maybe we'll have something for you. That was what they seemed to be saying. That didn't make any sense.

Richards: You see, it's like this: we have found that we can't talk anyone into wanting to stop using drugs, but if people want to stop, then we may have something to help them.

Loretta did not see how this answered her question, but maybe she was missing something. Anyway, she shut up. Her turn was coming next and she had probably already said too much. Besides, no one believed that the boy wanted to give up heroin and one committee member even implied that his only reason for being there was to look the place over in case he might need it sometime in the future when things got more uptight for him. The applicant never changed his story, though, and was finally given the usual directive to report back on Friday for a treatment recommendation, even though no one really expected to see him again.

It was Loretta's turn. It was getting late, five o'clock. Somehow she had not expected the meeting to take so long. She wondered if her children would be all right. They could make do. Anyway, she now had the experience of ten other interviews, eleven if you counted the guy who came in late, to go on. What could she make of it? It was a puzzle. If you said that you wanted to give up drugs because you wanted to give up drugs, they would not believe it. But if you said you came because of trouble with the law, they would accuse you of only wanting to get the law off your back. Either way they wouldn't believe you. They did believe the Spanish fellow, but then he put on a pretty good act. They did see through that act, though, and accepted the guy who was just out of Wintergate and he wasn't even strung out. Maybe you had to go to prison first to convince them that you were serious. Well, she wasn't back from prison; shit, she was trying to avoid prison, and she wasn't

Spanish. What the hell could she do? She had no more time to think, the interview had already got past the name, age, and address. Address! Both people who had done well were from Endfield, although they had neglected to mention this during their interviews, giving phony local addresses instead.

Loretta: Actually, I'm from Endfield. I just been staying with a friend here.

Screening Director: Then I'm sorry. We cannot help you. According to law we can only serve people who live in Riverdale or the surrounding county.

Jesus Christ! She blew that one. Actually she did live in Riverdale, had for the past six months, but Endfield was really her home town. She came to Riverdale because the Endfield pigs were after her old man and he had heard that pross in Riverdale was good now that so many girls had joined the NAU. It *was* good too, although the pigs were no better—six months and they got her. But could she change her story now? That pimp counselor from Methadone knew her. Shit, she had drank rum 'n cokes with him at the Sliding Gate. But he wasn't saying anything—like he didn't know her.

Loretta: I'm from Riverdale. It's just that I come from Endfield. That's where my people are.

Everyone seemed relieved and went on with the interview. That was curious. Maybe she had done something right after all. But what? Maybe they figured that coming from Endfield (where they did not have a drug treatment program) to Riverdale and lying about her address showed that she wanted treatment. Let them think that. Jesus, she sure hoped that the Methadone counselor kept his mouth shut. He could blow the whole thing.

The interview proceeded rather quietly. People were tired and didn't seem up to giving Loretta the shit they had given others. They did question her motivation, she couldn't seem to avoid that, but things seemed to be going pretty well until the Zeta House representative went into his song and dance about the House. Her, for the House? He couldn't be serious.

Loretta: But I have two children; who would take care of them?
Zeta House Rep: Who's taking care of them now? You're not. You're prostituting, hustling drugs—you're not caring for your children. We could make arrangements and then you could have your kids back after your graduation, when you would be a good mother again.

Shit, this bastard was serious. What was she going to do now?

Loretta: Could I have my baby at Zeta House?
Richards: You're pregnant?
Loretta: I think so.
Richards: Then that puts a new complexion on your case. We don't normally take pregnant women into Zeta House, although it has been done. In these cases we have to think about two people who have a drug problem: you and your baby. Usually we consider the unborn baby first. As you must know, it's rough going for a newborn baby with a heroin habit. Many of them die. Therefore we have a special program in which pregnant mothers are given reduced sustenance doses of methadone rather than the usual blockade doses of 70 mgs or more. When the baby is born (and we find that they do better than heroin babies), then we return to the mother's problem. Sometimes she will be detoxified from methadone and sent to Zeta House; sometimes she will be a suitable candidate for the Methadone Maintenance Program and she will be transferred there. In any event, you cannot get into this program unless you are examined and it is certain that you are pregnant. Come back Friday at two o'clock for our decision.

Loretta was not pregnant, she couldn't be, she had had the operation three years ago, but it seemed to be an effective lie. She had no idea what would happen once they found out that her tubes were tied, but for now she seemed to be in. She could deal with the other problem when it came up. Right now she might just have gotten enough play to deal with her court case, which was her paramount worry at the moment.

Evaluation

It was Thursday and Bill Richards was preparing for the Screening and Evaluation Committee meeting that would begin at eleven o'clock. Bill was always a little uneasy about this

DIFFERENT STROKES FOR DIFFERENT FOLKS 171

meeting. At the Wednesday meetings, with applicants there, the committee members stuck together, but Thursday meetings were different. There were no patients present and committee members acted more like spokesmen for their respective programs than like members of the Screening Committee. This made life difficult because NAU politics kept getting mixed up with the intended business of the day: making treatment recommendations for new patients and evaluating the progress of earlier applicants who were still in the process of getting into one or another of the treatment components.

Bill thumbed through the logbook. Besides the twelve new applicants this week, there were thirty-eight patients in continuing evaluation and investment. Fourteen of these had failed to show up for an interview at one or another of the programs the previous week or had quit coming to their investment group at ARCH. Unless they showed up this week, letters would have to be sent informing them that their applications had been closed. Three cases were patients at CSH and four were in the Riverdale Hospital ambulatory detox program. Three of these patients, the logbook showed, should be in the next day for a program recommendation. Eight people were undergoing methadone evaluation. The Screening Committee had sent them to the Methadone Program in weeks past, but Methadone did not automatically accept all Screening recommendations; instead, they had their own probationary status to be sure that the applicants sent their way were really suitable for maintenance. Nine more of the thirty-eight were in ARCH investment groups, four having been recommended to Zeta House and five to OPT. Before applicants could get into either of these programs, however, they had to prove their good intentions by showing up every day for a group run by ARCH.

The fifty patients under Screening and Evaluation jurisdiction this week looked fairly typical. There were, Bill noted, fewer hard-core addicts than the NAU used to get. After four years of Wilson Smith and the NAU, older hard-core addicts were either on the program or in prison, or so the NAU kept saying. Screening also saw fewer acid heads and speed freaks than they used to. This statistic bothered Bill since he thought the NAU should provide the kind of comprehensive program that would serve all drug abusers. But it did not.

Bill looked at the latest research report on Screening. It seemed to confirm his impressions. The report was two months old. Bill was just getting around to looking at it. The only place the reports proved very useful, though, was at NAU Coordinating Committee meetings where the professional staff used them to argue for their pet campaigns of the moment.

Bill used to be involved in a lot of campaigns. That was when he first started with the NAU, three and a half years ago. He had been right out of graduate school (M.S.W. in psychiatric casework) and was full of enthusiasm and theories about drug abuse. Three and a half years in the drug business, however, had changed all this. First there had been the conflicting theories coming from the various professional and ex-addict staff. Then there were the disappointments—the patients who had been doing so well who suddenly split, usually about the time their court stipulations ended. Bill had become jaded. He knew that. By and large, though, the ex-addict staff had been right; people won't get off drugs unless they have to and they won't stay in treatment unless they are forced.

It was time for the evaluation meeting. As usual, the committee began with those who had come in the previous day. LeRoy Jones was the first name on the list.

OPT Rep: Jones, which one was he?
Methadone Rep: The dude who said he didn't need no treatment.
ARCH Rep: He was only here because his probation officer said he had to come. We won't see him no more. Go to the next case.
Richards: No, we better make a recommendation.

Richards knew that chances were good that this applicant would not show up on Friday, but the committee had better have a recommendation ready just in case. Bill knew from experience that even the most recalcitrant applicant could have a change of heart after talking with his lawyer, and the most casual could see things in a more serious light after an arrest warrant came down. Besides, Richards had been caught before making treatment recommendations on his own. He did not like to do that. Unless he had committee support, his recommendations seemed to come back to haunt him, usually in the form of allegations that he was soft on addicts. The committee, therefore, made a recommendation for the Methadone Program, with the proviso that someone "run Zeta House" first. The Zeta House representative objected, as he often did, to making recommendations according to what the patient was likely to accept rather than according to what he needed, but as usual the final recommendation was a compromise: try to get the patient into the program he needs (usually Zeta House), and when that does not seem very likely, settle for what you can get.

Carl Cofrancesco, the garbage can, was easy. Zeta House was the only possibly choice. The man was in bad shape mentally and physically, unemployed, unattached, and willing to listen to a Zeta House recommendation.

The third candidate, Ernest Salter, was not so easy:

Richards: Is this man a hard-core addict? If not, he cannot be considered as a candidate for Methadone Maintenance.
Zeta Rep: Why should he be considered a candidate for Methadone Maintenance if he's hard-core? Shouldn't he also be considered a candidate for Zeta House?
Richards: I did not wish to imply that he is not a candidate for the House, only that he cannot be a candidate for Methadone unless we can establish that he is hard-core.
Zeta Rep: I know, but it just bothers me that every time the committee comes up on a black hard-core addict, they automatically assume that he's only a candidate for Methadone Maintenance. This overlooks the fact that they might also be a good candidate for the House.
Research Observer: I thought Zeta House was full. I thought you couldn't take anyone for a while.
Zeta Rep: We're never full. Sure we are up to fifty, but we can always make room for a good candidate. We especially need older black residents; with all the kids we have there's no one to provide any stability any more. There are graduations coming up. We could always make room . . .
Methadone Rep: But this man ain't going to Zeta Hose. There's no way. Shit, he just got out of Wintergate. He ain't going to turn around and go into Zeta House for two more years. That freedom tastes pretty sweet right now.
Zeta Rep: Sweet or not, if he doesn't got to the House he's just

headed back to Wintergate. That man's in bad shape. You know that. He's a junkie through and through. Give him six months—hell give him six weeks—and he'll be in as deep as ever. He's already using smack and he hasn't been out a week. And so what if he does get into the Methadone Program? He'll only lie up there, using methadone while he organizes his hustles. Wasn't he a dealer before he went up?
ARCH Rep: Sure was.
Zeta Rep: Like I was saying, put him on Methadone and he'll probably be dealing more coke to the NAU patients than he ever dealt heroin on the street. That man's head is in bad shape. He needs the House.
ARCH Rep: I agrees with you Pete; if we could get this man into Zeta House that would be beautiful. But there just ain't no chance he's going to stay there no time at all. He's got a woman been waiting for him for two years. He's got friends he hasn't seen in a long time; his people are all in Riverdale, and he's done his time. The law ain't going to be putting no pressure on him for a while. Now if we could get him to go to Zeta House, he would only split. Then he would have to wait six months to get into another program. He could get into a lot of trouble in that time, could bring grief to a lot of people. He's got a family to be thought about too. Now I think that if we could get him into the Methadone Program, that would be a feather in our cap. If we could get him into Zeta House, that would be two feathers in our cap, but I think we better settle for one feather. We's got the community to consider too. I knows what's going on out there in the community. I be's in the bars and I be's in the alleys and I knows that this man is already selling dope. Give him six months and he'll have kids selling dope for him in the high school cafeteria. If we can get this man into the Methadone Program, we better do it. There just ain't no chance of getting him into Zeta House.

    This speech settled the issue, as if it had not already been settled. The Zeta House representative never really thought of this applicant as a likely candidate for the House, but he did have to make his point. If Zeta House left it to the Screening Committee, they wouldn't get anybody in the House except screwed-up white chicks who belong in a mental hospital, and violent hoods who would be better behind bars. As it was, the House had to recruit half its residents from outside the catchment area just to keep some kind of reasonable balance in the resident population.

Jerry Paulson, the fourteen-year-old who got caught at school smoking pot warranted no more than the announcement that Richards had set up a conference for him with his parents and school guidance counselor. Anthony Morrelli, the gravedigger, and Sarah Cohen, the girl who had tried to commit suicide, were both recommended to Zeta House, although the committee gave some consideration to sending Sarah back to a psychiatric unit of the RMHC. The OPT representative was familiar with the case, though, and convinced the rest that this particular suicide attempt, although real, was not part of a persistent pattern and probably reflected immediate circumstances (breaking up with her boyfriend and the death of her father) more than any deep-seated psychological problem.

The committee recommended that Carlos Alvarez go to Methadone Maintenance as soon as he got back from CSH and that Patrick Shea go to OPT. The representative from OPT received approval from the other committee members when he asked if he could push the line about getting Pat's friends in at the same time. The committee did stipulate, however, that this was a line that "should just be run—it should not be a condition of treatment," as the OPT representative would have liked.

Ray Pritchard was another one of those cases for which the committee could make no satisfactory recommendation. He was young, he had no pressure on him, and he was in love with heroin. There were so many like him these days, and they continued to bother Richards. They also bothered the ARCH representative: "Is there nothing we can do for a man who's tasted heroin but decided in all honesty that he doesn't want to get strung out?" There was no answer and the committee went on; they recommended OPT for Ray and Methadone Maintenance Pregnant Women's Group for Loretta Thomas.

It was time for lunch and the Screening secretary brought in sandwiches and the announcement that Joe Jarvis had come for his "special hearing." Richards had Joe come in. The committee did not even need to discuss its recommendation—it was Zeta House or nothing. Joe objected, screamed that he was being discriminated against, but did not budge the committee. Hurling invectives, he left the room. Richards was a little apprehensive about what would happen when Joe and his mother got back to Suber, but he was satisfied that the committee had not turned Joe down completely and that their recommendation to Zeta House was appropriate. He took some comfort in the fact that the committee, to a man, had backed him and would present a solid wall should anyone try to bring pressure. He was equally confident that the Methadone Program would resist any attempts to circumvent Screening and place Joe directly on the program.

The committee turned next to the continuing applicants. Only one presented any real problem: Sheila Pond who had been in and out of the NAU five times. Sheila was not physically violent, but her mouth was a lethal weapon. No program had been able to deal with her. She was a classic junkie: former prostitute, in and out of jail and prison, using any drug she could get her hands on, completely unreliable, always lying, using everybody for her own ends. "Real bad," one counselor had described her once, "so bad she is beautiful." She was being kicked out of Methadone Evaluaton. "And now," the ARCH representative asked, "What is she supposed to do?"

Zeta Rep: She's supposed to go back to the street and stick a needle in her arm. That's what she wants to do.
ARCH Rep: I can't accept that. I thought the Methadone Program was to treat hard-core addicts. If ever there was a hard-core addict, Sheila Pond is it. Now if Methadone can't serve her, who can?
Methadone Rep: Well, Methadone can't serve that fuckin' whore. She'll ruin the whole goddamned program. Shit, Rockview [state prison for women] kicked her out before her [parole] due date. If the broad gets kicked out of prison, we're supposed to keep her?

The ARCH representative continued to object but the rest of the committee concluded that there were some addicts that even the NAU couldn't handle. Nevertheless, the committee did decided to offer Zeta House again although the House representative was less than hopeful about her chances there. Probably, he thought, the House wouldn't let her in. But that wasn't too important since there was little chance that she would ever make it to the prospect's chair anyway.

Having finished this week's list of names, the committee turned to general items of business. An hour and a half had already elapsed. Some of these items involved routine matters of getting applicants who were ready into one or another treatment component. Other matters were more provocative.

Methadone Rep: Why did the committee recommend Zeta House for that man who had a job when it recommmended Methadone Maintenance for that dude who didn't have no job at all? I thought we was supposed to try and keep people who have jobs working?

Zeta Rep: It was his attitude. That job was nothing; he probably only got it to get onto the program. What kind of a job was it anyway—gravedigger, wasn't it? He can dig his own grave. There's no future in it; any junkie could do that. Put that guy on Methadone and he would quit working and lie up on the program. He needs therapy and that's more important than any two-bit gig he might have right now.

The rest of the committee agreed and the recommendation to the House stood. Condition of employment or educational status was not of paramount interest to the Screening Committee, although these matters were of considerable interest to the NAU later on in a patient's treatment career. At entry, though, the program was primarily interested in the legal, family, and drug status of applicants because these told the committee something about how much pressure applicants were under and whether or not they were good Zeta House candidates.

The committee had finished its business for Thursday. Now all that remained was to see the applicants on Friday and give them the word. This did not take very long; usually not more than an hour or so. When the Friday meeting came, six of the Wednesday applicants were back, along with the three continuing applicants from CSH. The committee ran its recommendations with great dispatch and, as usual, little discussion. Carl Cofrancesco and Anthony Morelli objected when given Zeta House, but both agreed to show up at ARCH for their investment group as did Sarah Cohen, who didn't even register a protest. Ernest Salter and Loretta Thomas were sent to Methadone

Maintenance, which is what they wanted, and Patrick Shea was referred to OPT. Although the committee tried briefly to pursue the notion of getting Pat to bring in his friends, he insisted that he had already talked to his gang about the idea and got no takers. Anyway, he said, none of them were really very much into heroin and he would keep trying to interest them in the program.

The committee turned next to the three patients back from CSH and ambulatory detox. They took up the majority of the meeting time. Had the committee known for sure what to do with these candidates when they first saw them, they probably never would have recommended detox in the first place. As it was, however, detox gave the committee a short reprieve. The three candidates did not really fit any of the treatment programs. Two of the three had all the qualifications for Methadone Maintenance except age (one was nineteen and the other twenty): both were black, both had been using heroin a long time, and both were strung out with big habits. Unfortunately, neither was in much trouble with the law. One had no arrests at all and the other only had a two-bit breach-of-peace case pending, and neither had spouse or parents to put pressure on him. Zeta House was out of the question; they would not go there. Methadone was not open to them although that was where they wanted to go, and OPT would provide insufficient controls to keep them off the streets. Although the committee had actually recommended OPT for both because there seemed no alternative, they nonetheless tried again to talk the two into accepting Zeta House. The committee spent a lot of time trying to dispel myths about the House: "The doors are not locked, people do not hit you, you can have visitors and even weekend passes later on," and trying to convince the applicants that this was the best treatment for them. The two applicants did not budge, however, and the committee reluctantly made appointments for them at Out-Patient Treatment.

The third returnee from detox was even more of a problem. He was over thirty, black, had done some time in prison, had been strung out on heroin briefly, but *did not want to go onto the Methadone Maintenance Program*. He wanted to go drug-free but would not consider Zeta House since he had a wife and children whom he supported. As he told the committee, he had not been using drugs long, not more than a couple of years, didn't start until after he was thirty, and did not think he was really a hard-core addict. (The committee agreed; he was what the program sometimes called a woodwork case.) Not having been addicted to heroin very long, he did not now want to become addicted to methadone. If he did, he would be beholden to the program for his drugs. He preferred to be beholden to no one, but if he had to be addicted, at least a heroin jones would let him pick his own cop man.

The first time the committee saw this applicant (Peter Johnson was his name), they spent quite a lot of time trying to convince him that his heroin addiction was probably more serious than he thought and that methadone maintenance was not necessarily permanent, as some made it out to be. Nevertheless, Johnson presented a unique and persuasive case and the committee had taken him seriously. The first steps had been to arrange welfare for his family and get him started on ambulatory detox. Then they had to decide what to do next. There was no really appropriate program for him, just as there was no really appropriate program for nonheroin users, or heroin chippers. But clearly something had to be done and Richards had taken the problem to the NAU Coordinating Committee (composed of the NAU director, NAU clinical director, and heads of each NAU component: Methadone Maintenance, Out-Patient Treatment, Zeta House, ARCH, and Research).

Bill Richards did not really expect the Coordinating Committee to solve his problem. The same problem had been brought up there many times before, but he did want the matter kept open. As it was, the Screening Committee saw quite a few applicants who could not fit into existing programs. When they did not make it into treatment, Richards wanted it known that it was because there was no appropriate treatment for them, not that the committee was negligent in its duties.

The Coordinating Committee spent a whole session (two hours) on this one problem. (Richards got more than he bargained for.) Suber, however, was becoming increasingly concerned about the high percentage of dropouts between application and program entry and was also aware that the NAU, which was built during a time of crisis to serve confirmed addicts, was not serving a number of drug abusers who were applying for treatment. This was a problem, Suber thought, on several counts. First of all, Suber felt the NAU could, and should, provide treatment for all drug abusers. Left untreated, those just getting into heroin, and even many who were into other drugs, would eventually become confirmed addicts. The community, moreover, seemed to agree with Suber, as many groups were putting pressure on the NAU to be less restrictive about admitting new patients. The NAU could not tell these groups forever that their treatment capacity was limited and thus the most serious cases had to take preference.

The trouble was, Suber's clinical staff kept resisting his attempts to introduce "low-intervention" programs for those drug abusers who did not need the demanding programs currently in operation at the NAU. Although these programs might be appropriate for those currently in treatment, they were not appropriate for those who had only a minor investment in the drug life and retained conventional institutional supports, such as family or school, which intensive treatment could actually destroy. Although his staff could agree with this reasoning in principle, they resisted it in practice because they felt that any "cheap" program (one that demands nothing of the addicts) would only subvert the more intensive programs now in existence. If treatment is made easy for some, the staff contended, those who really need more intensive treatment will not accept it. Suber had argued that programs could be arranged in a hierarchy of intervention intensity with strict rules, like the six-month Zeta House splittee rule, which would not allow patients to go directly from a more intensive to a less intensive program and would require failures in a low-intervention program to go next to a high-intervention component. But this, the other clinicians had argued, would only be to set addicts up for failure. "Why let addicts into a program where you know they are going to fail? Addicts have enough failure in their lives already.

What we need to do is show them that for once they can succeed."

Suber knew that in essence the rest of the staff really didn't believe that low-intervention programming would work for anybody. But they did not have to take the brunt of community pressure and thus could ignore the problem altogether. But Suber could not, and so at this Coordinating Committee meeting he pushed his case, saying, in effect, that the NAU was going to introduce low-intervention programming whether existing components liked it or not. He was not sure yet how the program would be organized—as a separate clinical component, as part of an existing treatment modality, or as part of Screening and Evaluation—but he was sure it would be organized.

When Richards reported all this back to the Screening Committee, the members were actually pleased; the program was finally taking their plight seriously. Richards, however, was concerned lest he have to direct the new low-intervention program as well as continue his work as director in charge of Screening and Evaluation. He had his hands full already. He spent six or seven hours a week in Screening Committee meetings and another three or four hours preparing for them. The Coordinating Committee took two hours a week, and regular meetings with the Probation and Parole Departments killed another three or four hours. Correspondence, making arrangements for applicants to get started in treatment, and dealing with the crises which were perpetually besetting the NAU took all the rest of his time. He hardly even had time for an occasional speaking engagement, let alone regular meetings with other community agencies that could be sources of referral and which were always after Suber to be "more responsive to community needs." To supervise a new clinical program seemed out of the question.

Nevertheless, Richard suggested to the Screening and Evaluation Committee that he take as a private patient the man who did not want methadone. If Suber got his low-intervention program going in time, he could transfer the patient there and, if not, the patient could be transferred to Methadone Maintenance as soon as he showed the first signs of screwing up. Richards had little doubt that he would screw up sooner or later if he tried to make it drug-free.

This left the whole issue of the low-intervention program, and Richards' role in it, unresolved, but nothing was ever resolved, Bill thought, at the NAU. As soon as one crisis was over, someone started another one. Richards was getting tired of the constant round. But screening and evaluation were done for another week and it was time to go home.

9 Methadone Maintenance

The Methadone Maintenance Clinic of the NAU is now five years old. During those years the clinic has had four directors, at least one complete changeover in other staff positions, a markedly changing patient population (going from zero in the beginning to nearly 200 at its peak, and then back down to approximately 150), and marked shifts in program philosophy. As social scientists, our interest tended to focus on these long-term changes. We have found, however, that the program itself does not concentrate on these trends. It does not have a historical perspective. As one program director commented in an interview with us:

> I don't know why you're still interested in that. Yesterday Mark Halbrook paid me a visit. Remember him? He was one of the psychiatric residents who used to be here. He was telling me about the things he was doing when he was on the program. That was only a year ago, but it sounded like a thousand years. I had to work very hard to remember even the importance of those issues, much less their emergency, and I found it impossible to talk to him about recent program developments. There was no way that he could in any degree understand what is going on now. He was a member of another era.

Writing a description of the Methadone Maintenance Program, then, is difficult. A historical account would not be consistent with the way staff and patients see it, yet a static description would miss many of the issues and developments that were, in their time, keenly important to the program. Therefore, as a stylistic compromise, this chapter is organized around a series of incidents and issues which, when they occurred, were of utmost importance to the staff or patients of the program, even though each faded in time to the status of anecdote or was forgotten altogether.

Describing the Methodone Program in this way may give the impression that it developed as a series of crises. That impression is intentional. Although there were, to be sure, lulls between the storms, and much routine work went on all the time in the background, it was the storms, sometimes loud and raging, sometimes only quietly brewing, that gave the Methadone Maintenance Program its character. At times the program staff and members were filled with energy and optimism; at other times morale was low and pessimism was rampant. Never, however, was Methadone Maintenance dull and routine.

It should not be construed from this account, however, that the NAU, as a drug-treatment program operating in the crisis period of 1968–73, was, in balance, incompetently run or that its members did not work hard to make the program a success. In our judgment, and the judgment of others in the drug field, the NAU clinic is one of the best methadone programs in the country. Its patients have cleaner urines (only about 5 percent of the random urine checks show illegal drug use) and a higher rate of employment (as high as 90 percent for those who are physically employable) than any other program we are aware of. The Methadone staff, with Dr. Suber's support, has remained remarkably responsive to membership concerns and has encouraged and been receptive to more member involvement in program planning and execution than any other program we know of. It is probably no accident, therefore, that this methadone program has been in the forefront of dispelling the notion, popular in many quarters, that methadone maintenance is something that addicts must look forward to for life. At present, more than thirty Methadone Clinic members have successfully completed their course of treatment and are living independent, productive, drug-free lives. Many more are going through the process of methadone detoxification.

These successes, however, get submerged in the day-by-day business of doing drug treatment and being a Methadone patient. To those at the nurses' station or in the lounge, the program often seems a frantic confrontation of innumerable crises. It takes distance, both physical and professional, to see the Methadone Program as something else—something more ordered, more ordinary, more rational. For those who would like to read accounts of methadone maintenance written by people who have had this distance, we suggest: Raymond Glasscote et al., The Treatment of Drug Abuse (Washington, D.C., American Psychiatric Association, 1972, esp. pp. 30–35, 63–82, 139–44, 175–79, 216–21), or Ford Foundation, Dealing with Drug Abuse (New York, Praeger, 1972, esp. pp. 199–233). There are many other similar accounts in the literature.

Rapping

THE METHADONE MAINTENANCE CLINIC occupies half of a three-story brownstone located a few blocks away from the main RMHC facility, an ultramodern structure known to NAU staff and patients as the Center. Of all the NAU programs, only the Methadone Day Hospital (where new Methadone Maintenance candidates go for four weeks of group therapy and induction onto methadone) and Dr. Suber's office are actually located in the Center itself. The main NAU administrative offices, the NAU physician, and assorted personnel from other NAU components fill the other half of the building which houses the Methadone Clinic. The remaining NAU components are scattered throughout Riverdale.

The first floor of the Methadone Clinic has four rooms—the office of Dr. Klein the director, a nursing office, a methadone dispensing station, and a patients' bathroom. The second floor also has four rooms—a counselors' office, an office for conferences and group meetings, a patients' lounge, and a staff bathroom. The third floor has an office for the head nurse, which doubles as a meeting room and nurses' lounge, an office for the assistant director, which doubles as a meeting room, and an office for psychiatric residents. In back of the building is a small parking lot, and in front is a porch which is shared with the other side of the building.

It was on this porch that Loretta Thomas, Ernest Salter, Peter Johnson, and Carlos Alverez found each other late one unseasonably hot afternoon in May. All four were maintained members now and all had come for their medication. The line at the nurses' station was long, however, since many people had just come in after work for their daily dose of methadone, and

Loretta, Erny, Pete, and Carlos were hanging around waiting for the line to dwindle before they braved the crunch inside. As members of the same therapy group they had much to talk about.

Erny: You hear about Sheila Pond?
Loretta: No; what's my sister done now?
Erny: She says P.J.'s knocked her up.
Loretta: No shit!
Erny: P.J.'s been shacked up with Sheila ever since he split from Zeta House.
Pete: Dumb bastard. I wouldn't let Sheila in the same building with me without a chaperon. Shit, Sheila'd have a paternity suit going against Jesus Christ if she could get him alone in the same room with her for five minutes.
Erny: Well, P.J.'s been in the same room with her all right. She says she's going to bring suit, too. The brass are all uptight about it.
Pete: What the hell are they uptight about? It ain't like this is the first time Sheila's fucked anybody; P.J. either for that matter.
Erny: Tiny told me it was because P.J.'s old man is a big shot and gives a lot of money to Zeta House. If this thing makes the newspapers, he ain't likely to keep those fat donations coming in.
Pete: I bet they're uptight because Sheila's black and P.J.'s white. They're just jive motherfuckers.
Carlos: It may not matter too much what the reason is. Sheila just got her third dirty urine. The slip came back from the lab yesterday. They'll can her for that, sure.
Loretta: Sheila didn't have no three dirty urines. She's been taking some medicine her doctor gave her. It shows up like coke on the urine test, but it ain't cocaine.
Erny: The hell it ain't cocaine. Sheila shoots coke every time she gets a chance to get down.
Loretta: It wasn't coke! She just forgot to tell those honky bitches at the nursing station about the medicine she's been taking and they claim she got dirty urines. Shit, she even showed them the prescriptions. They wouldn't give her no rhythm at all. They just told her she shouldn't take no medicine unless Mansfield gives it to her. Shit, Mansfield wouldn't give you an aspirin for a toothache.
Erny: Well, it seems to me the lab should be able to tell coke from medicine. They know a week later if you've had one goddam gin

and tonic; why can't they tell when a dude's shot a spoon of coke the night before?
Loretta: But why should they want to know that? This program is here to get junkies to stop using heroin, not coke. The people in Riverdale don't care about cocaine. Why does the program always make it their business to try and get us to be like them white dudes who live in the suburbs. Shit, we're too old to start changing our lives now. Give up heroin? Sure! I agree that that's a good thing. But everything else? Hell no. Shit, if I had to give up pross, I couldn't even feed my family. You any idea how much my welfare check is?
Erny: It's enough to live on. My old lady lived on one when I was in the joint.
Loretta: Well, I don't call that living.

Carlos, by this time, was edging toward the door with the intention of going in for his medication. Not only did he want to get away from the others, but he was also hoping to get his med in time to make it to the bar for a couple of drinks before going on home to eat and rushing back to his group therapy meeting. Carlos was delayed, however, by Sherman Louis (Boss, as he had always been known on the streets and was still, as assistant director of the program). Boss was coming out to clear the porch. It was one of his periodic duties, initiated, as usual, by an irate phone call from Risa Dixon, the head NAU administrator. There was a rule that patients were not to gather on the front porch since the neighbors complained when they saw a horde of junkies milling around outside the clinic. Boss never liked the rule much, since it was so hard to enforce, but he did agree that the program should present a good public image and thus tried to clear the porch whenever Risa got on the phone to say that the neighbors were complaining again.

It was near the end of a long day, though, and Boss was tired. He had tried to get away earlier to unwind a bit over a drink, but the parade of members coming to him about one petty problem after another kept him tied down. It was with little finesse, then, that he asked the people to move on. It was with equally little finesse that Loretta told Boss to go fuck off. "If you'd get us a goddam air conditioner for the lounge, we'd go up there. Meanwhile, this is as good a place to rap as any."

"Look," Boss tried to explain, "we're working on that. We . . ."

"Seems to me you been working on that long enough," Loretta retorted, "who's this program for anyway? You're keeping your ass cool enough behind your air conditioner. Just remember, if it wasn't for the members you wouldn't have no goddam air conditioner at all. Shit, if it wasn't for the members, you wouldn't have a fuckin' job."

With that, Loretta turned her back on Boss and continued her conversation with Erny and Pete. (Carlos, by this time, had slipped inside.) Boss got mad. Loretta continued to ignore him. Boss grabbed Loretta by the shoulder and Pete bristled: "You take your fuckin' hands off Loretta or I'll stuff you down the goddam storm sewer."

That's all Boss needed. No one talked to Boss that way and got away with it. When he had been on the streets he was king; there wasn't nobody in their right mind dared lay a hand on him and those who were crazy enough to try never tried a second time. Boss's reputation as a tough dude, now that he was assistant director of the Methadone Clinic, was essentially intact. In fact, most of the patients figured that Boss got his job partly because he could keep the rest of the members in line and protect Klein. Now this reputation was on the line. "You want to come around back and try that?" Boss inquired. Pete had little choice. He had stuck his chin out; now he had to defend it. He and Boss left. Loretta ran for help. Loretta's first stop was the nurses' station. Most of the patients, by this time, had cleared out of the hallway and Carlos was standing by the dispensing window drinking his methadone.

"Boss and Pete's in a fight," Loretta yelled through the window to Mary Eastman, one of the two nurses on duty.

"What?" Mary answered incredulously.

"Boss and Pete's gone out back to have a fight," Loretta repeated.

"Shit!" Mary finally got the message, "go get the counselors. Where the hell are they anyway?"

"Tiny's in the john with Spooks supervising his urine," Carlos offered. "I don't know where Sparky is."

"Carlos, you get Tiny out here," Mary started giving orders. "Loretta, run upstairs and see if you can find Sparky, and hurry. Beth, cover the station for me and call Klein. He left for home about fifteen minutes ago. You better see if he can come back down here."

Beth Frazier, the other nurse on duty, called Klein and Mary headed out the back door followed closely by Tiny and Sparky, who stopped the fight practically before it got started. No one was hurt. Boss left and Pete came into the clinic for his med. He was still talking excitedly with Mary, Beth, Loretta, Tiny, and Sparky at the nurses' station when Klein came in. After a very brief conversation with all those assembled, Klein and Pete excused themselves and went off to Klein's office to finish the discussion.

The security guard from the Center, a portly gentleman in his early sixties, came in and Tiny and Sparky started gathering up the day's urine samples (the program collected thirty-two of the thirty-three random specimens the computer had designated for that day) and unused doses of methadone (there were six unclaimed bottles today). Nobody mentioned the fight to the security guard. Sparky, with the urine-specimen carrier, and Tiny, with a locked attaché case containing the extra medication, followed the guard to the state car that was parked out back. "See you at the Gate," Tiny called back over his shoulder as he, Sparky, and the guard went out the door.

Mary and Beth closed the dispensing window and began locking and tidying up the nurses' station. Klein, who had finished his conference with Pete, stuck his head in the door long enough to say good-bye before departing again for home.

Mary, who had been with the NAU for two years now, went about her work perfunctorily, but Beth, who was new to the program, still had to think about what she was doing. "What do we do about the six bottles that went back to the Center?" Beth inquired at one point. "Should I call over and have the emergency room hold them in case people come looking for them tonight?"

"Don't bother," Mary answered after thinking about it for a minute, "there won't be anyone in for them tonight. Four are p.r.n.'s for detox people. If they haven't come in for them by now, they can wait until morning. One is Barzini's, who Tiny thinks got busted today. We'll probably be taking his bottle to him in jail tomorrow morning. The other one is Sheila's. She hasn't picked up any medication in two days so I guess she can wait until tomorrow."

Mary and Beth finished their chores and were just turning on the burglar alarm when Bonnie Pratt, currently the program's only black nurse, walked up. Bonnie, who had been with the clinic since it opened, was off duty but had arranged to meet Mary and Beth for dinner. As the three started down the street, Tiny and Sparky drove up in Tiny's white Eldorado and the three nurses hopped in for the two-block ride to the Sliding Gate.

The conversation during two rounds of drinks and then dinner was all about Boss and Pete. "I think Boss ought to be fired," Mary concluded. "What right does he have fighting with patients anyway? He acts like he was still on the streets or something."

"Now hold on," Tiny counseled for the third time. "You and Beth are making a mountain out of a molehill. Boss wasn't going to hurt anybody. He just had to let Pete know who runs things around here. You know yourself that Boss takes a lot of weight off you nurses. Sometimes he has to do it his own way."

"Well," Beth agreed with Mary, "I don't think it's very professional."

"So it's not professional," Bonnie chimed in, "so what? You can't always be professional and be effective. Sometimes you got to be a little human too. Boss was just being human. Now don't get me wrong. I don't agree with what he did, but he did have his reasons and I think we should stick by him. Boss's got a tough job and he hasn't had much time to learn how to do it professionally. But he's learning. He needs our support."

Tiny and Sparky, although they were inclined to minimize the whole affair, sided with Bonnie. Mary and Beth still thought Boss ought to get called on the carpet for his unprofessional conduct. Once again Bonnie found herself on the side of the counselors—a bad habit, she thought, but what could she do? So what if she was patient-oriented? At least one nurse ought to be on the side of the counselors and patients. But now was no time to continue that argument; the others had to open up the clinic for evening groups.

Groups

Erny, Pete, and Loretta made it to group (held tonight in the second-floor meeting room) but Carl did not. Later, when confronted with his absence—a rule violation—Carl copped to the fact that he had figured it was wise to lay low for a while. He hadn't missed a group meeting for a long time, he said, so he figured he could miss this one without getting into trouble. And he was right; the only shit he took was from Erny who thought he should have been there to defend Pete in an hour of obvious need. What Carl never said, but thought nonetheless, was that he never had any intention of sticking up for Pete. If Pete was damn fool enough to tangle with Boss, he could just get himself out of it. Carl had a year to go, maybe less if he was lucky, before he would be eligible for detox and then graduation and he was not going to jeopardize that goal by getting involved in a dispute between staff and patients.

Loretta's position was different. She had not come to the NAU because she wanted to get off drugs; she came because she had to. Graduating from Methadone Maintenance was the farthest thing from her mind. She did, however, value the Methadone Program and during those first weeks in Meth Eval, and especially during the following four weeks in the Methadone Day Hospital, Loretta modified her views about drugs and the drug life enough to accept the idea that she was better off being a Methadone Program member than a junkie. Indeed, she even came to the point of trying to get her old man, who had split for Endfield the day after she started in Meth Eval, to join the program. What Loretta was still unable to accept, though, was the line run by the Methadone staff and a lot of the maintained Methadone patients that giving up heroin also meant giving up her whole life style. Loretta's group was always giving her shit about this, and once had even sent her to the Advisory Board because she refused to stop hustling. Aside from two months' bad standing, though, the only consequence of this was to complicate her life a little more; now she not only had to avoid the pigs but those program members who might rat on her as well.

Even though Erny Salter wasn't thinking particularly about graduating from the Methadone Program, like Carl he didn't want anything to interfere with his position in it. He liked the Methadone Clinic and with his wife's support (his wife was also a maintained member) was in the forefront of every campaign to tighten things up. Basically, this meant getting the fuck-ups, like Loretta and Sheila, to shape up so that they wouldn't give the program a bad name.

Pete was a maverick. He was outspoken on many matters, including almost every aspect of program policy. It was Pete's contention that the program, except for the methadone they dispensed, was essentially irrelevant. Groups, he thought, were a farce: "All they do is give crybabies a place to be heard." What the program really needed, Pete thought, was a larger vocational staff (the NAU had only one person devoting full time to this area at that time), which could do more to help members find jobs, and some kind of educational program for the Methadone members like they had for OPT members. That the NAU would allow Boss and some of the counselors to have important jobs without first completing at least a high school equivalency, was, in Pete's mind, ludicrous.

Pete's therapy group met once a week. It was led by Mary Eastman (each nurse and each counselor, as well as the assistant director, had responsibilities for one or more groups and Klein and Suber each led a good-standing detox group). Pete, like nearly everyone else in the program, thought that Mary was cold and indifferent. Although she was a good nurse, everyone admitted that, she showed little concern for individual patients. Mary opened the group meeting by asking: "Why don't you tell us what happened between you and Boss this afternoon?"

Pete: That motherfucker had no business hitting Loretta.
Erny: Now Pete, Boss didn't hit Loretta.
Pete: The hell he didn't.

Erny: He just grabbed her by the shoulder. He didn't mean no harm.
Pete: Well, he can just keep his fuckin' hands off people.
Mary: Loretta, did Boss hit you?
Loretta: No, but he didn't have no business grabbing me.
Mary: No business?
Erny: He had a business all right. Loretta wouldn't get off the porch.
Loretta: Well, I don't see why we can't stand on the porch. Whose goddam program is this anyway? We wasn't doing any harm, we was just waiting for the line to go down so we could get our med. Shit, it stinks in that hall when you get fifty people all lined up at once trying to get in and pick up their med. If you had any decent clinic hours around here some people might come at other times so there wouldn't be such a jam-up around five o'clock.
Mary: Boss was only doing his job.
Pete: Doing his job! You call hitting people doing his job? Shit, Boss acts like he's still on the streets. What kind of image is that? Hell, Boss is assistant director of the program. He should be acting like a professional.

Mary had to agree, and although normally she kept her opinions to herself for the sake of staff solidarity, this time she found herself agreeing out loud with the patients: "And a professional keeps his appointments, does not come to work drunk, and does not drink on the job."

Loretta: Well, all the counselors does that. It's not so bad as long as they does their jobs.
Pete: That's just the point; they're not doing their jobs. Part of their job is to give this program a good name and drinking in the parking lot, where every Tom, Dick, and Harry can see them, is not what I calls doing a good job. Seems to me Boss and the counselors should show more concern for their brothers and sisters than to act like that.
Mary: Well, Boss may shape up this time. Wait till Suber hears about this.
Pete: Fuck, Klein's going to cover up for him. I'll bet you $10 Suber never hears about our fight, and if he does, Klein will smooth it over.
Erny: You better just hope your fuckin' ass you're right. If you are,

you're home free. If Klein has to hush this up, the last thing he wants is you going before the Advisory Board.
Pete: I'll go before the Advisory Board gladly. I got more shit on those punks than I need to keep them from throwing me off the program. They wouldn't dare. But you're right. I probably won't even see the Advisory Board.

Although the group could have, and according to program rules, probably should have, sent Pete to the Advisory Board themselves, no one suggested such a move. Instead, everyone agreed that the incident would probably blow over as far as the staff was concerned. The only problem was whether one of the members would tell Suber. He was always talking with members.

The meeting moved at this juncture from bad-mouthing Boss to a perennial bitch: switching urines. One member of the group was still smarting under a dirty urine report he had received three weeks earlier. He claimed that the urine wasn't dirty and therefore someone must have switched his specimen with someone else's. Mary, although she was prepared to believe that counselors did sometimes switch urines in order to protect a friend, was not inclined to believe the allegation this time. After all, there were other ways than urine tests to find out if members were messing around and this member, according to all accounts, was a big coke shooter.

To the group members, though, the important issue was not whether the urine was really dirty but that counselors switched urines. Such activity, the members thought, was almost as bad as tampering with somebody's med. One of the members, in fact, recounted the incident when a member who had weekend medication privileges got two bottles of Tang with no methadone in them. When the first bottle hadn't held her, she marched the second bottle right up to Suber who had it tested and confirmed her suspicion that it was only juice.

The group wasn't going to resolve the issue of urines, though, and was discussing it in part as an excuse to get off the subject of Boss. Although there was a lot more to be said about the conflict between Pete and Boss, no one wanted to commit himself further until they found out whether Klein was successful in covering the whole thing up. If he was, that would be good for Pete, and if he wasn't, that would probably serve Boss right. Some day Boss was going to have to learn his lesson. The members, though, were not anxious to be the ones to teach him, partly because they were afraid of him, partly because Boss was one of their own, but mostly because they admired him despite his shortcomings.

Although no methadone member or staff mentioned the incident to him, Suber heard about it. Risa Dixon, who got the details from Beth, had told him. Suber was troubled. Although the incident itself as an isolated event was not of great concern, it was just one more in a series involving the Methadone counseling staff (Boss had been a counselor before becoming assistant director), that defined a disquieting pattern: ex-addicts had a hard time making it as staff in an outpatient setting. Ex-addicts seemed to function well in a therapeutic community where they were isolated from the streets, but they did not do well in programs that allowed them to spend their evenings making the rounds of their old haunts and socializing with their old friends. Suber had hoped for more from his ex-addict Methadone counselors. He had taken quite a risk in their behalf by hiring them in the first place and then promoting them to more responsible positions at the earliest opportunity. Incidents like this did not help his cause much and only gave those in the program, like Risa Dixon and the nurses who opposed hiring ex-addicts, another reason to say "I told you so." Since the incident passed, however, and Suber had no reason to intervene, he continued to hope for the best.

COMMUNITY MEETING

As the summer wore on, Boss and Klein, along with the Advisory Board, worked to document the rules and regulations of the Methadone Program. Up until then, the various rules, regulations, and procedures in the program had been scattered among many separate memoranda and minutes from Advisory Board or staff meetings, and the patients and staff seemed always to be arguing about what policy actually was. Klein hoped to stop the arguments once and for all by gathering everything together in one document that could be ratified by the patients and then kept as the standard against which patient conduct and staff actions could be judged. A draft of the document was finished, and the Advisory Board had called a community meeting so that all the staff and members could discuss it and, if all went well, perhaps even ratify it.

Community meetings were held in the RMHC auditorium; there was no other room in the RMHC big enough to hold the entire Methadone staff and membership. All the staff and most of the members came. Loretta, along with Sheila Pond and some other program loud-mouths, sat right up front. Carl sat in the back of the auditorium along with those who didn't want to be bothered with the whole thing but came because it was a program requirement. Pete and his group of troublemakers sat off in one corner and Erny and his wife sat in the middle of the room. Klein, Boss, and the members of the Advisory Board sat up front on the stage. Beth, the nursing staff representative to the Advisory Board, had been chosen to read the document:

Standards and guidelines for members of the Methadone Maintenance Program

This program accepts the fact that those having good reason to want to give up a life of drug abuse will do so if given the proper vehicle. In our case, a program strong enough to counter the pleasure of drugs is the vehicle. Program strength means nonpermissiveness toward regressive behavior like stealing, hustling, prostitution, and drug use. This strength, coming from the member rather than the staff level, appears to be effective in cultivating awareness of the significance of problematic behavior.

Spooks, who was sitting next to Carl, offered him a hit off a bottle that was making the rounds of the back row. Carl declined the offer. Beth read on:

Our credibility is important if we are to meet the needs of those who seek our services. Members must feel that they are part of an institution geared to help them in a serious and humane manner. Our credibility will be established by a no-nonsense attitude based on the knowledge that heroin is the most potent chemical man has ever abused and, to overcome its seductive rape, one must wage a never-ending struggle. It is impossible to win this struggle if an individual has to also fight the stigma brought upon him by misfits who are insincere about getting drugs out of their lives.

Good Standing: Henceforth only members in good standing will be eligible to attend and vote at community meetings. Members shall be in good standing . . . ,

"Hey, what kind of shit is that?" one of Loretta's friends who was not in good standing interrupted. "Who put in a rule like that?" A chorus of members shouted her down. Beth continued:

Members shall be in good standing if they fulfill all program, committee, and group commitments as set forth by the Standards and Guidelines, abstain from all drug abuse, conduct themselves as responsible adults, exert every effort toward being gainfully employed, personify dignity at public functions, exercise restraint in expressions of violence toward fellow members and staff, show concern for individuals less fortunate than themselves, resist the impulse to resort to old habits of shoplifting, stealing, prostitution, hustling, etc., and DEMONSTRATE SERIOUS INTENT IN MAINTAINING A NON-ADDICT LIFE STYLE.

Advisory Board: Bad standing shall be decided by the Advisory Board, which is empowered to deal with any problem members may have, whether brought to the board's attention by the member's group or by Methadone staff. The power to impose helpful probations, as well as execute penalties for infractions of the rules, is what makes the Advisory Board effective. Members whose actions show that they do not wish to remain a part of the program may be discharged from the program by the Advisory Board.

Numerous not inaudible asides ("bullshit," "you got to be kidding") could be heard from various parts of the room, but Beth held the floor and kept reading. She covered a section describing procedures for electing members to the Advisory Board and proceeded to a lengthy list of major and minor infractions and their consequences. Major infractions, like selling one's methadone, getting arrested for a felony, or having more than three dirty urines in a thirty-day period, could lead to dismissal from the program. Minor infractions, like physical violence, selling stolen goods on program premises, or missing too many group meetings, would lead to bad standing for varying lengths of time. The section concluded with a short paragraph specifying dirty urines. Some of the members in the front row tried several times to interrupt, but the rest of the members shouted them down each time. Klein was pleased. Boss had been telling him that the bulk of the membership supported a tight program, but Klein had had trouble believing it. Beth continued to read:

Take-Home Privileges: No one will receive take-home medication privileges until he has been on the program at least six months, four of which must have been in continuous good standing. Full-time employment, twenty hours a week of regularly scheduled volunteer work, or twelve hours a week in school are necessary before take-home privileges can begin and must be maintained if the privilege is to be retained.

Selling one's take-home medication is very serious business. Even rumors of this act are as damaging to the program as the act itself. Therefore, all members with take-home privileges must exercise utmost care to avoid any situation which could generate the rumor that they are selling their medication. Evidence that a member has misused his take-home privileges can lead to immediate dismissal from the program; rumors alone can lead to a suspension of the take-home privilege. If any member wishes to scotch rumors, he may either go quietly to the program director, assistant director, physician, or nurses to set a trap for the rumor monger, or he may bring the perpetrator personally to the Advisory Board for a hearing and possible disciplinary action.

A number of members interrupted to ask Beth exactly what kind of trap the Advisory Board had in mind. "Oh," she answered, "like quietly leaving your take-home med with us so you couldn't possibly be selling it. Then if someone says you are, we would know they were lying." Beth returned to the document:

Detoxification: Anyone accepting Methadone Maintenance as a program of treatment must be *active* in the program for *at least one year* following day status before he becomes eligible for detoxification with medical advice. Continuous good standing for *at least* two months is a prerequisite for any good standing detox request.

Detoxification in good standing will be executed under the direct supervision of a detox group leader and the program physician. The physician's medical knowledge of detox procedures, along with other expert consultation, will continue to be the sole guide for the nursing staff in dispensing medication to detox members.

Anyone wishing to detox without meeting these conditions will do so against medical advice. AMA detox will be accomplished in thirty days. No exceptions. Members who are dropped from the program by the Advisory Board will be detoxed AMA.

All hell broke loose. Concern about detox was strong and had been festering among the membership and, to some degree, among the staff as well, for some time. But, this was the first time that the staff and the membership had confronted each other in community meeting about the issues involved in methadone detox.

The membership, as a whole, was against thirty-day detox: "That's just sending people back to the streets to shoot dope."

"It ain't fair."

"It ain't right."

"You can't kick a methadone habit in no thirty days. Shit, good standing detox takes dudes months and even then some don't make it so good."

"It's your own choice," Boss charged into the melée. "There ain't nobody makes you opt for thirty-day detox. Either you chooses it or you're such a fuck-up that we have no choice but to let you go. As I see it, you got to work real hard to get kicked out of this program. Seems to me misfits don't deserve no bed of roses. If people worked half as hard at being responsible members of the Methadone Program as they do at hustling and being junkies, they wouldn't have no trouble around here at all."

The members were still opposed; detoxing fast enough to make it in thirty days was too painful for anyone to endure. Therefore, thirty-day detox people *had* to supplement their methadone with heroin just to keep from getting sick. As everyone knew, most of these people didn't even stick around for the whole thirty days but just quit and went back to dope. While some of the staff argued that this was what the misfits wanted anyway, the members knew better. Some people simply wanted off methadone and thirty-day detox was the only route the staff left them; for them, it was too short a time to come off successfully.

Mary Eastman worked her way into the conflict: "The trouble is, you all want detox before you're ready. Detox is just a fad; you all want it because you think it would be nice to be in a group with Klein or Suber. Well, you'll all get your turn. Meanwhile you shouldn't be so impatient. Detoxing is hard. Not everybody makes it, even in the good-standing detox groups. People shouldn't even try to detox until they're ready."

"What the shit is this 'ready,' anyway?" one of Pete's friends wanted to know. "Since when does someone who has never taken drugs know when a dude is ready to pack it in?"

"You don't just quit taking drugs," Mary came back, "it takes therapy."

"Therapy?" Erny Salter could contain himself no longer, "they don't do no therapy in those detox groups. All they do is sit around and complain about how sick they are, how their backs ache and how they can't sleep and such stuff. Then the doc runs in with an increase in their methadone or gives them pills to make them sleep or feel better. If they was getting therapy, I would say, right on. But they ain't, so why don't we just cut the jive. Seems to me any of us could detox by ourselves once we gets our shit together, gets a job, or gets back in school."

"That's bullshit and you know it." Now Mary was getting mad. "If getting off drugs is so easy, why don't addicts do it by themselves on the street? There's methadone out there. It's cheaper than heroin, too. If you're so smart, why did you ever come on the program?"

Klein interrupted. Tempers were starting to go above the boiling point. "It's true," Klein said, "that there is not enough therapy in detox groups; there's not enough therapy in the whole program. But detox is experimental and it will take a long time to work out the bugs so that it's really efficient. In the meantime I think we should all concentrate on our therapy groups rather than on detox. I think there's a lot more we could be doing in the way of getting people ready for detox."

Both staff and members agreed that more therapy was needed. Some members argued in favor of more individual therapy and vocational training, and the staff urged more family therapy and relevant community involvement. It was Pete, however, who most forcefully expressed the opinion of a growing number of members.

He said: "This is all bullshit. What you're all trying to do is make us dependent on the program. Shit, we was dependent on heroin before we come here. Switching one dependency for another isn't therapy. Real therapy would make us independent —independent from heroin and independent from methadone and this here clinic. Six months is all it should take. Any dude who is serious should be able to get his thing together in six months if he has medication to take care of his habit and some kind of relevant program to help him learn how to make a living some other way than going back on the streets or hustling welfare. Then, when a dude gets himself together, I say he should get right off methadone; the faster the better. The longer he drags it out, the more dependent he becomes, and the harder it's going to be to cut the ties with the program. It's no wonder people in the detox groups are having a hard time of it. Now they're methadone junkies and they have come to like being members of the Methadone Program; they get a lot of status from it. Shit, they goes out on speaking engagements all the time and parades in front of businessmen and white kids in the suburbs and says 'look at me, I'm a Methadone Maintenance member. Ain't I great?' Well I say that they ain't great, they're just one notch better off than they were on the street. What they need to do is get their asses out of here—as far away as they can—and become really great."

The meeting had reached an impasse. Klein had hoped the members would ratify "Standards and Guidelines" but it was obvious that they would not tonight. Klein, therefore, did not push to have the matter put to a vote. Instead, he closed the meeting with what he considered to be a compromise. "I think we should have the Advisory Board do some more work on the document and then call another community meeting. Perhaps the Advisory Board can look more closely at the issues involving detox." As the meeting ended and the members wandered out, many expressed satisfaction: "See, what'd I tell you, this is still a member-run program."

A few, mostly from Pete's crowd, expressed another view: "That's the last time we'll see that paper. I'll give you ten to one the staff just goes ahead and does what they wants to without ever calling another community meeting."

Staff Meeting

It had been six months since the community meeting at which "Standards and Guidelines" had been proposed. Detox was still an issue, although its salience had subsided somewhat, due in large measure to the neutral ninety-day detox which the Methadone staff finally initiated. Quite a few patients rushed to join the new program, so many in fact that a waiting list had to be established for this detox also. (There had always been a waiting list for good-standing detox groups.)

It was time for the weekly Methadone staff meeting. The nurses' station had been closed (it was closed for two hours every afternoon to accommodate staff meetings and conferences) and the Day Hospital counselor had just come over from the Center. Everyone was waiting for Dr. Suber, who had been invited over especially to discuss problems surrounding program expansion.

The main agenda topic was the new Methadone Clinic, a second clinic, which should have opened two months ago but was still being delayed. The staff was demanding some action and Suber had agreed to come over to discuss the problem. Such matters were usually confined to NAU Coordinating Committee meetings; indeed the second clinic had been discussed there several times. The details of these discussions, however, had not made their way back to the Methadone staff because Klein had resigned to take a job in another city and Boss had been fired. Dr. Suber was therefore glad to step in and help hold

things together until the new director could come on board.
Waiting for Suber, the staff had a chance to fill each other in on the current state of the program. This was the way most meetings at the NAU got started. George Long, the brand-new assistant director (not an ex-addict) mentioned that Erny Salter had just been elected chairman of the Advisory Board. Everyone seemed pleased. One of the nurses reported that Carlos Alverez had applied for good-standing detox. Mary Eastman expressed surprise. "Isn't he a little premature?" she asked, but Tiny eased any concern that Mary or any of the other nurses might have when he noted that being on the waiting list didn't mean that he was being detoxed. By the time Carlos' name worked its way to the top of the list he would have plenty of time to get ready. Beth announced that Peter Johnson had just zeroed out in neutral detox; he was the first program member to complete the regime. Some of the staff congratulated Beth, who was overseeing the program, although Bonnie was the only one who expressed any regrets that Pete would now be leaving the program. Sparky, who was the current Methadone Representative in Screening, mentioned that Loretta Thomas's old man had finally applied to the program. This was good, the staff felt, and probably Loretta's handiwork. Loretta had become a solid member of the program. Her volunteer work at the jail and her generally cooperative behavior demonstrated a marked improvement in attitude.

John Mansfield, the Methadone physician (a part-time position), hurried into the room and apologized for being late. No one seemed very upset, but John explained why he was tardy anyway. He had just admitted Sheila Pond to the hospital with what looked like a cerebral aneurysm. Her chances, Mansfield reported, were probably no better than fifty-fifty.

"What's a cerebral aneurysm?" Sparky inquired.

"That's when a blood vessel bursts in the brain," Mary offered.

"Actually," Dr. Mansfield refined the explanation, "a cerebral aneurysm is a weak spot in an artery in the head. The artery bulges out like a balloon. Sometimes they burst and blood flows all over inside the head. That's what happened to Sheila."

"It got anything to do with Sheila being on methadone?" Bonnie wanted to know.

"I don't know," Mansfield answered, sharing Bonnie's concern. "So far as we know, aneurysms are hereditary. Perhaps methadone aggravated it, we just don't know. There's a lot we don't know about methadone."

"Ain't it a bitch," Tiny observed, as much to himself as to the rest of the group, "and Sheila was finally doing so good too."

Suber breezed in. He was a half-hour late. No one had expected him any earlier and thus registered no surprise at his tardiness. "The day Suber makes it to a meeting on time," Bonnie Pratt once observed, "this program is in real trouble. Suber's late because he always takes time to stop and listen to folks' problems—any folks: nurses, counselors, or patients."

Suber had in fact stopped along the way, although it had not been a Methadone patient or staff member who had detained him this time, but Risa Dixon. Suber listened patiently as Risa brought him up to date on her latest crisis, a pending site visit by a management-consulting firm which Washington had contracted to review administrative procedure in drug programs receiving federal funding. To Suber, the site visit was more of an annoyance than anything else, but to Risa, who had enough trouble just keeping the state's accountants off Suber's back, it was a potential catastrophe.

Suber started the Methadone staff meeting by outlining the problem. Washington had granted a budget increase to expand the Methadone Program to two clinics. This increase, however, had been predicated on an enrollment projection of nearly 300 members by this date, and 400 a year later. Actual enrollment was 157, down from a high, a year earlier, of 194. How could Suber justify opening a second clinic, he concluded, when the numbers didn't warrant it?

"But the numbers do justify it," George Long, the new assistant director, offered cautiously. "These quarters really can't accommodate more than about 100 comfortably. With a second clinic, we could divide our current population in half. Then we might have a little room to breathe."

"But I can't justify two clinics for 150 patients," Dr. Suber responded. "This clinic itself is too expensive to fall within the new federal guidelines."

"Fuck the federal guidelines." It was Tiny who was speaking. "We all know you can't run a quality program with those guidelines. Shit, we ain't just a methadone dispensary like they run in Detroit or New York."

"I know," Dr. Suber agreed, "but it's places like Detroit and New York that set the pace. They have such big waiting lists for methadone in the big cities that they have little choice but to run programs with a minimum of psychosocial supports. I know we're different and I'm proud of it. I have always been able to justify our program on the basis that we're in the forefront of introducing innovative treatment in our clinic. We have many firsts to our credit, but I can carry this kind of justification only so far. It disturbs me that our enrollment in Methadone is so low."

"It's probably only a temporary thing," Beth offered. "We are down now because we have had so many graduates all of a sudden and intake has been slow. Summers are always slow."

"Things'll change," Tiny picked up where Beth left off, "as soon as it really starts getting cold out there on the streets. December and January are always our biggest months."

"But this is what bothers me," Suber went on. "November is usually a big month too, but applications this year are way below what they were in November a year ago. Sparky, you sit on Screening. What do you think?"

"I don't know," Sparky stalled for time so he could think of something important to say. "It's true, though, that we ain't seeing very many dudes down at Screening these days."

"The trouble is," Tiny interrupted, "the police ain't puttin' pressure on people no more. Since Smith left the Vice Squad, they ain't been making half as many arrests as they used to."

"And what's the story about the warrants the police aren't serving?" Mary wanted to know. "I was talking to a probation officer just last week who said that the police have a thousand outstanding warrants that they haven't served. What good does it do us to get probation to violate our splitees if the police won't even pick them up?"

"That might change," Suber answered. "I've been talking with the chief and I think the police are going to start doing a better job again soon. He maintains that the problem is that bad speed bust they got caught on last spring. They've got to be more careful in the future, but once they get the Vice Squad reorganized, we should see an upturn in police activity again."

"It's about time," Tiny concluded. "There's a lot of folks doin' drugs out there; more than ever before."

"The trouble is," Sparky was finally ready to contribute to the discussion, "the ones doin' drugs these days is all kids. Even if we got them to the NAU, they wouldn't be old enough for methadone."

"Then maybe we should again consider lowering the age for the Methadone Program to eighteen," Dr. Suber offered.

"And give the babies their methadone in bottles with nipples on them I suppose," Tiny retorted disgustedly. "We've been going over dropping the age to eighteen for two years. I thought we had settled that issue."

"I'm against it too." Dr. Mansfield entered the discussion for the first time. "Methadone is a serious drug and I don't think we ought to dispense it lightly. I certainly don't think we should give it to anyone under twenty-one until it has been proven that nothing else will work."

"I don't think we really have to be going into that argument again anyway," Tiny went on. "Most of the people doing heroin these days, so far as I can tell, is over twenty-one anyway. I would say that most of them is twenty-three or twenty-four. Once the police starts puttin' the heat on these people, we will have plenty to fill two clinics."

"But," Mary turned to a new topic, "screening is still a problem. Half the people who apply to the NAU still don't make it into treatment. How can we expect to keep our numbers up when Screening does that kind of a job?"

"Things at Screening are changing too," Suber confided. "It's probably no secret that Richards is resigning as director of Screening. I have someone new in mind for the position who has a lot of good ideas about how Screening can be reorganized to begin doing some real outreach work."

"In the meantime we might do more in the prisons," Sparky offered. "There is lots of dudes up there who should be coming out soon. I bet that every one of them would jump at the chance of hooking up with Methadone if we could arrange an early release date for them. What we ought to be doing is setting it up with Corrections so these dudes could come out of the joint and go straight onto the Methadone Program."

"Don't think we aren't working on that possibility," Suber went on. "I've been talking with Corrections for over a year about it. The commissioner is all for it. The only trouble is, the governor won't give him the money to get the program started."

"I know about this plan," Dr. Mansfield interrupted, "and it still bothers me. Somehow it seems unethical to me to blockade people on methadone who aren't even strung out. I know what you're going to say, and I guess I have to agree with you, even though I do it reluctantly. But do we know for sure that these people would go straight back to dope if they are not maintained immediately on methadone? Maybe some of them wouldn't. I was willing to take the risk when we were talking about only a dozen or so work-release patients. But now we're talking about a lot of people, and I'm sure that some of them could make it without methadone. How do we balance this risk against the risk that the majority will return to heroin when they get out of prison if they don't receive treatment?"

"The Sieve Committee can handle that," Tiny said rather flippantly. "We can tell when someone's serious enough to change his life so that he can stay away from dope. I can tell you, though, that not many just coming out of the joint are that serious. We wouldn't run no risk."

The rest of the staff, with the exception of Bonnie Pratt, agreed. Experience had taught them that addicts are probably best off if they go straight to methadone when they come out of prison. Once they get their lives back together, they can come off methadone. In the meantime, they will have had the protection of methadone for those first trying days back on the streets.

The meeting went on, but by this time most of the essential points of the discussion had emerged. Only Bonnie Pratt raised any objections to going ahead with the second clinic when she suggested that maybe it would be best to stick with only one. The rest of the staff seemed embarrassed by the very suggestion and dismissed it abruptly. "No," Tiny summarized for everyone, "there's a lot of dudes out there who should be in the Methadone Program. They'll be here too, soon as Screening gets on the ball and the police gets back on the job."

10 Zeta House: A Humanizing Community

A few months after the NAU opened its Methadone Clinic, it organized Zeta House, a twenty-four-hour a day, live-in therapeutic community based on the model of Synanon. The staff were all ex-addict graduates from other Synanon-type houses. Originally, Zeta House was quite separate from the NAU. It was located many miles away from other NAU components, it had its own board of directors and corporate status, and to a large extent it ran its own affairs. Gradually, however, Zeta House came to play a more dominant role in the NAU, first by converting significant organizations (ARCH among them) and individuals to its therapeutic philosophy, called "the Concept," and second by placing its graduates in staff positions in other NAU components.

The evolution of the NAU's outpatient therapy program offers a good example of this development. It began as a fairly conventional social work clinic. Gradually, though, as this relatively easygoing approach to drug treatment seemed to be failing, the OPT staff introduced more and more structure into their program, eventually organizing a day program and a short-term residential facility. At this point it seemed reasonable to Dr. Suber and the Zeta House staff that OPT go all the way and embrace the treatment philosophy of the Concept. The director of OPT resisted, however, and continued to put forth therapeutic models of his own as rationales for his program. For a while the OPT staff supported their director but eventually even they began to defect; some went over to the Concept, others became disillusioned and left the NAU altogether. Although the director of OPT finally gave in and publicly accepted the Concept, his position by this time had become so eroded that he eventually had no alternative but to resign.

To describe both Zeta House and OPT in this volume would be to a large extent redundant. Although OPT was, for a while, very different from Zeta House, these differences faded over time. Currently, both the philosophy and the practice of drug treatment in OPT are very much like those in Zeta House. The following chapter, although centered on Zeta House, should nevertheless serve to describe the present approach of OPT as well.

Because of Zeta House's independence, research there was less a matter for design than a matter for negotiation, and although the House remained open to some kinds of research, its staff always reserved the right to admit researchers of their own choosing for projects which suited their own purposes. Basic statistics on residents were kept and appeared to the research unit to have been compiled conscientiously. "We have nothing to hide," House staff said many times. "We want everyone to know what kind of a job we can do." The House also cooperated, very willingly, with a before–after psychological study conducted by a medical student to measure the "junkie personality" and see if residence in the Zeta House therapeutic community could actually modify this personality profile. The House also approved a one-month stay by a college student, who served as a participant observer, and a follow-up study of Zeta House graduates by a student nurse.

What Zeta House would not allow was NAU research staff to interview residents directly or discuss internal House affairs with staff. Interviewing residents, Zeta House maintained (and Dr. Suber concurred), would be countertherapeutic. Private discussions about intrastaff affairs was not even open for discussion since it would violate that tenet of the Concept which forbids family members from saying anything negative about another family member when the other member is not present.

Sources of data about how residents and staff perceived the House were thus limited and we had to pursue them wherever and whenever we could find them. One source was interviews with Zeta House graduates. A second source was conversations, almost always spontaneous and usually informal, with people who split from the House. Although both of these sources were retrospective, they did provide a varied body of data about what being a resident in Zeta House is like, both to those who stick with Zeta House and master the Concept, and to those who do not. The one subject about which we were never able to gather sufficient data, however, was the day-to-day processes of staff interaction and decision making. While we have much information about when and, according to the Concept, why such things as orders would be given or punishments meted out, we do not know how such decisions were reached nor how the staff felt about them once they were executed. These issues, therefore, do not find their way into the account that follows.

The Prospect's Chair

IT WAS one of those gray, foreboding November days in Riverdale when everything looked as if it were viewed through frosted bathroom glass. Tony Morelli, who huddled uncomfortably in the back seat of the Zeta House station wagon, was torn with emotion as he watched the scenery change from the familiar urban sights of Riverdale to the nondescript gas stations and quick-service restaurants of the suburbs and to the open countryside where Zeta House was located. Tom Murphy, Zeta House's resident director, was at the wheel and said nothing until the station wagon rounded the last bend in the road before entering the Zeta House driveway. Then Tom pointed to the sign, which Tony otherwise certainly would have missed, and read aloud: "Zeta House: A Humanizing Community."

The House was not noticeable from the road, being more or less hidden by a line of trees, but commanded considerable attention once one came into the driveway. The dominant structure was a late-nineteenth-century country inn, built in the Victorian style. Unobtrusively off to one side, but attached to the main building was a flat-roofed structure that looked something like a 1930s country dance hall. Zeta House residents, it was apparent, had been making a valiant, if as yet not completely successful, attempt to change the building's appearance by stripping off the more pretentious trim and repainting the buildings in more tasteful hues.

Tony had only a moment to take all this in before the station wagon pulled to a stop and he had to begin assembling his gear: a guitar, a knapsack full of clothes, and a paper bag filled with books and a high school equivalency study course which he hoped to finish while at Zeta House. "Could you help me with these?" Tony asked as he was getting out of the car. "You brought it, you carry it yourself," was Tom's reply. Some months later, Tony, in a letter to a friend, described what happened next as he entered the House:

> I walked in, put my stuff down, and 90,000 people came out of nowhere and grabbed it and started ripping it apart. "Got any drugs on you?" one of them said, and I said, "No!" "Then go sit on the chair." So I sat on the chair and no one talked to me again for two hours.
>
> I remember very distinctly that there are 106 bricks in the chimney across the room. I counted every one of them. I tried to look like I was doing some really serious thinking, but actually I was trying to catch what was going on out of the corner of my eye. The only really interesting thing I saw, though, was somebody wearing a Zeta House learning-experience sign around his neck, sweeping the floor. "I'm glad I'm not him," I said to myself. Eventually I got to know the guy. I hated his guts.
>
> I was still sitting on the chair when this chick who couldn't have been more than sixteen, but acted like she was twenty-three, walks up to me, looks me square in the eye and says, "Prospect Anthony Morelli?"
>
> "Yes," I said, and she said, "Come with me." I got up and started to follow and she said, "Empty your ashtray." "Oh shit," I thought, "this bitch is something else." She was too.
>
> First we went into a little room where I spent about thirty minutes answering questions. Then we went into another room full of people. I saw Tom Murphy (the guy who drove me out to Zeta House), a big fat black dude, Arthur White (I later learned he is the executive director; Tom is the resident director), Bob Rosenbaum, Jerry Rickey, and Jimmy Sitrowsky (you remember these clowns), and a couple of people I didn't know but took to be Zeta House residents. One was a pretty good-looking chick; the other was a black dude, not too old, name of Timmy.
>
> Timmy started asking me questions, just probing a little. I'm answering the questions right off—figured I'd been through all this before. Then one of these cats informs the staff that I had been in drug programs before, and they sprang a super set of questions on me. I copped to just about everything. They asked me silly hypothetical questions like, "On one side there's a pile of cow shit and

on the other side there is you. We are going to put you both in the garden. Which is more important to us at Zeta House?" I answered, "Of course I am, because I have a brain and I'm smarter than cow shit." And they said, "Yeah, but this cow shit is going to work twenty-four hours a day, seven days a week. How long are you going to last?"

The next question had to do with what might have happened to me had I gone to prison (a very real possibility) instead of coming to Zeta House. "You know, you're kind of a good-looking kid and you're standing in your cell when four lifers come in and say 'OK kid, give up your asshole,' and they hold a razorblade up to your throat. What are you going to do?" "I'll break all their arms and legs," I said. "I'll fight right down to the bed; I'll fight right down to the last smidgen of Vaseline." In the end, however, I copped to the fact that I probably would have been on the bed before they could get their flies down. Anyway, it was all very degrading.

Finally, someone asked if I really wanted to come into the House. I said, "Yeah, I really do."

"Well, we're offering to support you for maybe two years—give you cigarettes, give you food, give you a place to sleep—which is better than you've had up to now."

Somehow Zeta House didn't seem quite so bad when they put it that way. I had to admit it was better than prison or Uncle Harry's basement, where I was staying before going to the House.

"We want you to do something that's hard for you, to prove to us that you really want to come here," said Tom. "Do you like to sing?"

"Oh," I said, "I have a fair voice."

"Then stand up on that chair" one of them said, "and sing *Mary Had a Little Lamb* loud enough to break that light bulb over your head."

It was pretty ridiculous but everything was so ridiculous by this point that I jumped right up on the chair and began to sing. If I had hesitated even a quarter of a second, it would have been a hundred times harder. If I had delayed a full second, I'm sure I would have been right out the door. It was a virtuoso performance and I actually thought the bulb was beginning to crack a little when I got to the last "Mary had a little lamb," and would you believe it, I couldn't remember the last line. So I stopped and I said, "Excuse me, does anyone know what comes next? What about a cue sheet?" Nobody thought that was very funny.

All they said was, "Sing it over."

So all of a sudden it hit me, "Whose fleece was white as snow." So I threw my arms out and sang it so loud that they were either going to take me seriously or I was going to kill myself. Would you believe it, Tom came up and put his arms around me. That was the first and only time anybody at Zeta House ever touched me. I was very nervous, very uptight, thought Tom must be some kind of a queer but he said "Brother, that was really fine. Welcome to the family." He went on to tell me that now I was a brother of everyone else in the House. So there I was, in the House. I was pretty lonely, and I was scared.

The next thing they did was cut my hair. I tried to save one lock and somebody spotted me.

"What's that for?"

"I promised it to my girl friend," I answered, and they said, "How did you know we were going to cut your hair?"

I said, "I read it in *Life* Magazine." Nobody thought that was very funny and they took the lock of hair away from me.

Next, Timmy lead me to where I could get some straight clothes. I had a choice between a neat pair of imitation cobra-skin pants and a pair of old corduroys. I picked the old corduroys. Then I was informed about where I would sleep and who I could and could not talk to. People who knew each other on the street are not allowed to talk to each other for at least a month. They call it "being on a ban." Some of my older friends, like Bob Rosenbaum and Jerry Rickey, could speak to me because they had been in the House long enough to be able to handle talking to some of their old cronies, but I could not talk with them unless they spoke to me first.

Gathering Data

Learning about the concept and the rules and routines of the House is called gathering data. Tony began gathering data the next morning at seven o'clock when his first guide for the day met him and showed him how to make his bed and put his room in order. The two then went to breakfast along with the rest of the House. Tony ate heartily. He was surprised at how good the food was.

Tony was not given a work assignment for the first three

days. Instead, a succession of guides escorted him about, showing him how things were done. Tony was never on his own; someone had to escort him even to the bathroom, and although he did not stay close enough to watch, he did stay close enough to hear.

After breakfast, Tony's second guide led him to the morning meeting which, this morning, was being led by Tom Murphy, although more often one of the coordinator trainees would handle it. Tom picked up the announcement and pull-up sheets from outside the expediter's office as he went by and scanned the items for those that should be included at this meeting. (Any resident who had an announcement to make or wanted to make a pull-up could sign the sheet, but the staff member who ran the meeting decided which items were actually worth bringing to the meeting.)

It was 8:15 and the meeting opened with one resident reciting the Zeta House creed:

> We are here because there is no refuge, finally from ourselves. Until a person confronts himself in the eyes and hearts of others, he is running. Until he suffers them to share his secret he has no safety from it. Afraid to be known, he can know neither himself nor any other . . . he will be alone. . . .
> Where else but in our common ground can we find such a mirror? Here, together, a person can at last appear clearly to himself, not as the giant of his dreams, nor the dwarf of his fears, but as a man, part of a whole, with his share in its purpose.
> In this ground we can each take root and grow, not alone any more as in death but alive to ourselves and to others. . . .

Next, Tom allowed various residents to make their announcements and then turned to Paula Kronbach, a senior resident, for her pull-up. "I've noticed that a lot of people are not emptying their ashtrays lately," Paula began. "I think this is sloppy behavior which shows an attitude of not caring for others in the House. Let me see the hands of those people who are not emptying their ashtrays." About ten people, including an expediter, raised their hands. "Well, I suggest you people get a grip on it. We can't take pride in a slovenly home."

"Thank you," some of the residents said, and Paula sat down.

Tom Murphy launched into a long stern lecture:

I'm surprised that there was only one pull-up on the sheet this morning. It would seem to me that people are holding back. There's been a lot more than dirty ashtrays wrong around here lately. If things don't start shaping up, you'll be eating those butts pretty soon. It seems to me that a lot of you don't care any more. I don't see that old concern for the House and the members of the family. Maybe some of you should start thinking about leaving. Zeta House is giving you everything, and what are you giving in return? Nothing. You're just taking. You're acting like a bunch of machines trying to get through. Get it together. If you don't want what Zeta House has to offer, there are plenty out there on the street who do. If you think this is a freeway, just whip off at the next exit. But it will take you right back where you started—the streets—and that's what you deserve if you don't keep moving in the right direction. Is there anyone who would like to get off right now? There's an exit right around the corner.

No one raised a hand.

The Zeta House newspaper, including the weather report for the day which had been compiled without the aid of U.S. Weather Bureau resources, was next. Outside news of the kind that comes through newspapers or TV is of little use to Zeta House residents and it is thus discouraged.

In a somewhat lighter vein, the residents sang a couple of songs, including one which was the day's menu set to music. It was 9:10. The meeting adjourned and people separated to go to their departments for their daily work assignments.

Tony's next guide explained that each resident at Zeta House has a job. How long one is in the House and the amount he has grown determines how responsible a job he will have. New residents start out as workers in Service, which does repairs and renovations; Kitchen, which prepares meals; Expediting, the administrative unit responsible for coordinating absolutely everything that is going on in the House and seeing to it that House rules are obeyed and House standards kept; Business, which handles correspondence and records; Medical, which attends to minor medical problems and schedules appointments with the doctor or the dentist; Community Relations, which arranges speakers for various engagements; or Procurement, which hustles things the House could use from charitable citizens and organizations in the community. Workers are under the charge of a department head who in turn must report to one of the three house coordinators. Some of the departments, like Medical, have no workers, and some of the bigger ones, like Kitchen or Service, have many workers and an additional position, a ramrod, between the workers and department head. Tony's first work assignment, to begin the following Monday, was in Service. Right now, however, Tony was free to continue gathering data and Timmy, his next guide, began rapping with him.

As Tony listened, he went over to the coffee urn, picked up a mug, and started to fill it with coffee. "What are you doing?" Timmy asked.

"I'm getting a cup of coffee," Tony answered.

"With *what* are you getting a cup of coffee?" Tony's guide asked further.

"This here mug," Tony answered.

"Who told you you could use that mug?" Tony was admonished. Timmy went on to explain that mugs were a badge of status reserved for staff and department heads.

Different guides took turns giving Tony data. This was the custom. Not only was everyone in the House supposed to relate to everyone else as "one big family," but every attempt was made to avoid cliques, which were dangerous for a number of reasons. First of all, the people who were likely to form a clique were those who had been friends in the streets and a clique in the House would only facilitate talk about drugs or the former street life, negative talk as it was called in the House. Cliques also made agreements not to rat on each other easier. And finally, if one member of a clique split, it put a lot of pressure on the other members of the clique to leave the House also.

Tony's next guide was carrying a copy of a book called, *The Teachings of Don Juan.* Tony had heard about the book, that it was about a Mexican Indian sorcerer and peyote, but he had never read it. Tony asked about the book and his guide said, "Oh, it deals with an old Indian priest and some of his philosophies of life."

"But isn't it about peyote?" Tony asked.

"Yes," the guide answered, "but you'd be better off not thinking about that right now."

Paula Kronbach, the resident who had pulled everyone up at the morning meeting, was Tony's next guide. Tony was pretty leery of Paula, especially after her performance earlier, and Paula felt it. Nevertheless, she went on to discuss Zeta House rules:

> There are two cardinal rules here; break these rules and you are immediately expelled. No one takes drugs—you must even ask before taking an aspirin—and no one uses physical violence. You don't even threaten it. I once saw someone raise a clenched fist just to emphasize a point, and he got a general meeting and a bald head. You can express all the anger you want at anyone in the House, even toward senior residents and staff, in hostility groups. At all other times, you must not show hostility. It is also a rule that you must follow directions, without hesitation and without complaining, given by any member. There is another rule that if you do something wrong you tell somebody higher up about it and take your punishment. If you don't, guilt will build up and it will stop your growth. Also, there is no sex among residents. One resident who had been in the House for a year and a half got a bald head last New Year's Eve for kissing another resident. When you get into reentry, you can start thinking about your sex life again.

Paula explained various other do's and don't's having to do with cursing, being on time, making a proper bed, leaving no dirt around, checking in and out of the House when one got privileges to go outside, and the absolute rule against negative talk. Paula concluded her list with the rule that there was to be no bad rapping about a third party unless that party was present.

Punishments for infractions of the rules, Paula went on, vary according to the seriousness of the infraction, the reason for the violation, the frequency of violation, and how tight the House is at the moment. Right now, Paula explained, as Tony could probably gather from Mike's talk at morning meeting, the House was getting pretty loose and thus everyone could expect harsh punishments for a while. Until the House was tight again, everyone would have to be careful. Paula went on to explain about pull-ups and pointed out another example of a learning experience: the resident Tony had seen the day before with a sign around his neck. Today he was wearing a big cardboard box painted black which had the words "atomic reactor" stenciled across the front and back. The box had holes cut in it for head and arms. It looked altogether uncomfortable. After having gotten his sign off the day before, Paula explained, Charles Brown had been working on dishpan duty when someone said, "Charlie, go over there and do such and such." Charlie turned around and threw his sponge in obvious disgust.

Haircuts, Paula continued, are reserved for serious or persistent infractions of the rules. Even a confirmed graduate, still living in the House, Paula went on, got a haircut because he came in drunk one night and paraded his inebriation in front of all the other residents. Perhaps it would not have been so bad if he had slipped quietly up to his apartment (graduates do have drinking privileges), but the fact that he was so insensitive to the rest of the members of the House showed that he had not completely matured. They shaved his head, Paula said with a smile, and busted him to "dishpan," which meant that he had to wash all the heavy pots and pans in the kitchen. He could have gotten "spare parts" which would have meant he would have to do all the dirty jobs, like washing the cars or cleaning up the dog action in the hall, whenever he was called on day or night.

Paula went on to explain research in the community and how a person could be expelled from Zeta House altogether, but by this time Tony's powers of concentration had waned considerably. Paula took Tony to lunch and from there another guide took him to his first afternoon seminar. "Seminars," the guide explained, "are designed to broaden our intellectual scope. Sometimes they bring speakers in but more often the staff just organizes discussion on various intellectual topics. Sometimes we have debates or a Zeta bowl, like the College Bowl on television."

Tony described his first seminar as follows:

The second day I was there they had a seminar on astrology. I figured, OK, I'm suppose to get up and talk about this when the question-and-answer period comes. And I did it too. Some of the residents were having a hard time taking astrology very seriously so I went into this long discussion about Einsteinian relativity in which you picture the universe as a piece of Saran wrap with marbles embedded in it. All these powerful forces—gravity, electromagnetic energy, etc.—I explained, have an effect on the human body. Perhaps astrology is based on Einsteinian relativity. Nobody understood a word I was saying and I got killed.

"What the hell are you talking about? Who do you think you are? What kind of image were you trying to put out with that anyway?"

So I resolved then, OK, I'll say nothing at seminars if talking gives the wrong image. Now you've got to understand that as negative as they said I was coming across, I was really trying hard. I went to bed that night thinking I really was a deranged junkie. I kept trying to drum this into my head, but in fact I knew that I wasn't. I knew they were trying to wipe the slate clean. Everything I had gotten in life so far, they said, had been worthless. I could not admit that. I thought I had learned a great deal from almost all my experiences but therein started the friction.

There was another seminar the next day and Kyriakos, a probation officer from Riverdale, was the speaker. He talked about treatment and what a good job Zeta House was doing; and Jim White, who made the big effort and showed up for this seminar, said how helpful probation had been to the success of the House. Well, when it got around to questions and answers, I said to myself, don't let that old image pop out, just shut up and play stupid. Would you believe it, I got killed the next day for saying nothing.

"Why didn't you say anything?" they asked. "You wanted to say something, we know you wanted to say something. Was that really you sitting there saying nothing?"

I said, "Oh, it was really me and I had lots to say, but . . ." It didn't make any sense to me at all at this point.

Tony spent the rest of the afternoon gathering more data. He watched and listened as a procession of resident guides filled him in on various aspects of House routine and on how important the Concept was to them. The Zeta House philosophy, a dynamic way of life, they explained, was like a new life to a junkie. The old life style of the streets could only mean death; the Concept meant life, not just getting away from drugs but a new life as a whole individual who had control of himself and grip on his environment. Anyone, they explained, could benefit from the Concept, but it was a junkie's salvation.

After dinner the residents received their hostility-group assignments. Tony had heard about confrontation groups, that they were pretty heavy, but he had never actually been in one before:

Coordinator: Well, does anyone have any hostil. . . .

You dirty motherfucker. What the fuck do you mean telling me to get off my ass and do some work. I'll work when I get fucking good and ready. You got balls . . .

Listen you cock-sucker, when I tell you to do something, you do it and you do it quick. You don't sit on your fat ass blinking your eyelashes at me . . .

You can just suck my black ass you fat bastard. Go fuck yourself with your orders. You hear, just fuck yourself. And as for you, you prick, don't you fucking come over to me and tell me . . .

Listen bitch, just stop complaining. All you fucking do is complain.

Tony almost jumped right out of his chair. He knew that Zeta House residents were not allowed to show hostility to other members of the family *except* during the hostility-group sessions, but it seemed to Tony that this was a bit excessive. (Later Tony would come to accept the loud shouting of hostility groups as a matter of course and come to know that a lot of hostility did indeed build up during the week which was in need of some outlet.)

Saturday began very much like any other day, except that everyone got up a half an hour later. There were no afternoon seminars, however, and work crews knocked off about 2:30 so that the residents could get the House and themselves shipshape for the Saturday night open house which would begin around 7:15 when the jackets and ties went on and final preparations were made to greet the guests who would begin arriving at eight o'clock.

As the guests arrived (fifty to seventy-five showed up some evenings and there were about ten regular visitors), residents greeted them and engaged them in conversation until nine o'clock when the seminar began. The seminar started with a sentence which one of the members of the House wrote on the blackboard, and invited everyone to discuss. Guests were usually shy in these matters and, despite the moderator's cajoling, residents usually wound up doing most of the talking.

The topic this evening was: "Taking drugs is a symptom rather than a disease." During the discussion, members of the House explained that the goal of Zeta House is not just to get residents to stop using drugs but to rehabilitate the whole person —body, personality, and character. One of the coordinators went into more detail, writing the following list of goals on the blackboard:

1. Stop taking drugs
2. Disavow unhealthy street values
3. Become aware of feelings
4. Deal maturely with feelings
5. Become an internalizer
6. Deal with the environment to achieve healthy goals
7. Accept and take responsibility for oneself
8. Become an independent, useful member of society
9. Teach the Zeta House philosophy to others

Then the coordinator continued:

The way Zeta House reaches these goals is to completely strip the junkie of all his street ways and negative memories, and then, as you would with a new baby, start building a new character. The environment at Zeta is harsh, austere, and authoritarian. This is necessary in order to strip away the old personality. As residents stay in the House, however, they discover the concern that everyone in the House has for them. Even through punishment one learns this concern. Since our old habits could lead only to death, we learn that breaking these habits is the extreme act of love. Not everyone appreciates this concern and goes on to graduate from Zeta House as a new human being. Some residents slip along the way and go back to the streets from whence they came. Sometimes a second experience in the streets, if he survives, is sufficient to make the errant member of the family more appreciative of what Zeta House was giving him and, like the prodigal son, he will return. If they come back with the proper attitude, the family will readmit them.

At about ten o'clock, after the seminar, people broke up into small groups to dance or engage in conversation. Saturday night open house has two functions: to let the community find out what Zeta House is all about, and thus to make friends for it, and to give the residents a chance to interact successfully with squares. All residents must attend open house and must try to mix with as many guests as possible. As soon as a resident gets too comfortable with one set of guests, someone will be sure to tell him to spread the action.

Sunday is a day off. Brunch runs from eleven until noon, but if people choose they may skip brunch and sleep in. Some residents play pool or Scrabble; others lie around reading or sewing. Sometimes small conversations develop and on nice days people may get up a ballgame. Dinner is at four or four-thirty and bedtime, as usual, is at midnight. No one, except some expediters and a coordinator, carries on his usual job on Sundays, but volunteers are called for to cook the meals or perhaps wash the cars.

Harry, the chief expediter, did ask for volunteers to wash the cars this Sunday. Tony, who still didn't know any better, raised his hand as did Jerry Rickey. Everyone else played touch football. Tony thought that volunteering might get him a few brownie points. He could not understand why Jerry, who seemed to be in a good position in the House, had volunteered. Jerry explained: "You will learn that it's good to volunteer every so often in order to keep your belly tight. This way when you hear the lectures on extending yourself, you don't have to feel any guilt."

Pressure

When Tony reported to the service crew for work on Monday, Harold Washington, the department head, gave everyone a lecture. Partly the lecture was for Tony's benefit, but partly it was for the rest of the residents as well, who constantly had to be kept on their toes.

Work is hard, but work is good for you. The only work any of you guys ever knew out on the street was pimping and chasing the bag. That kind of work does not build character. The work you do here does build character. My job is to keep a foot up your ass all the time. If we don't do that, you'd get lazy and slovenly. Those are street habits and we have to break you of them. You're going to hate us for it, but that's good. You can drop all the slips you want, but you're still going to do as you're told, and you're going to get every last atom of dirt cleaned away if it takes you until midnight to do it. Nobody grows without work and nobody works without pressure. We'll keep up the pressure; you'll do the growing. Some day you'll thank us for it, but right now it's sufficient that you just do it. When your ramrod says do something, you jump. You don't ask why, you don't make excuses, you just do it. You can't hide from it here in Zeta House, you can't go shoot up when the pressure starts to build. But that's good. Until you learn to conquer pressure without resorting to dope, until you learn to meet pressure head-on and surmount it yourself, you'll never develop character.

By the end of the first day's work, Tony concluded that if pressure builds character, he'd be Winston Churchill before he got out of Zeta House. One of the first things he did on his work crew was ask one of the other residents on his crew for a cigarette. He was blown away immediately. "We only get seven packs of cigarettes a week at Zeta House. We can't be wasteful of them. Everyone is responsible for his own cigarettes." (Tony had forgotten and left his pack of cigarettes in the dining room, for which he would no doubt get into trouble, and had thought nothing about asking to borrow one. He intended fully to pay it back.) To make matters worse, the resident who had blown Tony away then gave him a cigarette. Tony tried not to take it, but the resident insisted. It was the awfullest-tasting cigarette he had ever had. Later, when there seemed to be something like a pause in the work, Tony asked his ramrod if he could go to the dining room and get his cigarettes, but was told no. He had no more cigarettes until lunch time.

Tony scrubbed down each bathroom a minimum of three times. Just when he thought he had one clean enough so you could eat right out of the bowl, the ramrod would find some minute speck of dirt and make him wash the whole bathroom again—not just the speck of dirt, the whole bathroom.

He went on like this the whole day, making mistakes, getting blown away, redoing every job which to anyone else would have appeared to be perfect. He was down to his last bathroom, and what Tony thought surely must be its last inspection, when the ramrod spotted the mop sprawling soggily in the middle of the hall floor.

"What the hell is this?" the ramrod asked. "A snare to catch your brothers?" Before Tony could even answer, the ramrod launched into a tirade about leaving his mop lying about so casually.

Tony knew that he had not left the mop there; he had given it to Jeffrey Smith, who was watching the whole thing without saying a word. Evidently, Jeff had left the mop on the floor, but he wasn't saying anything now that the ramrod had spotted it.

As soon as Tony could get a word in edgewise, he said, "But . . ." and the ramrod said, "Is that spelled with one T or two T's?" If it's spelled with two T's, that's hostility and you can save that for your hostility group. If it's spelled with one T, then that's a reaction, and you can get a learning experience for that." Tony, furious, picked up the mop and put it away. He gave Jeff a look he hoped would cut his guts out.

After dinner, Harold Washington called a special meeting of the service crew. Evidently, Tom Murphy or Jim White, God knows how, found something amiss. Harold made the service crew go back and do everything again. When the crew finally got finished, at twelve midnight, Tony was so tired that not even his rage could keep him awake.

Wednesday evening was the regular time for static groups and the group leader for that night (Strengths, as they were called) drew Tony aside to describe the nature of static groups:

> In static groups you are only supposed to relate to the group; no hostility, that's reserved for hostility groups. One person relates at a

time. When the group has spent enough time on that person's problems, I will call on another member, although anyone can ask to relate something if he wants to. When you relate, the group will question you and try to get behind the words and emotions which are hiding your real feelings. Sometimes the group may go into your past history, but usually we emphasize the present.

Complete honesty is demanded of everyone. No one, of course, can achieve complete honesty right off, so we will have to strip away your defenses and force you, at first, to reveal all facets of your thoughts and take complete responsibility for your life. Group members are good at uncovering lies, coverups, and rationalizations and at getting you to accept yourself completely. Don't be worried. I will guide the group and make sure that your first experience is a positive one.

The main thing that Tony noticed when the meeting got underway was that all the topics the Strength brought up seemed geared to probe the members' feelings of guilt. Once the Strength turned up some guilt vibes, he then acted like he had known the "secret" all the time and proceeded to draw the individual out until he confessed: "until he got it out of his belly."

The most striking example was a member who got very uptight when the discussion turned to homosexuality and even more uptight when the discussion turned to him and he was forced to admit to homosexuality as a teenager. The group Strength and other members then taunted him and asked, "How does it feel to be a woman? I've never been a woman, how does it feel?" Later, after the resident was thoroughly humiliated, shaken, and visibly hostile, the group Strength admitted that he also had had homosexual encounters as a teenager. This, he said, was not unusual and now was part of his past. It did not mean that he was a homosexual now, although it was something humiliating which he had to accept responsibility for and live with the rest of his life. Tony was not asked to relate this week; his turn would come later.

The next day Tony began to get a little better hang of his job, but his anger at Jeff Smith did not abate. "Yes," Tony thought to himself, "I certainly am going to drop a slip on that motherfucking nigger." Later in a letter to his friend, Tony described the incident as follows:

> Participation in groups is the most important thing at Zeta House. We have two hostility and one static group meetings a week. I think they should probably have more groups, but maybe three a week is all people can handle.
> The first week I was there I developed this terrible hostility toward Jeff Smith, a guy who let me take the weight for his leaving a mop in the middle of the floor and the ramrod tripping over it. You're not suppose to let hostilities build up in you so I decided right off to drop a slip on Jeff Smith.
> When I came in the meeting room, there was Jeff just waiting for me. I didn't even wait for the Strength to start the meeting. I just lit right into Jeff. Now, as you know, I have a pretty good obscene vocabulary. I must have gone on for at least three minutes without ever repeating myself. I used things like "demented eunuch, and your mother has a breast amputation." When I got around to, "Your grandmother wears combat boots," I thought I was going to crack up. I was really flying. It was all very ridiculous and infantile. I felt like a first-grader again who's just warming up for a playground fight. Anyway, Jeff can do little more than the usual motherfucker, dirty motherfucker, cock-sucker, dirty cock-sucker, son of a bitch, and so forth. I was doing so well, though, that the whole group started paying attention to me.

The next day the group Strength called Tony aside and told him how he had used the group the night before for his own selfish ends rather than as a vehicle for personal growth. This was a negative attitude, a holdover from the street, which would have to go. If everyone in the House were as selfish as Tony had been, the House couldn't survive ten minutes. Tony was surprised and crushed. He would have to be more careful about this in the future, paying special attention to his intellectual wise-guy image.

For the next month only minor incidents came Tony's way. He was constantly being blown away: "Excuse me, Mr. Morelli, did you leave that light on?"

"Yes," he would answer.

"Then turn it off, dum dum! Electricity costs money."

There was one general meeting, a haircut, with everyone in the House in attendance, for a resident, George Harris, who had had sexual relations with another resident and had finally been found out.

"Did you have relations with this girl?"

"I sure did," answered George. There was nothing else he could say since the girl was standing right there. He had lived in mortal fear for three weeks that she might cop to her guilt so when it happened, he was not surprised. They shaved George's head, busted him to spare parts, and removed all his privileges. He also had to wear a big scarlet letter F around his neck for the next two weeks.

Tony never wore a learning-experience sign; his nemesis was the atomic reactor. He was never quite able to accept other residents telling him to do something, especially when he thought that what he was being told was wrong. All he got for his trouble, however, was chafed underarms and a sore neck from wearing the big black box.

But Tony learned quickly and made satisfactory progress in the concept. After two months, he was made expediter. Although he felt more important with a job carrying responsibility, he also realized that he was in essence little more than an errand boy and policeman. He would clean the coordinator's office whenever it became free and stand ready to fetch people when the coordinator called. He also made periodic runs of the House to see if everything was in order.

As an expediter, Tony had longer work hours but more free time on the job. He was also confined to an office and had to miss some of the House events like Jerry Rickey's birthday party. For the first time, Tony felt isolated, physically and emotionally, from the other residents. He had often felt lonely before, mostly for his old friends, but now the loneliness became almost unbearable. To make matters worse, now he also had to be the bad guy who was always on the lookout for mistakes, always quick with the pull-ups, always assigning members to fix things that were out of order. Slowly Tony began to feel above the House, watching it closely, but no longer really a part of it. He began to feel like a cop.

Splitting

It was after Tony became an expediter that he began writing clandestine letters to Harvey Schultz, his friend on the outside. The letters had to be written secretly because residents were not allowed to write to friends for many months after they entered Zeta House. After about three months, residents could write letters to parents, but writing to his father did not fill the void. Tony therefore simply slipped a letter to Harvey into each letter he wrote to his father, with instructions to him to forward the letter to Harvey.

At first, Tony felt extremely guilty about his duplicity. He told himself, though, that he would eventually be able to write the letters legitimately; he was just getting a little head start. And besides, he thought, the letters were only about the House and thus would help to spread the Zeta House philosophy. In a few months he would get telephone privileges and after being in the House for seven or eight months, he could start receiving visitors. After ten months he would probably get permission to visit home, accompanied by an older resident. After twelve or fourteen months, he could probably get limited weekend privileges.

Tony's guilt, although it eased somewhat as time went on, never completely vanished. He thought at first that he would probably get caught, but as the weeks went by and no one indicated the slightest suspicion about what he was doing, he realized that he might not get caught after all. Several times in static groups Tony had a tremendous urge to confess, but he could never actually bring himself to it. Had the subject of sneaking letters out ever come up, he thought, he surely would not have been able to keep it in. But the subject never came up.

Meanwhile, Tony continued to make what appeared to be satisfactory progress in the Concept. He worked hard and was a good family member. Although the Concept was not yet completely a part of him, he felt that it was coming. Now that he had a chance to relate a little more directly to older residents and Zeta House staff members, he began to see how much some people treasured their Zeta House experience and the new life it promised.

It was a warm spring afternoon in late April or early May when Tom Murphy asked Tony if he wouldn't like to knock off early and go outside. Tony jumped at the opportunity, not only to relieve the tedium of his job but to talk intimately with Tom Murphy, who was, more than anyone else in the House, his ideal. Tom had graduated from Zeta House two years before. He seemed so poised, so self-assured, so mature. Tony dug the hell out of him. It was against the House rules to leave his job, but when Tony mentioned this, Tom only laughed and told Tony that people are worth more than rules.

Tom recounted his life story: the days in the streets, the years in prison, and finally the two years as a resident at Zeta House. Tom had had it tougher than Tony. Tom's father had been an alcoholic (he was dead now) and his mother a prostitute. Although his mother was now too old to practice her profession regularly, she did, Tom suspected, still turn a few tricks for some of the winos in New York City's Lower East Side. Tom saw his mother occasionally, although his visits were growing less and less frequent.

From as early as he could remember, Tom had been a creature of the streets. He had always tried to avoid his father, and his mother's working hours had never coincided with the hours a young boy was normally awake. School had meant something to Tom for a while, but it was not sustaining. Most of the time, as a young boy, he ran with a gang. His gang even achieved a fair amount of local prominence when he was younger, but as the members grew older they drifted apart, mostly to reform school. Tom spent more than half his teenage years in institutions.

As Tom reached manhood, he tried to make it in the rackets but by then he was too notorious and untrustworthy to get more than very minor assignments. It was during this time, when Tom was in the Tombs awaiting trial on a B&E, that he had his first taste of heroin. He got the heroin as payment for homosexual services and took it because he figured he might as well exact as heavy a toll as he could out of the bastard who took advantage of him.

Tom snorted the stuff and got violently sick. This might have ended his drug career right then and there had he not, upon leaving the Tombs, fallen back in with some of the members of his old gang who were heavily into dope. At first Tom wanted no part of heroin, but time played its seductive game and within a year Tom was a hard-core junkie. Two runs through Beth Israel Hospital for detoxification, several more trips to the Tombs, and a bit in the state penitentiary brought Tom to Zeta House.

Zeta House was the only real home Tom had ever had and the only real family he had ever known. It literally meant the world to him and he would sacrifice anything for it. Just like everyone else, Tom had found those first months in the House difficult, even crushing, but through it all he felt, for the first time in his life, that someone cared about him, that they were concerned about his growth and development. Tom had a lot of bad attitudes and habits to get rid of and the process was painful, but he had come out of it, he thought, a far better human being. Not everyone who went through Zeta House appreciated this. It was particularly hard for those who had led a soft life, who had had everything given to them. They had trouble appreciating the value of the Concept. Some people didn't stick around long enough to even know what was ultimately available in the House, others just slid along learning to master the routines without going through the harsh and painful process of personal growth. What worried Tom most, perhaps, was whether Zeta House was relevant for those, like Tony, who had not grown up in the hard life of the streets.

Tony could not share Tom's concern. Tom's self-confidence and emotional control were impressive, and his ability to be both tough and compassionate at the same time were qualities which Tony very much wanted to emulate. Although Tony could not yet emotionally accept the notion that the harsh authoritarian structure of Zeta House was an expression of love and concern, he could understand it intellectually. Maybe now that he could interact more intimately with those who had successfully mastered the Concept, he too could become part of the movement. "And it is a movement," Tom told Tony:

> Beginning with the first Concept House, Synanon, in California, the movement has spread throughout the land and is even making inroads into foreign countries. Encounter groups are now the main type of therapy in all kinds of drug treatment programs, and new residential communities are springing up daily. OPT, after a long struggle, is now a Concept program. Zeta House has established Concept programs in the men's and women's reformatories and in the federal prison at Junction City. Plans are also afoot for Zeta House to start a residential community in conjunction with the VA Hospital to treat the returning GI's who got addicted to heroin in Vietnam. Once we take over the NAU Methadone Maintenance Clinic, the Concept will be the only form of drug treatment in the whole area.

Tony was infused with Tom's enthusiasm and redoubled his determination to absorb the Concept completely. But such was not to be his fate.

It was Sunday and Tony had just come in, along with some of the other residents, from playing ball. As Tony was cleaning up, an expediter informed him that there was to be a general meeting. The meeting was for Tony.

Dr. Morelli had been disturbed by the letters Tony had sent him for Harvey. Although they had been sealed separately, Dr. Morelli opened them anyway and read them. They seemed cynical and smart-alecky. Dr. Morelli knew that informing the Zeta House staff about the letters would probably get his son in trouble, but he figured that if he did not, his son would be in trouble in other more fundamental ways. Dr. Morelli therefore sent the letters to Jim White, the Zeta House executive director, along with a note explaining how he had received them and why he had not brought them to Zeta House staff attention earlier. He hoped that his actions would not make things difficult for Tony but that bringing the letters to light would facilitate Tony's complete recovery. Dr. Morelli had never shown the letters to Harvey Schultz.

The general meeting was a ritual. Tony did not even listen to what transpired. He was crushed. Just as he was about to really make it, this had to come up. As far as Tony was concerned, it was an unimportant issue. But Zeta House did not see it that way; they shaved his head, busted him to dishpan, and took away all privileges.

It was one o'clock in the afternoon, two weeks later when it finally happened. The House was giving a Fourth of July picnic. Tony was not allowed to join in. He was in the kitchen washing dishes and in general feeling very sorry for himself, when he happened to look out the window and see three people streak by on motorcycles. "What am I doing here anyway?" Tony thought to himself. "What in the world has Zeta House done for me? It doesn't matter what I do, I'm always catching hell, and no matter how hard I try, I never get rewarded for my efforts. The only rewards they know here are completely negative."

"Perhaps," Tony thought, "some people can dig this place, but not me. For those who have know nothing better, Zeta House may look pretty good. Purgatory would probably seem like heaven to someone who had lived in hell all his life. But my experience has been different. I never was a down-and-out hard-core junkie groveling in the streets. To me, Zeta House looks like hell. Why should one choose hell of his own accord? It will probably come soon enough all by itself if we just let nature take its course. In the meantime, there must be something better than this."

Tony took off his apron, left it in a heap on the counter, and threw his wet sponge to the middle of the floor. He then walked up to the expediter's desk and said, "Hank, I'm going to leave."

Hank didn't even look really surprised and simply answered, "Well, there's nothing to hold you here. There's the door. All I can say is I would cut off my right ball in order to stay in this place, but you're free to leave if you want to." Hank was one of those hard-core junkies off the streets who saw Zeta House as their last chance. He too had been busted some weeks earlier and was again working his way up through the job ranks.

"I don't know, Hank," Tony said, "maybe I'd better think about it for a little bit first." So Tony sat down. He lit up a cigarette and thought, but somehow he knew this was it.

Within two minutes he heard, "Tony Morelli, please report to the staff office"—not the coordinator's office—but Jim White's office. This was the big time.

Tony knocked on the door: "Who is it?"

"Tony Morelli."

"Come right in."

Tony walked in and there were Jim White, Tom Murphy, and others of the top Zeta House brass. "Have a seat Tony," Jim White said, and everyone looked very amicable. "We understand that you're thinking about leaving," Jim White said.

"Yeah," Tony answered, "that's right, just talked to Hank about it."

"Well, why do you want to leave?" Tom Murphy wanted to know.

"I have finally decided," Tony answered, "that I'm just not the type of individual that you can help. I don't feel that I'm doing anything more here than wasting your time and mine and I think the place for me to go now is to school."

"Well," Jim White answered, "that's real fine, but who's going to support you while you go to school?"

Tony knew he was going to get killed if he said it, but he said it anyway: "My father will support me. My father has promised to pay for college when and if I ever go there. Now I think I'll go."

"But you don't even have a high school diploma," Tom Murphy pointed out," and college doesn't begin until September."

"I've thought about all that," Tony replied, "I plan to get a job and take my equivalency test this summer and enroll in a community college this fall. If I do well there, I'll transfer to State next year."

"So you're going to go running back to daddy," Tom said. "It's going to cost you $20,000 or more to go to college and you're just going to let your old man pay for it. If I had that kind of money, I'd go to college myself. But I don't. Maybe I'll save up for it someday, but when I do I'll know that it's something that I have earned. Why don't you think about earning it?"

Tony did not answer but simply said he was going to leave.

Now the conversation got decidedly more heated. They called Tony a lot of names. Tom said, "You wouldn't have lasted a day on my block in New York."

Tony replied, "probably not, but I probably wouldn't even have gone to your block in New York."

The discussion continued in this vein with six people really laying it on Tony and Tony getting more nervous all the time. But they were getting nowhere, that was obvious.

"You never ate off the greasy rock, kid. You don't know what it's like to sleep in the gutter. You've never had it hard on the street. Go on out there and see what the street's really like. You'll learn soon enough and you'll be running back to us. So go on, leave, we've got no objections at all. I just hope you're not dead before you finally get a grip on yourself," Tom Murphy intoned. "What do you think you're going to do about the probation you still have hanging over you? Is your daddy going to take care of that too?"

"I'll take my chances with my PO," was all Tony could say.

"Listen, Tony," Jim White cut in, "we're only saying all these things because we care about you. We care about you as a person. We don't want you to go out there and kill yourself with dope. We don't want you to blow your probation and get sent to prison. We don't want you to go out until you feel like a whole human being again. We love you. We really do. We love you as a brother."

"I don't think you really love me," Tony retorted. "If you had loved me, you would have shown me more concern when it really counted. Besides, I don't think I'm a spineless, chicken, pussy punk like you say. If I were, I would have eased right out the door without saying boo to anyone. As it is, I stayed to take my licks. That took balls, to come here and face you people like this."

"So what is your decision?" Jim White asked.

"I plan to leave."

"Then go sit on the prospect's chair," Jim White ordered.

To Tony's surprise he did exactly that. Soon someone came in and gave him his guitar and knapsack with his personal belongings just stuffed into it. Tony checked his things. They had given him the Zeta House toothbrush, but they kept the Zeta House razor and did not return the one he had brought with him. Of the shirts he had brought, he got two back and three sets of somebody else's underwear. There were no pants, none of his books, and his high school equivalency course was missing. Somebody handed him his ring and his watch but not the two dollars or so loose change he had had when he came into the House. He only had four cigarettes left.

Everybody looked at him as he went out the door—mothers, brothers, sisters, fathers—everybody at the picnic watched as Tony was led to the station wagon carrying all his gear.

"There's one for the morgue," he heard someone in the background explain. "Well, it was obvious he wasn't going to make it at Zeta House anyway."

Forty heavy minutes later, Tony was dropped off in Riverdale with a guitar, a knapsack, two cigarettes, no money, and an almost certain probation violation. As far as the House was concerned, Tony was a splittee and a failure. As far as Tony was concerned, the House had let him down. Some splittees find their way back to heroin and some even back to the House. Tony did neither. A year later he finished his high school equivalency and enrolled in college. The police never served his warrant for violating probation.